DREAMING IN GERMAN

Author's Note

This memoir is based on events recalled through the imperfect lens of memory. I have changed a few names, but have tried to tell the truth I remember.

Throughout this book, I have used the words "communist" and "socialist" to refer to the Socialist Unity Party government that ruled the German Democratic Republic or "East Germany." I realize this government was neither truly socialist nor communist, just as it was not a democratic republic. As is usually the case, those in power dictated the language of the times.

If you would like to see family photographs, maps and a family tree, please go to www.dreamingingerman.com

www.triplewaterpress.com

ISBN 978-0-578-08832-7

Cover Art: "Heimweh – Longing", Encaustic Mixed Media Collage by Claudia Poser using a photograph by Siegfried Poser

DREAMING IN GERMAN

A MEMOIR

CLAUDIA POSER

How can I live so far away

from what I loved, what I love?

Pablo Neruda

SUSPENDED

I fight to stay awake as long as I can, because sleep is a waste of time. The lights outside my window cast a lacy pattern through the horse chestnuts that line Siemensstrasse. At long intervals, I hear the hiss of tires splashing through puddles, followed by a faint sweep of light that pans from the wall across the wardrobe across the foot of my bed. I tuck my teddy bear tighter under my arm. The rain drumming on the roof and splashing down the window makes me feel cozy. I burrow deeper under my feather comforter.

Our house is one of a long row of identical two story houses with steep tiled roofs. The outside walls are painted different colors: shades of gray, light green and cream. There are small patches of grass in front, bordered by low, trimmed hedges. Houses like this continue around the corner and line the several blocks I walk each day to St. Antonius Kindergarten. One day when we crossed Virchowstraße on the way to the playground, my mother explained that the streets are all named after scientists: Virchow, Siemens, Volta, and Nernst. I love knowing that someone thought hard about our street names. It tells me the world makes sense.

Until I was thirteen, I knew exactly who I was. A West German girl born to parents who were refugees from the East. I knew where I belonged. Krefeld, a small industrial city on the left bank of the Rhine, was the firm center of my universe, but it wasn't my only home. My mother and I spent long weeks with relatives in the East, behind the Iron Curtain, in the shadow side of History, whenever possible. Even divided, Germany was my country where I grew up rooted.

I can pinpoint the moment that fractured my life. On November 14, 1966, a week after my thirteenth birthday, I climbed the metal steps into my first airplane. We were moving to America. I was preoccupied trying to hide my nerves and excitement behind the blasé exterior I'd recently adopted in the belief that indifference bestowed an air of sophistication and maturity. Still, I couldn't help watching as the plane took off, the Rhineland dropped away, its looping river and wet meadows, its dense rows of apartment buildings receding into the past. The plane glided through the dense clouds and my view of home vanished under a white shroud.

Next to me, my mother checked her bag one more time. Had she stowed our passports properly? Satisfied, she sat up straight, and gnawed her lower lip. She caught my eye and pointed out the window. I brushed her off. Yes, I saw. Clouds. Even though the plane was nearly empty, I worried that everyone would know I had never flown before.

My father had already loosened his tie and unbuttoned his top shirt button. He suggested we spread out, each take our own row, so we could stretch and maybe even sleep on the flight to New York. He'd been shuttling back and forth between our home in Krefeld and Clemson, South Carolina where he'd been sent to be sales manager of his textile machinery company's American branch. When the owner's son offered him the job almost a year before, he tried to moderate his excitement. My father had fallen in love with America as a prisoner of war, when he picked apples in the mountains of Virginia. But he knew my mother, who still pined for her hometown in East Germany after seventeen years in Krefeld, would be a hard sell.

"Move to America? No. I don't want to be that far away from home," she said at first. She meant East Germany, of course. My father didn't give up - he never did when he had a plan - and my mother weakened under the assault of his intense desire. She agreed to give South Carolina a try when he promised we could reconsider after five years.

I thought moving to another country sounded glamorous. All around me, Europeans learned each other's languages and sent students on exchanges. The girls in the novels I read went to boarding schools in Switzerland or France and emerged worldly and multilingual. I'd learn perfect English, see the world, and return exotic. How could I have guessed that I would never really be able to come home?

My father's suggestion to sleep on the plane was ridiculous. He knew that neither my mother nor I could relax in a strange place heading toward an unknown future, even if he could sleep anywhere. I moved to a row toward the front and pulled out the book I had brought for the trip. The author (*Dostojewski*) and the title (*Schuld und Sühne* - Crime and Punishment) crossed the spine in gold letters. Inside the cover my grandfather's library label spelled out his initials, GS, and 'Eilenburg'.

The plain leather binding meant this was one of the books he had rebound after it was damaged in the American artillery attack that destroyed the house in '45. I chose this book, because I wanted to look grown up, ready for the world.

Soon I was absorbed, though irritated. Why couldn't this fellow Raskolnikov pull himself together? He was filthy and obsessed with an old lady, instead of cleaning himself up and looking for a job. Weren't people in control of their destinies?

The stewardess brought dinner. I delighted in the tray with its nestled porcelain dishes, the smaller than standard silverware. Everything fit perfectly into its allotted space. Of course, I tried to look like I ate on airplanes every day.

After the meal, I leaned back with my eyes closed, my head filled with images from the night before. Our steps echoed on the bare parquet in our apartment. Most of our furniture waited in Hamburg to be loaded onto a ship to Charleston. I could locate the missing pictures by the shadowy shapes they'd left on the walls. The parakeet cage on my room's marble windowsill was gone; we had to give Putzi away because we didn't think she'd survive the loneliness of six weeks in quarantine. My mother's best friend and her daughters came over for one last goodbye. Ulli and Bine, close to me in age, were my daily playmates. We would fight and make up and fight again. I was annoyed that hugging them made me cry. I was trying so hard to be brave.

Once the stewardess removed my tray, I flipped up the armrests and settled in with my feet up to read some more. I wished for a different book, one that didn't require so much concentration. Sometime during the flight, my eyes and brain worn out from roaming St. Petersburg with a madman, I thought about the future. *Amerika.* I pictured the oversized cars we occasionally saw in Germany - candy colored, dripping with chrome, sharp-finned, and way too big for any of our parking spots. My father had shown me a photo of his company car: a Chevrolet Impala, metallic green, no fins. He also tried to explain that South Carolina was not like the USA we saw on TV. No skyscrapers. No big cities. He brought back a Sears catalogue from one of his trips. I studied the huge book carefully, looking for clues. I came away confused. America was supposed to be rich, progressive, and the source of new ideas. Yet there were pages and pages of frumpy women's clothes - shirtwaists with Peter Pan collars and blouse and sweater sets with matching knee length skirts. The older girls at my school wore minis in geometric prints, the latest French and English styles.

An even gray light flooded in through the windows. I floated high above the Atlantic, unable to make out the future. Suspended.

Later, I would remember this night and picture myself afloat between lives. America would turn out to be deeply different from Europe in ways I would need years to understand. My adolescent worries couldn't scratch the surface. Living in another country would change me bit by bit without my consent. I was still malleable, young enough to be a chameleon, reflecting back the culture around me. And this unconscious adaptation - surely it was a survival reflex? - transformed me into a woman straining to bridge the rift between my German and American lives.

I tried to turn back, but I no longer fit and the home I longed for had vanished along with the child I had been. Instead of returning, I migrated North, then West, until I settled in Minnesota, in the heart of German immigrant country. For over thirty years, I tantalized myself with regular trips across the ocean, each time bruising my spirit anew. In my heart, I treasured that five-year-old self, snug in bed, at one with the world. I yearned to recover that feeling, but the more I strained to feel the warmth and hear the trickling rain, the more I knocked against the windowpane of memory. I was trapped a lifetime away, aching with longing. Where was home for me now?

THE KNOWN WORLD

Can I recreate the girl suspended between lives on that plane? Can I call up a sense of her lost home?

I have a photo taken the year I was born, in 1953. In it I may be invisible, but I take up a lot of space. My brand-new wicker pram, tarted up with white sidewalls, chrome fenders and a fat low-slung body, stars front and center. The curved hood, more useful in Krefeld for protection from rain in its multiple forms than from the occasional ray of sun, presents its back to the camera. My parents, Ingrid and Siegfried, face the photographer beaming as if they had won the grand prize in God's lottery. My mother's hands both wrap around the shiny handlebar, a move that forces her elbows to stick out. One arm rests against my father's suit coat. He stands a tad behind her, one foot forward, his hands clasped behind his back. Do they look German? They are dressed for Sunday, she in a summer dress with a white belt, he wearing a tie that angles off to one side. He is a few centimeters taller, and they are slender though they have lost the hungry look of the early post-war years. Their hair is abundant and close to black. Both of their brilliant smiles underline prominent noses. "A strong nose is a sign of character," we say in our family. Behind the happy couple with the baby carriage, I recognize the Rhine promenade in Ürdingen, a suburb of Krefeld and the site of many Sunday afternoon walks. A shady tree, a stretch of meadow, a low barge drifting along the broad water. The landscape of my childhood.

Other writers will tell you that a happy childhood is hardly worth your while, or that such a childhood is a myth constructed through self-delusion and denial. Are they speaking from envy? From the distance of America my German childhood glows with colors of bliss. Perhaps that's an instance of self-delusion? When I step back from the primal textures of memory, I'm astounded to realize that my parents were poor. Not grinding-no-hope poor, but refugee poor. They lived in one room with a two-burner stove and a curtain to hide the sofa bed. I never understood how small this space was until I had a daughter of my own. As my mother and I sat in my Minnesota living room watching little Sophie scoot across the carpet on hands and knees, my mother said, "You never did that."

"Never did what?"

"Crawl. You never crawled."

I had just finished reading a parenting book that claimed crawling was crucial for brain development. How could I not have crawled?

"There wasn't room. You went straight from sitting to walking."

That explained the baby pictures. I was the fattest one-year-old imaginable. Instead of a double chin and a fold of fat on my thighs, every layer of my baby fat came in triples. I never suspected the problem was lack of space. It took until I was three to wear off the extra padding. After that I looked normal. People even thought I was skinny because I had a narrow face that was dominated by dark eyes inherited from my mother.

As my father's fortunes improved, we traded our single room for the second floor and attic of a small row house. In 1950s Germany, women who lived on the ground floor of any building had sidewalk duty. Usually, they started by mopping the floors inside. Then they carried their buckets out. First they swept the sidewalk clean of branches, leaves and cigarette butts. Then they poured their wash-water out over the paving stones and scrubbed them with a brush. My mother must have been thrilled that we'd be living upstairs. We spread out into two rooms and a kitchen on the second floor, plus another small room and the bathroom tucked under the eaves. That apartment is the site of my early memories.

I am five years old, lying in my room with my teddy bear tucked under my arm, wide-awake. I'm buried up to my nose under my feather comforter because it's cold up here in the attic. It's only warm on Saturdays when my father carries a metal bucket filled with coal briquettes up from the basement and stacks them in the bathroom water heater. He starts the fire in the afternoon, so we can have a bath before dinner, but the warmth lingers until bedtime.

I picture my parents downstairs, in the pool of lamplight, my father propped on the couch, my mother upright in the new easy chair, each lost in a book. I see them like this when I come downstairs to tell them I can't sleep. Children my age are supposed to go to bed at eight o'clock and get 11 hours of sleep. That's impossible for me, because my brain doesn't know how to stop and I rarely get tired.

When my parents go to the movies, I'm allowed to sleep in their bedroom, in the vastness of their double bed, so Frau Jakobs, who owns the house and lives downstairs can hear me if I need help. I've never called her, but I know all I have to do is knock on the floor. I like being left alone. It makes me feel grown up. When my parents come back, my father carries me up the stairs to my own bed, and my mother leaves a treat for me on my nightstand. Sometimes it's burnt almonds; sometimes it's non-pareils. I will be allowed to eat a handful during *Kaffeeklatsch* or for dessert after dinner. My mother is very strict about candy, so I wish they'd go out more often.

But most nights, I lie in my own bed, biding my time. I remember my day, make up stories, sing songs, and listen for sounds from outside. Sometimes, I hear people out on the street, coming home, singing or talking, but the trees and the frequent rain muffle their voices.

Maybe in the morning my parents will send me across the street to the store to buy them cigarettes. I clutch the coins they hand me and check twice in both directions before crossing. When I open the narrow door, a bell jangles. Frau Callefice comes in from her kitchen, drying her hands, and asks what I want. She remembers my name, but I'm a little scared of her, because her voice is deep as a man's and she has a mustache. She's a Krefeld native, not a refugee like us, so I have to strain a little to understand her dialect. She hands me the pack of cigarettes, then throws in a bonbon, with a reminder to ask my mother if it's ok before I eat it.

I remember the night before the Callefice girl got married my parents didn't even try to put me to bed. It was the young couple's *Polterabend* - a rowdy evening with peculiar traditions. My father held me up to my window so I could watch their friends arrive for the party and break old plates and chipped crockery on the doorstep. "*Scherben bringen Glück*" - shards bring luck - they yelled. Inside the lit doorway, the bride and groom watched, wine glasses in their hands, dancing and shouting swirling behind. The destruction bothered me. Why break things on purpose? My father assured me that they were only breaking dishes too old and chipped to be of use. We watched until Frau Callefice appeared with a big broom and began scraping the shards into a metal dustpan and dumping them into a bucket.

I snuggle into my pillow and think about the other errand I'm allowed to perform: picking up hard rolls at the bakery. The bakery sits on the corner and has huge plate glass windows on both sides. I love the light that streams into the room and bathes the rolls so they glow. Sometimes, the baker or his wife gives me a small pastry. I liked to come here, until my mother bought me a pair of *Lederhosen* on a vacation in Bavaria. She thinks I look cute in them, and she had me convinced it's fun to wear pants, until she sent me to the bakery in them. The baker joked that my name must now be Klaus instead of Claudia. I told him no, and he teased me. He would not give up. From then on, even when I was wearing the skirt my grandmother knitted for me, he greeted me with "Here comes Klaus." I told my mother I no longer liked my *Lederhosen*, and I didn't want to pick up rolls at the bakery anymore. When she realized my real reason, she promised she'd only send me in the afternoon when the baker's wife minds the store and the baker takes his nap. I always check to make sure I can see it's her, before I open the door.

Finally, sleep comes within reach. I trace the outlines of the horse chestnut shadow with my eyes, whisper the words to my favorite lullaby one more time: *Die Blümelein sie schlafen schon längst im Mondenschein* - the flowers are already asleep in the moonshine, and drift off clutching the bear, secure in my ignorance of the future.

*****

I adored my father. Later, in South Carolina, when I wanted to despise him for ripping me from my home, echoes of my early adulation muddied my passion. How could I hate the center of my childhood universe? Even though he traveled for work and was often gone for weeks at a time, our lives revolved around him. When my father was home, we acted like the textbook German family. Meals and bedtimes were punctual. On workdays, we ate breakfast together. Afterwards, my father and I both put on our shoes and rain gear. He left on his bicycle in the direction of town, and I walked the other way to meet my friend Birgit so we could hold hands on the way to *Kindergarten*. My mother nudged the living room curtain aside to watch us go. She'd spend the morning straightening the apartment and then walk into town to buy the day's food. We had a refrigerator just big enough to hold two glass milk bottles, a pound of green beans, some cold cuts, a piece of cheese, and if things were stacked just right, a one pound Sunday roast. She had to shop every day. Of course I never wondered whether she got bored. Like every coddled child, I assumed she loved her life because I was satisfied.

When I returned at noon, the house was tidy and my mother stirred pots in the kitchen. I climbed down the stairs shortly before one and waited on the front steps until I saw my father coming, his bicycle appearing and disappearing between the horse chestnut trunks, his hat bobbing slightly, his raincoat tails fluttering behind. As he got closer his face with the brilliant blue eyes and delighted smile came into focus. When he spotted me, he lit up. Once he arrived a few meters away, he swung his right leg over the crossbar, coasted to a stop, and flipped down the bike stand. He bent down and hoisted me up level with his face. I wrapped my arms around his neck and inhaled the scent of shaving soap, before he let me slide back down.

Inside, we walked through Frau Jakobs' foyer and then up the dark stairway sniffing and trying to guess at dinner. The smell of boiling potatoes was constant. In summer we might detect cucumber salad and scrambled eggs, in winter sweet and sour lung hash or fried eggs and cabbage. The kitchen was tiny, with a door facing the top of the stairs. My mother knew we were coming. She watched for my father out the window, so she could have dinner on the table, cooling to just the right temperature as soon as he walked in. She clattered in the kitchen, filling pots with water to soak, calling out to my father over her shoulder: "Did your meeting go all right?" She slipped off her apron and waited at the top of the stairs. My father described his morning, but interrupted himself as he reached the landing and kissed her cheek.

They continued to talk about my father's work as we settled into chairs and filled our plates. His sales territory was the Far East, so I heard stories about India and Pakistan, Bombay and Karachi. When he traveled he carried his camera, so I had images to go with the words. A donkey hitched to a mill, wearing circles into a dusty track. My father smiling from the hump of a camel, snake charmers with bulbous flutes facing cobras rising from wicker baskets. More mysterious were words like "calender" and "dyeing range," words I couldn't connect with images. In my twenties, when I was a university student majoring in Textile Chemistry I nearly swooned with recognition on a tour of my first Finishing Plant. Huge rollers conveyed lengths of fabric through dye baths and rinses, and more rollers ironed them flat. But as a child I just accepted that these were big pieces of equipment my father sold, and enjoyed the stories of his dramatic negotiations with customers who tried to outwit him with tales of lower prices from competitors.

Once my father's topics sank to the table exhausted, the conversation shifted to my mother's and my concerns. I recited newly learned scraps of poetry, and delivered the latest *Kindergarten* news. My mother talked about what's on sale, what we could afford, what she planned to do in the afternoon. As she and I cleared the table, my father napped on the sofa. After twenty minutes, my mother sent me to wake

him, which I did with a sloppy kiss. I waved goodbye from the front
door as his bicycle receded.

On weekday afternoons, my mother bustled around cleaning. On
Mondays, wet clothes piled up in a wicker basket, the big pot in the
kitchen boiled with cotton underwear. The smell of simmering soap
filled the rooms. Tuesdays, she ironed my father's shirts and pulled the
stiff underwear back into shape as she folded. I helped with the sheets
and towels. Wednesday and Thursday meant shopping and sewing.
Fridays, buckets of sudsy water lined the hallway, and the afternoon
crackled with scrubbing and polishing to get ready for the weekend.

The shopping, the cleaning, the sewing - especially the sewing -
had to be finished before my father came home. I bristled at the thought
of having to drop everything for a man, even if he was my beloved
father. When I asked my mother why she couldn't finish a hem just
because of his return she blamed it on his mother. Omi Hedwig was a
master seamstress. My father had to compete with threads and patterns
for her attention, even in the evenings. Omi Hedwig had to make money,
because Opa Willy didn't earn enough to support his growing family. A
huge family, by German standards. By the time my father's youngest
sister arrived during the war, my father had five siblings! I never could
make sense of it. Even three children appeared reckless to me. My
mother never exactly said she thought her in-laws were irresponsible, but
she wondered out loud why they kept having babies. My father kept
silent on that topic, but he dreamed of a mother who had nothing on her
mind but her family. My mother chased through the afternoons, busy,
rushing to get everything back in its place before six thirty.

At five o'clock though, we took a break. My mother settled us at
the table, a cup of coffee for her, some cocoa for me, and a plate with a
few cookies to share. Sometimes she read to me, or showed me how to
crochet. Sometimes I drew while she tried to sneak in a few pages of the
book she was reading. I preferred to have her attention. We ended our
Kaffeeklatsch reluctantly - she moved to finish up the work of the day, I
either helped or returned to my solitary play.

At seven, after my father returned, my mother had one more task
to accomplish. She arranged cold cuts and cheese on plates, sliced bread
and layered it into the breadbasket. She billowed the white tablecloth
above the table and let it settle squarely. In winter, she cooked a pot of
black tea and filled a crystal pitcher with rum. In summer, she polished
my father's beer glass and set the dark brown bottle on the table.

Bedtime arrived soon after supper. My father carried me into the
kitchen and plopped me down on the counter next to the sink. I pulled
off my shirt. With a washcloth, he rubbed my arms and belly, then my

neck, all the while hunting for dirt. I hated having my ears washed, so he tugged and tickled and told tales in a sing-songy voice about ear monsters and children who grew trees in their ears, because they never let their parents wash in there. He dried me off with a towel, scrubbing and teasing, then pulled my nightgown over my head. Then he flipped me upside down, boosted me into the air, so my feet walked on the ceiling all the way to the attic stairs. My mother intercepted us to give me a goodnight kiss, and we climbed up to my room. He put me down and I bounced into bed, tucking teddy in next to me. I gurgled with laughter until he shushed me with a lullaby. Then he kissed me goodnight and turned to go. I reminded him to leave the door ajar and the hall light on. He did, even though I knew how much he hated to waste electricity.

Sunday afternoons we went on outings or visited with friends. My father wore a suit with a white shirt and tie, my mother and I put on our best dresses. If we were invited for 'coffee,' we stopped first at the railroad station - the only place stores were allowed to open on Sunday - and bought flowers. Then we rode the streetcar to our destination. Birgit and the other native Krefelders spent Sundays with cousins and grandparents. My parents had cobbled together a group of friends their age who had also fled the East.

Every month or two, my father packed his suitcase full of white shirts and clean underwear and disappeared into a chauffeured company car. We waved from the sidewalk, then retreated into our all female house.

The rules sagged and time shifted. I arrived home from *Kindergarten* to find my mother tackling a big project like taking down curtains to wash, bubbling with the prospect of uninterrupted activity. She greeted me with: "What do you feel like eating for dinner?" I liked soup, which my father didn't count as real food, and I liked the square bread my mother bought when we were alone. It reminded my father of army rations; he wouldn't touch it. Or maybe we could have fried leftover dumpling slices? Pudding Soup? In the summer she'd even let me eat a big bowl of grated carrots with sugar on top, or sliced bananas with *Quark,* a soured fresh cheese I loved. We ate whenever she finished detaching the curtains.

After our meal, we dawdled. We folded paper hats, or drew bunnies behind a forest of tulips. Then my mother worked on a new dress for me. I wanted the dress, but I hated trying it on. I shrank inside the stiff fabric, trying to avoid the pins. Even when they didn't stick me, they pierced me with cold. I turned this way and that on the footstool, so she could adjust the fit. She accidentally fastened the dress to my undershirt while trying to adjust darts. When she lifted the hem and pulled up while I extended my arms, my undershirt peeled off and dangled from the new dress.

Once she started sewing, she forgot me, more or less. I fetched my can of beads and settled in, on the floor, next to her. Every few beads, I licked the string to ease it through the holes. Slowly, the light faded. My mother switched on the lamp. "I'm hungry, " I said. "When can we have dinner?" She roused herself out of her concentration and led me into the kitchen. We roamed through the refrigerator, stacking wrapped cold cuts and cheese on the board. Then she sliced bread. One for me, two for her. She scraped a thin coat of butter over the dark sourdough, then had me select. Swiss on one half, liverwurst on the other. She cut my bread into bite-size pieces, arranged it on a wooden board, then fixed her own. We carried our sandwich boards back into the living room and ate, the sewing piled on one end of the table.

Afterwards, I returned the boards to the kitchen while she picked up her sewing. If I played very quietly, she sometimes forgot the time, and I could stay up a half hour longer. Then she washed me very fast and tried to hurry me up to bed.

Some of my father's trips lasted six weeks or even eight. Our arrangements wore on us then. My mother tired of having only me to talk to, and I missed my evening games and Sunday outings. She took me to the park or zoo on Sunday afternoon, but she couldn't make silly rhymes and she wouldn't run to catch me. Worse, she shrieked with worry when I climbed a tree or leaned too far over a bridge railing.

For the few days before my father returned, we led a frenzied life. Everything had to get finished. The new dresses, hers and mine, needed to be hemmed and ironed. The curtains were back on the rods, the floors gleamed, and the bathroom shone down to the corners. We shopped for special food - fried herrings or smoked mackerel - and planned what we'd wear to the airport.

The afternoon of his arrival, I had to nap, since going to the airport would push me way past bedtime. I fidgeted on my bed, singing and talking. Finally, just as dusk spread into the corners of my room, my mother appeared in the doorway with permission to get up. I pulled on my new dress, turned to let her zip it, and followed her downstairs. I watched her finish dressing and even got a dab of perfume on my wrist. We put on our raincoats, rushed down the steps and waited behind the front door until the company chauffeur honked outside.

At the airport, I dragged my mother toward the bright doors, into the hall that pulsed with fluorescent lights. We stopped at the barricade. Beyond, customs officers waited behind wooden tables, pacing and chatting with each other. I climbed on the barricade, but my mother's hand grabbed the back of my dress as she hissed for me to keep my feet on the floor. The doors on the other side of the hall opened and a mixture of German men in crumpled white shirts, Indian men in Western dress, and women wrapped in brilliant saris flooded the tables. For a moment I stared at the blood red drops on the women's foreheads, but then I remembered why I was here. I searched the faces until I spotted my father. He looked worn, his shirt wrinkled and his hair sticking up in the back. His tie hung askew a little below his neck and he carried his raincoat slung over the arm that held his briefcase. His suitcase weighed down his other hand. I waved, throwing my whole body into the motion, like an ecstatic dog. It worked. His eyes brightened and he straightened as if he'd had an infusion of energy. He exchanged a few words with the uniformed man at the table and strode toward the exit, toward us. He put down his suitcase at the same time I jumped. I felt myself flying as he lifted me with one quick motion. Then my mother's arms wrapped around both of us, and his attention shifted as he kissed her hello. All the way back to Krefeld, we chattered without pause.

At home, I badgered him to unpack his suitcase. He fished presents from between shirts and socks. A gauzy black scarf edged with a procession of gold elephants, its center sprinkled with more elephants like fat stars, went to my mother. I got a leather drawstring purse, decorated with green, red and yellow camels, elephants, and goats. An exotic odor lingered inside. I giggled for no good reason, and jumped up and down in my father's lap.

After a snack of his favorite foods, he picked me up and said, "You're too tired to even wash, we'll just go straight to bed." I protested, but before I picked up steam he settled me on his shoulders. "Watch out for your head!" he shouted, as he bounced up the steps. I giggled again, and trailed my hand across the ceiling. The bed was soft and cozy, and I knew just how tomorrow would go.

If anyone had told me then that soon after our move I would be furious at my father - deeply angry, not the kind of passing passion that erupted when he sent me to my room for a fib - I would have tapped my head to say you're crazy.

*****

Nobody told me I was lucky to be born well after the war. I knew it, the way I knew my eyes were brown. The evidence surrounded me. On Sunday afternoons, when my parents gathered for coffee with their refugee friends, their talk drifted to stories of hunger and cold, stories of ingenuity and survival. My father recalled patching and repatching a worn bike tire on the 10 km ride to his uncle's farm, just so he could work for the day and be paid with a place at the farm's dinner table. "It was worth it. I was full for the first time in months."

As the adults dug into butter cream torte and piled whipped cream on fruit tarts, they looked into the middle distance, and said, "Remember fake whipped cream made from wheat kernels? Or sprinkling a bit of salt on a piece of rye bread? My mother used to say 'Close your eyes and pretend it's liverwurst.' Or how we baked a simple flour and sugar cake on Sunday, and that was all we had for the day? We'd spend most of the day in bed, we were so weak."

I listened; the butter cream heavy in my mouth. After everyone had finished prodigious portions - West Germans spent the late fifties and early sixties gorging themselves to compensate for the hunger years - the talk turned to bombing raids and coal shortages. Sometimes I stayed, fascinated, the way I indulged in the grimmest fairytales to see whether I could take it. But more often, I sneaked off with the other children to play.

Even as a young child, I needed to know more. I wanted to believe the war had been so terrible that nothing like it could ever happen again. But what if it did?

I saved my worries for late afternoons, during *Kaffeeklatsch* time. My mother was beautiful when she relaxed. Then the deep furrows between her dark eyebrows smoothed out and her intense brown eyes sparkled. A gold tooth glinted at the edge of her laughing mouth. Her dimples appeared. Even her tightly permed hair let loose at those times and sent a strand or two straggling onto her forehead. When I saw the light in her eyes, I begged her to tell me stories about *früher* - earlier. What I wanted to know was how a child survived a war. I wanted to know exactly what to do if this happened again.

I had trouble grasping how much of my mother's childhood the war occupied. At first, there were signs of what was coming: a Jewish girl in her class leaving to emigrate, for reasons my mother hadn't really understood, and I didn't either. I didn't even know what a Jew was. I'd never heard the word mentioned before. My mother tried to explain that Jews had a different religion, and that the Nazis hated them and tried to kill them. Why would religion matter that much? She didn't know either. I tried another tack to get at this mystery. "But how could they tell who was Jewish?"

My mother stumbled over that one. "Well, they could tell by looking at people," she tried.

"But how?" I asked. She told me I would understand better when I got older. That, of course, infuriated me. I was certainly smart enough to understand, if someone would only tell me all the details.

My mother's stories couldn't really explain the full horror of recent history. That had to wait until I was ten. German television produced a documentary of the Third Reich that year - an exhaustive show that ran in many segments on Sunday afternoons. My father insisted I watch it with him. The first Sunday, I remember he perched at the edge of the couch, absorbed in a film clip of that insane gnome called Hitler shrieking one of his speeches. As the screen cut to show thousands saluting, my father mumbled to himself, "How could we have been taken in by this?" The way my father sagged, all confidence drained out of him, his eyes moist - I couldn't bear to see him like this. I tried to leave the room, but he stopped me.

"This is important. You need to know." It sounded more like a plea than an order. I forced myself to return to the couch. I thought Hitler and the Nazis looked too ridiculous to take seriously, but the series progressed through *Kristallnacht* and streams of bombs and burning cities. I cringed more and more. How could people be so cruel and stupid? And then, the liberation of the concentration camps. I wanted to look away, but I could not. Has anyone ever been prepared?

Afterwards, I emerged into the bright sunshine of the early sixties shaken to the core. I knew we were skating on a thin layer of civilization that could crack anytime and dump us back into chaos. As long as I lived in Germany, I could regard Hitler and his war as a human problem, a calamity that held a universal warning. I wouldn't be forced to wrestle with the question whether Nazism grew out of a German cultural character flaw until much later.

My experience with life in East Germany - I couldn't have described it as totalitarianism then - colored my understanding of life in Nazi Germany. On every trip, I experienced social control and fear. I did not expect stories of heroic resistance. I knew that would only land you in jail. I learned that my grandparents had opposed the Nazis – my mother had told me how my grandfather, Opa Gustav, had been arrested and my grandparents' apartment had been ransacked because Opa Gustav wouldn't stop having his daily beer with a friend who was Jewish. What a relief to know my beloved grandfather had tried to do the right thing. I didn't think to ask what happened after the Nazis released him.

My father's story wasn't quite so simple, though he had the excuse of youth, and had seen the error of his ways just in time. His family avoided politics, and his mother had tried to stop him when he'd been accepted to a Nazi boarding school for aspiring pilots at 15. He burned with ambition. Only the best and brightest and physically perfect could aspire to fly. He pleaded with his mother until she gave in. (He never achieved his dream. A few years later, air force doctors noticed a glaring physical defect: his little toes grow on top of his foot. Those toes saved my father's life. The death rate for German pilots nudged close to a hundred percent.) Close to graduation, an SS recruiter called on him. My father missed the visit - he'd gone into town, probably looking for girls. One of his lucky days, my father said. Then, he acted on a hunch - his revulsion based on nothing more than rumors. He dashed back into town the next morning and signed up with the regular German army. When the man from the SS returned, he could honestly tell him, "Too late."

Instead of having to come to terms with enthusiastic Nazis in my immediate family, my legacy was more complex. I grew up wondering how much resistance I could muster in case of a government run amok. From the way I quaked when we had to register with the East German police, I suspected passive resistance would be the best I could manage. Would I even be able to scoot along the margins of resistance, the way my grandfather had?

That children went to school during the war surprised me. My mother was 10 when Hitler invaded Poland and 17 when it was over. That was too long a stretch for me to imagine. I pictured war as one continuous battle, with streams of bombs dropping from the sky, so you'd have to dodge them on the pavement. But no, my mother said, especially at the beginning, life didn't change very much for her. Some of the male teachers left and some of her friends' fathers, food was rationed, but she and her schoolmates still had Latin and Writing. They had to join the BDM (the female branch of the Hitler Youth). They had to participate in summer work brigades - farm work - and in the winter they learned crafts and folksongs. Not much different from the Young Pioneers in their blue neck kerchiefs that we saw all over East Germany.

Later in the war, their life did change. Whenever the air raid sirens sounded, they scrambled for the basement. They camped out down there, among the winter potatoes and the coal bins, for hours, doing homework, trying to sleep. As the war progressed, the basement became more and more crowded. First, some Soviet deportees moved in while they worked at my grandfather's factory. Opa Gustav owned a jewelry case manufacturing business, the factory building connected to the apartment house the family owned. He knew conditions at the workers' camps were dismal, so he'd insisted the workers be quartered at his house. Later there were refugees from parts of Germany that were occupied by the advancing Allies. Most of the time, the "all clear" finally sounded and everyone went upstairs and climbed into cold beds for whatever snatch of sleep they might catch.

One night in April 1945, when the Americans shelled the town with artillery, the house took a serious hit. A mortar shell crashed through the roof and the floors of three levels, setting the house on fire. Only the basement ceiling held. Everyone had to climb out through the basement window to the street. My great-grandmother, who was fat even during the war, got stuck in the window. Half the family clamored in the basement, the fire brigade poured water toward the flaming house, and Opa Gustav crouched on the street pulling on his mother. His brother pushed from inside. All my mother could remember was this moment of panic. She couldn't recall how they got her great-grandmother out, but she guessed they finally just pushed and pulled hard enough. Once the fire died, they sifted through the wreckage. All the china and crystal, all the dining room furniture was gone. Yet the bedroom set from the next room remained intact except for the glass in the wardrobe's doors. That had shattered with the impact. Now I knew why my grandparents' massive wardrobe had milky yellow plastic in its carved walnut doors.

"Was Omi upset about loosing her crystal and china?" I asked.

"Oh, no. She said she'd never liked that fancy stuff anyway. And besides, we were all alive." She did add that later, during the hunger years following the war, Paula wished she'd had the foresight to stow her valuables in the basement so she could have bartered them for food on the black market.

The summer of '45, the whole family camped out in the rooms that were untouched. During the day, the girls used hammers to knock mortar off the bricks they'd salvaged from the rubble. By the end of the year, Opa Gustav had arranged to rebuild the house.

The stories about war did nothing to make me feel confident that I could handle such a catastrophe. They left me certain that you needed luck to survive. But luck I already had. I was alive now, after the war, in a time when the world had just learned a lesson it could never forget. Nationalism had been exposed as a curse. Everyone had learned war brought no glory, only misery. I hoped that would be enough.

The past, which cast such deep shadows, only intensified my sense of privilege. What a thrill to have escaped, just barely. And what a gift to grow up armed with the knowledge that chaos and evil lurk in the world without having to endure it myself. In the fall-out after the War I'd even managed to end up on the right side of the Iron Curtain.

What else could I call it but luck?

*****

    I lived in a time of optimism, a world of progress and change. West Germany in the fifties simmered with the energy of transformation, even as the ashes of war remained visible. The neighborhood around Siemensstrasse had miraculously escaped the heavy bombing that had ravaged Krefeld's downtown, but every time my mother and I went shopping, we passed a rubble field and a massive air raid shelter. Twisted iron bars studded the hulking concrete shell. Streaks of rust stained the walls; I imagined they were tears. Would I have quaked, huddling inside, listening for the approaching whine of airplanes?
    On the other side of the street, the rows of apartment houses remained gap-toothed. Only the first story lingered in several cases – the windows bricked up for safety. The neighboring buildings, oddly untouched, rose up like monuments to what had been destroyed. Broken bricks traced the outlines of old rooms and remnants of wallpaper turned the wall into a checkerboard. I used to try to guess which room had belonged to a kitchen, which one to a bedroom. The trick was to shut off my thoughts before wondering what had happened to the people.
    But once we reached the station, we entered the construction zone. We had arrived at Krefeld's most elegant shopping street, the Ostwall - a broad strip of park separated its two lanes. Rows of brand new stucco boxes lined one side. The other side appeared quite presentable as well, as long as you didn't look up. Bombs had blasted away the upper stories of many buildings, but at the base a sound masonry frame remained. When the owners rebuilt, they had little money, so they started by clearing the rubble and fixing up the first floors to restart their businesses. At street level the stores looked up-to-the-minute modern with their plate glass and fresh signs, but if your eyes strayed you found the rest of the building either altogether missing, or partially crumbled. The ratatat of jackhammers echoed in the street. You could never just walk down the sidewalk. There was always an obstacle - the characteristic plywood walls that proclaimed a construction site. Sometimes the plywood formed a tunnel and I had to follow my mother single-file, sometimes the sidewalk disappeared altogether, so we had to cross the street. Because of the frenzied reconstruction, I believed constant improvement was the way of the world.
    Despite the plywood and noise, shopping with my mother brimmed with sensual pleasures. The Ostwall's flowerbeds bloomed with intense colors most of the year. Sidewalk restaurants planted fields

of bright umbrellas for their customers. For a snack I begged for a cone from Fontanella's Italian ice-cream parlor or for a raisin bun from one of the many bakeries. Outside the *Kaufhof* - the newly rebuilt department store - I wanted to stop at the tables piled with sale merchandise. I also loved to listen to the men with auctioneer voices who demonstrated kitchen gadgets to gathering crowds of shoppers. My mother didn't have much patience for their spiels. "It's all junk we don't need," she'd say as she pulled me away to lead me to the outdoor market. There, farmwomen in kerchiefs sold mountains of fresh fruits and vegetables. Sprinkled in between the farm stands, bakers and butchers offered their wares. Sometimes, they cut samples and tucked them into my hand. I especially prized pale pink slices of *Jagdwurst* - a mild cold cut that looked like bologna except for the embedded jewels of rich organ meats. I knew how to prolong the pleasure of taste by letting small bites rest on my tongue. We returned home from our shopping trips, our string bag bulging with produce, our feet pleasantly tired.

Every year brought less rubble and newer, shinier buildings. I took it for granted that the damage gradually disappeared. By the mid-sixties, the rubble lots had vanished and the city's architects dreamed even bigger. They tore down the city theater, built in haste after the war, and merely serviceable, and replaced it with a bold design. I thought its copper roof and tinted glass façade the epitome of modern architecture.

Like the city, our family made progress. When I was five or so, before we moved from the old apartment to a newer, larger one across town, my mother and I bought very little beyond necessities on these shopping trips. We mostly window-shopped. My mother studied the designs at Krapohl's exclusive children's shop so she could duplicate them with a pattern from Simplicity and a remnant from the small fabric store near the market. She knew which bakery's raisin buns were cheapest, and if she did buy me a cone at Fontanella, it contained only whipped cream. Soon after we moved, my father was promoted to Sales Manager for his company's textile division. My mother still liked to sew, but she splurged on high quality fabric now. We bought cones with two scoops. I preferred hazelnut and lemon. Our shopping expanded to include occasional indulgences, like a tiara from Woolworth's for my *Karneval* costume, or a slice of fresh coconut from a market stall.

Our new apartment lay at the edge of the city, near cabbage and rye fields. A shepherd drove his flock down the middle of our street every morning and evening, so his sheep could spend the day grazing on the stubble at the edge of our apartment complex. Some mornings, we heard the clip-clop of horses drawing farm carts past our kitchen window. But the high-rise office building with its swooping concrete entrance just across the street was another sign of progress. By the time we left for the US, the shepherd had retired and the open fields had transformed into large blocks of subsidized housing all the way to the edge of the British military barracks a half-mile away.

We rarely saw any sign of our British occupiers. When I rode the bus to school, we passed the tall brick walls that surrounded the compound and could make out only rows of roofs. Once in a while, an officer's wife would get on the bus, clutching the hand of a timid child. They'd pay without a word, and stand on the bus, looking out the window, silent. I wondered at their odd clothes - the girls always seemed to wear pink hats - and why they looked so uncomfortable, but decided it was probably because they rarely came out from behind their walls, so they must be nervous about getting lost. I knew it wasn't the British we had to thank for our rise from the rubble, even if we were in the British zone. My mother often said we needed to thank the Americans and something called the "Marshall Plan." I didn't know until later what that was, but I was grateful that I lived in a place that got better every day. Especially since I knew what a narrow escape I'd had.

*****

How did I get so lucky? I lived in the West, but I didn't long for home like a refugee. After all, I'd been born in Krefeld. East Germany, once we got past the border and tucked into relatives' homes, was a nice place to visit, but I shuddered at the thought of growing up there. Only one other member of our family had escaped to the West, my father's sister Nanne. She lived in southern Germany with her family. Whenever I got together with my West German cousin Ulrike, I felt like we shared a delicious secret.

Yet, my mother's longing for home was a palpable presence. *Zu Hause* - back home - was the first word in many of her sentences. Like every lost home, *zu Hause* was better in every way. The people were warm and honest instead of cold and manipulative like the Rhinelanders. The bread tasted earthier, the cold cuts were spicier, and most of all *zu Hause* my grandparents would be there to lend emotional and financial support. The weather was drier *zu Hause*. This was indisputable. In Krefeld you could count on using your umbrella most days of the year.

There was just one problem. *Zu Hause* was shut away behind the border, made uninhabitable by the communists who were 'puppets' of the Russians. When my mother received a letter from *zu Hause*, she held it up to the light to show me the telltale signs that proved the letter had been steamed open and read by 'them.' Sometimes, the letter itself referenced an enclosed piece of paper money that was absent. A few years after East Germany collapsed curiosity compelled me to visit the *Stasi* museum in Leipzig. The *Stasi* was the East German secret police. I was amazed to find a room devoted to machines that steamed open, copied and resealed letters. According to the display, *Stasi* personnel read and archived copies of 15% of all mail sent to and from West Germany every year. Underneath my astonishment at this waste of resources, I detected a glimmer of relief. We hadn't been paranoid.

My mother and I visited East Germany often, my father never. From the time I could ask questions, I knew that my father had gotten in trouble with the Russians before he fled, and feared the East German police would arrest him if he returned. Yet my father spoke of his home as Gera, not *zu Hause*. The only time I ever spied the look of longing on his face was when a butcher from Gera set up shop a few blocks away and began to make and sell *Rostbratwürste* - char grilled Bratwurst - on Saturdays. Then my father and I would stand in line, inhaling the spicy smoke. While we waited, he reminisced. How many *Rostbratwürste* he once ate when he was twelve, how much he had longed for them during and after the war. When we reached the head of the line and he bit into his crispy brown sausage, he briefly closed his eyes. A bit of juice dripped on his chin. Ah, yes, this tasted like the sausages of memory.

Maybe it was my mother's frequent trips home that kept alive her longing. Or maybe it was that my father's life was more engaging. He was working, his career was going places, and he traveled the world. Meanwhile my mother was at home with just one child and a limited social life. Then again, my mother and father were very different. He woke up every day expecting the best to happen. My mother made mental lists of everything that could go wrong.

I knew my mother would never have fled East Germany on her own. My father held the key to my escape. I asked to hear how my parents met. Since my grandfather owned a business and was therefore considered a capitalist, the communist government wouldn't allow my mother to go to university, especially to study something as unnecessary as Art History, her heart's desire. She applied to a Craft Institute to train as a weaver, but was rejected and offered a spot at the Textile School in Greiz instead. In East Germany in 1946, you had to take what the state offered you. My father had returned from being a US prisoner of war at an awkward time and couldn't get admitted to study Law. The East German planners assigned him to study Textile Engineering. My mother usually chuckled at this point in the story, because we both knew that my father was clumsy with mechanical objects. The state threw them together and they fell in love.

Because they met in the late forties most of the stories of their romance revolved around schemes to acquire food, special treats my mother brought back from visits home, special occasions when for once they had enough potatoes to throw a party. I sometimes paged through an old photo album with pictures they had taken of each other back then and stared at my father's protruding cheekbones and the way my mother's dresses hung off her shoulders. Yet I could see from the light in their eyes that they burned with happiness.

Even the drama of my father's arrest hinged on how little food they had. One of the students in their circle of friends acquired two bottles of cognac on the black market and brought it to a party. My father and three of his friends downed the cognac, and partly because of their empty stomachs, the unaccustomed alcohol went straight to everyone's head. Stumbling home that night, my father and several of his friends passed a campaign poster for the first post-war election. Even then, the nature of elections in East Germany was growing clear. The outcome was predetermined, the election mere window-dressing. My father grabbed a poster by its dog-eared corner and ripped it off the wall. Police materialized out of the darkness, arrested him and turned him over to the Russian authorities.

They kept him in jail for ten days trying to get him to admit to being part of an anti-government conspiracy and then released him on probation. My mother came to the jail every day to check on him.

"Weren't you scared they'd arrest you too?" I asked.

"Of course, I was scared," my mother said. I couldn't imagine her acting so fearless.

After his release, my father's probation officer, a pretty blonde woman from the Ukraine, pressured him to spy on his fellow students. My father had a vision of his future: a lifetime of informing on his friends. He knew he had to leave.

Opa Gustav had contacts in Krefeld, because that's where he ordered his velvet and silk before the war. He made some inquiries to assure that my father could continue his studies at the textile school there. My father escaped by sneaking into West Berlin on the subway and investing half of his life savings in a plane ticket to the Western Zone. My mother never had any doubts that she would follow. As she was packing her suitcase, she couldn't understand why Omi Paula hovered around her, crying. "I told her to stop it. It was getting on my nerves. I guess I didn't really think about what I was doing." My mother looked surprised at her own ignorance. She had left home without a backward glance. Following my father. Just like I would.

*****

The Cold War slithered at the edges of my childhood paradise. As far as I could tell as a child, happiness lay secure inside my family. Danger and misery threatened from outside. Almost nightly, the TV news anchor's voice snapped out the words *"der kalte Krieg"* as he blamed the Cold War for some new escalation in inter-German tension. I hoped no bombs would drop, though my mother did lay in a supply of canned and dried foods during the Cuban missile crisis. But I knew we would pay. The East German government had chicanery down to a fine art form. Were West Germans getting so well off that they could afford to send cast-off clothing to their East German relatives? Force them to have the clothes disinfected and certified. That way we could feel insulted and inconvenienced at the same time. Was East German currency worthless on the world market? Force the West Germans who insisted on visiting their relatives to buy a minimum amount of East German money per day, at the official exchange rate that pretended the two marks remained equal. What choice did we have?

The East German border guards - usually rude, always intimidating - escalated their harassment whenever international tensions notched up. I don't remember my first border crossing, I'm told I was six weeks old, but I must have experienced that terrifying ritual close to fifty times before East Germany fell. I carry layers of border crossings tattooed on my neurons. Until I was a teenager, I never questioned why tension and fear were the price I had to pay to see my relatives. So many of our friends were fellow refugees that official East German harassment was just a fact of life.

We usually bought tickets to Leipzig, the closest major railroad station to Eilenburg. The three or four hours to reach the border dragged, time lengthened by nerves. Outside the train windows, whitewashed houses and gleaming tractors crossing tidy fields rolled by. My mother and I became adept at making paper hats and snowflakes, memorizing poetry, even singing when we had a compartment to ourselves. I can still summon a typical crossing in excruciating detail.

During the last stop on our side, the West German patrol boarded the train. Their green-grey uniforms were made of soft wool. They flowed down the aisles, sticking their heads in each compartment to make sure we had visas. The doors thudded shut. I felt myself tighten up. I couldn't read anymore, I had to stare out the window.

The train crept past the first layer of barbed wire, then glided through the bare strips of land where mines lay hidden. Guard towers hovered on stilts above the tracks. If I dared get close to the window and twisted my head, I could see soldiers up there holding machine guns.

We coasted toward the rows of barracks. White paint blinded the windowpanes. As if the train didn't want to call attention to itself, it slowed to a stop without a sound. The East German border guards stood in a row, uniforms tight, knee high black boots polished, German shepherds tense at their sides, facing toward the train. A loudspeaker barked: *"Willkommen in der Deutschen Demokratischen Republik"* - welcome to the German Democratic Republic. "No one is allowed to leave the train except under explicit orders. Evacuate the bathrooms and stay in your compartment until the inspection is complete."

My mother sat forward in her seat, wrapping her fingers around each other. The creases above her nose deepened. I barely breathed. Someone whispered, "Look, they're making people get out with their luggage."

That's how we knew the guards were in a bad mood. A line of people piled up outside the barracks. A woman who had gotten on at Kassel peered up at her fat suitcase. "I'll never be able to shut it again."

A man on the aisle tried a joke. "Once they've taken all the contraband, it'll be a lot lighter." All eyes turned to punish him.

We sat for an hour, waiting with our papers in our laps. A few times someone muttered complaints in a low voice, as if they weren't sure it was safe. I tried to pick up my book, but I kept reading the same paragraph over and over. My stomach rumbled. I wished I'd eaten another sandwich instead of saving it for after the border. Even with the windows open, the air smelled sweaty. A young man stood up and stuck his head outside. He told us they had still only gotten halfway through the train. A rumor spread from car to car. "They've decided to inspect the rest of us on the train. We won't have to get off."

I tightened myself around my middle and concentrated on the dairy company advertisement above my mother's shoulder. Fat cows munching a Bavarian meadow beneath puffy clouds. I wanted to be the cows.

Doors tore open. Officers stomped down aisles. We heard them shout from a few compartments away. Passport Control. Have your passport and visa ready! How long are you staying? Customs. Do you have any forbidden books? Magazines? Records? Register your foreign currency. Where is your visa?

We straightened, papers in hand, eyes fixed on the door. Flinched to attention as the guard barged in. His eyes flashed. He slammed stamps on papers. When my mother fumbled with her passport, he scowled. "Hurry up." He slapped the stamp down and thrust the passport back into her hand. He turned on his heel and marched out.

The customs officer stuck her head in the door, scanned the racks and tables for magazines. Her fierce expression and uniform hat looked like a disguise. She was short and plump and could have been someone's aunt.

"What's that?" She pointed at my book. I held it out. What if she took it? She narrowed her eyes and turned the book over to see the cover.

"It's just Greek mythology. A children's version ..." My mother's voice trailed off.

"All right." She slammed it shut and handed it back. Her eyes had lost interest in me. They were checking over the stuffed luggage racks above. She hesitated over the biggest case, then thought better of it, and spit out a "Gute Reise" - good journey - on her way out. The currency exchange official traded our money matter-of-factly in her wake. The harsh voices receded down the aisle. Finally the train door slammed.

I felt like I had been released from a spell. I breathed in - I hadn't realized I had barely dared to inhale - and tested my arms to see if they'd move. In the next compartment, someone giggled. Sandwich papers rustled. The old man in the aisle seat offered a bag of grapes. I tore off a branch, and popped one in my mouth. Warm juice exploded on my tongue.

"It wasn't so bad for us this time," he said, and settled back into his corner. My mother cracked an eggshell on the table and peeled shards into a paper bag. Between bites we sprinkled salt over the crumbling yolk. The guards reassembled on the pavement, snapping out jokes, forcing laughter. The train started with a jerk, then slid forward. Puffs of sooty smoke spread above us. The tracks on this side were loose from wear. We swayed from side to side as we gained speed.

The passengers finished their food and reorganized their luggage. Magazines came out of hiding. At the first East German stop, locals flooded the train. Their voices were rougher, less polite than at home. A young boy off to camp pointed at a string bag and shouted to his friend, "This must be a West train. Look at all those oranges!" Others just eyed the bulging bags and our exotic clothes.

I looked out the window and saw horse wagons creeping down the narrow streets. Huge fields stretched away from the tracks. Chunky women in aprons and kerchiefs bent over potato furrows, weeding by hand. Small villages swept by. The houses looked uniformly gray; some of their roof tiles were overgrown with dark moss. Barn doors hung open, askew. The bigger towns, the ones we stopped in, looked like a black and white movie. Full of boxy grey houses, paint peeling off window frames, and sooty train stations. The people waiting looked bent and angry. They shouted at each other "hey, you, watch out" and "you idiot, you cut me off!" as they rushed to the train. But at the railroad crossings the children stood, holding their bicycles, waving to the train. Their Young Pioneer kerchiefs glowed bright blue.

A half-hour before Leipzig, my mother gathered my books and cleaned up our sandwich papers. I buried my excitement during the long trip, but when I realized we were close to seeing my grandparents, I regained my energy. My mother had to tell me to hold still twice as she tugged on my sweater. She piled our hand luggage on my seat. Then we stood by the window and she announced each suburban Leipzig station as we sped through. She pointed out the zoo and told me again how the animals had howled after the war, because there was nothing to feed them. I didn't like hearing that story, because the animals, trapped as they were, had no hope of helping themselves. A young East German man offered to carry our suitcases to the door. I jumped up and down, ready to get off.

Opa Gustav stood, his hands behind his back, belly forward, at the track's edge. His summer suit strained at the buttons, and his eyes strove to spot us. He drifted by as the train came to a stop. My mother flung the door open before the squeals died down. She lowered me carefully down the steps by one hand. She did not let go as she followed, until she saw Opa stepping out, his arms wide out to receive me. Released, I shot forward. I heard Omi Paula fluttering behind Opa as he lifted me up. At last, I felt safe.

I still marvel at the way the East German state perfected intimidation. The minefields and guard towers came about through necessity, I know. Before their installation millions of people hemorrhaged into the West, depopulating the East. How could the government build a socialist state without people? They had to be kept from leaving for their own good.

But why use the border to harass visitors? I suppose the government resented the refugees who wanted to come back to see their families. Or perhaps, intimidation was a habit, an addictive power trip. They didn't treat us any worse than they did their own people. I caught border-crossing anxiety like a virus from the adults before I could talk. It didn't matter that I always got to the other side. Preverbal terror lodged in my body, and all my logic was powerless against it. Whenever we arrived, I dropped limp with relief into my grandparents' world, sure that Opa Gustav would protect us even here.

*****

In East Germany, insides and outsides didn't match up. My grandparents' house on Nordring looked neglected from the outside, just like all the other houses in town. The dirt brown stucco had chipped off in places, exposing patches of brick. Bullet holes from the American artillery attack in '45 still pockmarked the surface; the facade had survived the shelling and fire. The wrought iron balcony railings hadn't seen a coat of paint in years. Rusty streaks dripped down the façade. Just looking at the building made me feel tired.

The light blue paint and lace-curtained glass on my grandparents' apartment door hinted that you were leaving East German public space. Inside, the apartment had high ceilings and tall windows. I loved the ornate tile ovens, shiny blue tiles with a garland and angel border for the dining room, cozy green tiles in the living room, even though they were rendered obsolete by the radiators under the windows. Most of the Art Nouveau furniture from before the war had survived. Shelves of books lined the walls, and Omi Paula grew snake plants and cyclamen on the windowsills. It felt cozy and so old fashioned it could have been a museum to German domestic life in the thirties if my grandfather hadn't had a passion for technology. Opa Gustav had bartered and finagled to obtain a TV and a record player, a refrigerator and a juicer. The apartment was full to the brim with textures, colors and the comforts of home. I slipped into this space relieved to forget the outside ugliness.

At least as long as I didn't look out the living room window. Out there, two streets formed a useless triangle of land. For a few years, the city government installed playground equipment, a merry-go-round and a sandbox. It should have been a bright spot, and in some ways it was. The merry-go-round had seats painted in primary colors when it was first installed. But the grass never got mowed and soon turned into patchy weeds that looked dull under a film of street dust. Children shoveled the sand outside the box, and no one ever refilled it. The playground withered from neglect and after a few years disappeared.

I hate being in ugly places. It hurts my eyes and drags down my soul. So why did I love to visit Eilenburg? When we arrived, Omi Paula took over. My mother was young and I was her first child. She raised me by the rules. But when she came home, she became a daughter again, relaxing against her mother's experience. The first night, we gathered in the kitchen. Omi didn't worry that it was getting late. I would get to bed eventually. We gathered around the table where my mother had spread out our gifts: several pounds of coffee, cigarettes for Opa, nylon stockings for Omi. It always amazed me that these things we could buy on sale everywhere in Krefeld were so precious here that Omi and Opa both grinned with pleasure. I loved that feeling of satisfying their wants so easily and always wondered why my mother didn't buy even more.

The next morning when I awoke, Opa was already at work. Omi too had gotten up early, to go stand in line at the bakery for hard rolls. They lay in a nylon bag on the table. My mother sipped a cup of coffee. I settled in for my breakfast and listened as she and Omi traded news.

A long-time family employee poked her head into the kitchen. She greeted us with one of her round-faced smiles, but quickly moved on to important news. One of the women workers had run into town on her break. They had cauliflower at the HO - the state-owned grocery. Cauliflower! They hadn't had any vegetables in months. Omi pulled off her apron. I asked her if I could come along. My childish mind converted the struggle to snatch rare foods into a treasure hunt. We rushed out of the house and hurried the three blocks to the grocery. The rumor had to be true. The line on the sidewalk was at least thirty people long. Omi asked me to get in it, while she went up to the window to see whether there was any chance the supply might outlast the line. She came back undecided. We'd just have to try.

The line grew behind us, as we inched forward. Eilenburg was small enough so many of the people in line knew Omi and each other. I heard lots of "Guten Tag, Frau Sieg" from both directions, and Omi smiled and nodded back. I felt conspicuous in my white pleated skirt and lemon yellow sweater. The women checked me out, and then continued the conversation. "You must have visitors from the West," they would say. I assumed they could tell from my clothes. West German clothes with their space age fabrics, bright colors and up-to-the-minute fashion stood out in the East where factories turned out clothes according to the dictates of planning, not consumer demand.

I had plenty of time to look around while we waited. Rows of grey and dirty brown buildings. Huge placards and banners draped from the upper stories provided the only splashes of color along the Leipzigerstrasse. Red letters on white backgrounds proclaiming the glory of socialism and Russian/German solidarity. *Dem Sozialismus gehört die Zukunft* - the future belongs to socialism. *Von der Sowjetunion lernen, heisst siegen lernen* - *l*earning from the Soviet Union is learning to win. *Lang Lebe der Marxismus-Leninismus* - long live Marxism-Leninism. I always had the impression as a child that socialism was too serious to allow the fun things that livened up West German cities. The ice cream stands and outdoor cafes, the flower beds and sculptures. In the East, there wasn't time or energy for aesthetics or pleasure.

We made slow progress into the store. When we reached the counter, we saw there were only a few heads of cauliflower left. Their greens wilted a bit and the white flowerets were tinged with brown. The customers jostled each other, trying to get to the counter in time. One of the saleswomen said: "None of that. When they're gone they're gone." She moved with deliberate slowness, and chose who got waited on next. She recognized Omi and picked her. We got one of the last. The people behind us groaned. By the time we walked out, the store was empty except for a bin of shriveled onions. Omi carried her cauliflower like a trophy.

Usually, my grandparents managed to circumvent East Germany's unpredictable distribution system. Opa Gustav cultivated friendships with the butcher across the alley, the private greenhouse grower who puttered on the remnants of his family's estate, the sales clerk at the toy store, and the electrician who managed to hang on to a small private business at the margins of the collective economy. He bartered using bolts of velvet, wood, or his considerable connections. When Opa spotted scarce goods, he couldn't ask himself whether he really needed them. The thrill of the hunt mooted the question. It looked exciting, if exhausting to me. Survival in East Germany required a complex web of relationships and constant maneuvering. When the government crumbled long after my grandfather's death and goods became abundant overnight, East Germans not only struggled to learn how to make buying decisions, they also lost a sense of interdependence, of cooperation for survival.

I fidgeted my way through Opa's lunchtime nap, anxious to go to work with him. We walked down the hall from the kitchen to the office door, holding hands. I liked the way my hand vanished inside his. I even liked how his calluses scratched my fingers. When Opa first opened the door, large piles of packages wrapped in gray paper and blue string blocked my view of his desk. I followed him around the pile. The shipping clerk bent over her worktable, wrapping product. When she noticed me with Opa she turned around.

"*Ach*, you brought Claudia to help us today." She bent toward me, offering a hand. I stared at the bright red lipstick she always wore.

She even painted the mole next to her lip with it. That and her bright blonde hair scared me a little. I curtsied when I shook her hand.

Opa glanced at his desk to see if there were any urgent notes. When Opa was ready, he led the way on his daily tour of the factory. His belly strained against his blue work coat. He liked to walk with his hands clasped behind his back, like Napoleon. I followed behind, amazed at his ridged, yellowed fingernails. We made our way through the thicket of boxes into the cutting room where a worker sliced up stacks of velvet and imitation leather on a giant cutting machine. It was designed like a paper cutter, but so big, she had to reach over her head to pull down the blade. The steel gleamed. I had been warned repeatedly that it was very sharp. The thought of what would happen to my finger if I touched it produced an icy shudder in my shoulder blades. I kept my distance and fingered the rolls of velvet on the other side of the aisle. Emerald green, ruby red and sapphire blue, they glowed in the dim light that filtered in through the small window.

Opa was already entering the assembly room. It was a large room with big windows facing the alley. Women sat on stools at long tables. Each one wore a patterned nylon apron - every single apron sent by a relative or a friend's relative from the West. In East Germany, the truly disadvantaged were the people with no one from *Drüben* - over there. Pots of caramel-colored glue bubbled on hot plates. A thick sticky smell filled every crevice of the room. Each woman had a permanent station. Plants and pictures of children lined the windowsills. Thermoses and snacks shared space with watchcase pre-forms and piles of imprinted velvet patches. All day, they talked as they worked, mostly about their children and what you could buy or swap for and where. When they saw Opa, they interrupted that flow to call out greetings and problems they'd been saving for him. The stamping press for imprinting the gold leaf logos was stuck. They were about to run out of earring cards. There was something wrong with the wooden pre-forms for the last batch of protractor cases. Opa bent his head down to listen to each woman. He asked questions to make sure he understood. Cracked a joke or two. Then moved on. I followed along, greeting the women I knew with a handshake.

Liesel was my favorite. She grinned when she saw me coming, and had an extra chair at the table for me. Like the other women she wore a nylon apron, hers was patterned in pink flowers on a navy background, over her street clothes. She moved with such energy that I thought of her as younger than the others, but when she smiled wrinkles crinkled at the corners of her eyes. Liesel found some defective parts for me and gave me a smooth, pointed tool. I later learned it was called a bone folder. Then she showed me how she glued the same parts and turned them into a ring case. Sometimes she gave me piles of black velvet pieces that had been imprinted with gold leaf. My job was to scrape the extra gold leaf off until the "*Waldhütte*" logo was free of debris. I worked and listened to the women. Sometimes they complained about empty stores and high prices, though more often they made trying to get the goods they wanted sound exciting. Getting special food or clothes was the central drama of their lives.

Quitting time was at four, and even though I would have stayed longer, everyone vanished exactly then. Liesel sent me back to Opa's office, where he was still on the phone, trying to coax someone into supplying him with the wood he needed. He smoked and tapped on his desk as he talked. Above him, in an oval frame, hung a photograph of Gustav Sr., his ample belly graced by a watch chain. Opa put down the receiver and sighed. He leaned back in his chair to finish his cigarette. I brushed fabric scraps and gold leaf off my pleated skirt and went back to the apartment.

I didn't wonder until years later how my grandfather managed to keep his company private. When the Russians installed the socialist government, they first concentrated on collectivizing agriculture and then moved on to exerting state control over large manufacturers. At less than fifty employees, *Sieg & Söhne*- Sieg & Sons -slipped through below the radar. But in the fifties, my grandfather came under increased scrutiny. He wiggled through every loophole he could – at one point he had his operation reclassified as an artisan's shop – until his health failed in the late sixties, several years after we moved. Only then did he sell out for a pittance to secure a retirement income for my grandmother.

Once in a while, I imagined what my world would have been like if Germany hadn't been divided. In my dreams, I waved my magic wand, and pictured the whole country basking in the West German prosperity I knew. In that world, my grandfather would be a rich factory owner. I pictured myself dressed in velvet, rich as a princess. But my imagination stalled there. I knew my mother felt cheated out of her inheritance, but I was satisfied with my life in Krefeld. Whenever I fantasized, I got sidetracked into picturing the immense pleasure I'd feel if I could lift the cloud of frustration I felt hanging over all of East Germany. I didn't think I'd live to see that day.

In the evening, Opa sat in his chair, a cigarette sending up a curl of smoke from the pedestal ashtray next to him, and read the paper. He muttered to himself "*So ein Mist*"- what manure - and "*Quatsch*" - nonsense - as he worked his way through the front page. The newspaper was thin, and looked denser than the one we got at home. It took me a few years to realize why it looked so different. There were no ads. I asked Opa once why he got the paper when he knew it was all propaganda. He had to stop and think. He finally said he did it for the local news and so he knew what the Party was up to. It was from the newspaper he found out that the Party had decided to lower wages. They didn't say it that way; they called it an adjustment for greater socialist productivity. And they didn't explain the reason. Opa said it was because East Germans were getting too rich compared to their Eastern Block neighbors. They outearned the Poles, Hungarians and Czechs. He tried to figure out a way to juggle the books so he could pay his employees more than legally allowed.

I envisioned Opa Gustav as a protective shield. His sphere extended not just over the apartment and the factory; I trusted that his resourcefulness would save me even if I encountered trouble elsewhere in Eilenburg. Not that I ever did. When I went anywhere alone, say to Tante Anni's farm across the river and up the hill, I scurried like a mouse, eager to get inside the next safe haven.

*****

The sisters, Tante Anni and Omi Paula both had high voices that trembled when they got emotional, but Tante Anni's sliced a little sharper, maybe because she'd had worse luck. Her husband had left her for his secretary and their only son, Günter, had been killed in the last battle of the war on the streets of Berlin. I admired her for surviving her tragic life. Opa avoided her, because her sharp-tongued laments got on his nerves, but I didn't mind giving her a little sympathy. In return she liked to slip me treats and talk me up to her friends. Tante Anni lived with her younger brother Otto on the farm where Paula, Anni, and Otto had grown up.

After I turned eight I was judged old enough to walk to the farm alone, but only from the Mulde Bridge. The streets to the bridge were too narrow and dangerous. Trucks thundered down the hill and sped through the center of town. Omi had other errands to do, so she pushed her bicycle along between the trucks and me, a clattering shield. On the other side of the bridge, a pedestrian path led off the main road directly up the hill. She kissed me goodbye, pointed her bicycle back across the bridge, and settled on its seat. Her raincoat bulged as she picked up speed.

When I reached Halleschestrasse 7, I opened the door to the right of the big gate and stepped into the yard. The dog barked and wagged and the chickens scattered as I pushed through the bunch of them. Tante Anni saw me walk past the kitchen window and came to the door to let me into the house. She wore one of the nylon aprons my mother and I had picked out from the sale rack at the discount store in Krefeld. Muted colors proper for an old woman. The buttons strained over her barrel shape. A hairnet restrained her still dark hair into a bun. My arrival sparked a glow in her sad eyes. We hung up my coat and I asked what I could do to help. What I most loved about the farm is that it was the one place where I felt able to do real work.

First I fed the chickens. Tante Anni handed me a chocolate brown enamel bowl and a tin cup. Inside the chill of the pantry, I dipped the cup into the feed three times. As soon as I appeared on the stone doorsill, a wave of clucking, bobbing birds raced towards me. We danced back and forth, the hens following the seeds I tossed until I was out of grain. The bowl and cup clattered as I set them back on the shelf.

Next, I searched for eggs. Tante Anni had shown me the hens' favorite nests. Most of them were near the chicken coop, but I climbed into the haylofts first. That way, if I slipped, I wouldn't lose many eggs. Tante Anni needed the money the collective paid her on delivery. In the far left corner, a hen sat, puffed up, trying to warm a nest. I rushed toward her, arms spread, hissing, the way Tante Anni had taught me. The hen cackled, her neck jerking. The she pulled in her feathers and raced past me. On the compressed straw, in a small hollow, lay a single white egg. I wrapped my fingers around the warm shell and lifted it into my basket. I climbed into the eaves and found eggs in unexpected places. When I returned to the house, my basket was full.

"Can I pull a few carrots?" I asked.

Tante Anni grinned and nodded. "Only as many as you can eat though." I promised. I knew Tante Anni needed the vegetables from the garden to can for the winter. I crossed the courtyard and walked through the back barn, past the pig stable where a huge hog grunted. Here the paving stopped and turned into a patch of overgrown grass. Rows of gnarled fruit trees surrounded the old bee house. I had seen a picture of Opa wearing a beekeeper suit, tending the wicker hives. In the late forties, when there was no food, they needed the honey. Now the door hung open on a bent hinge. When I peeked inside, I saw the hives and equipment still stacked inside under layers of dust. The vegetable garden stretched in a few tidy rows behind the shed. I loved the feathery carrot greens, each one promising a mystery. You never knew when you began to tug whether you had chosen well until the carrot emerged. Sometimes what looked like a huge orange top was revealed as a knobby stub and some of the tiniest greens produced lovely tapering roots. I barely wiped the soil off on my skirt before chomping down on them.

Onkel Otto was Omi and Tante Anni's younger brother. He was short and hunchbacked and had a squeaky voice. My great-grandmother had fallen down the stairs while she was pregnant. The fall had broken Onkel Otto's spine. As a child he had spent months in traction at the hospital, and later he kept to himself to avoid being teased at school. He liked to spend his time with animals and children. When his chores for the farm cooperative were done, he'd take me to the rabbit barn, and hold the rabbits for me, one by one, so I could feel their soft fur.

At lunchtime, Onkel Otto and I took off our dirty shoes and put them on the rubber mat by the door. Tante Anni knew I loved green bean soup, so most often that's the smell that greeted us in the kitchen. Onkel Otto took off his blue work jacket and settled in at the oilcloth-covered table. I carried the soup plates and the tin spoons. Tante Anni brought a bottle of vinegar. The thin mutton broth floated with home canned beans, chopped onion and potato chunks.

Between slurps of soup, Onkel Otto and Tante Anni discussed the farm cooperative. In the late forties, the government had confiscated the farm's fields, but the house, barn and garden remained family property. The co-op housed calves in one of the barns and employed Tante Anni and Onkel Otto. They struggled to keep their property from getting ruined by careless helpers. Tante Anni was in charge of dealing with troublesome workers - Otto liked to stay in the background. He nodded, said "ja, ja" and relied on her to confront problems.

When they were done with business and soup, Onkel Otto lit his pipe. He leaned back and sighed from behind his cloud of smoke. Above him, next to the wooden clock, hung a picture of Tante Anni's son, Günter. He wore a German army uniform and an optimistic smile. His hair was blond, his features even. He didn't look like Tante Anni, but I didn't know if he looked like his father, because I'd never seen a picture of him.

Tante Anni liked to talk about Günter. While Onkel Otto left to take his nap, she went into the front room and got some of Günter's old books. We leafed through them together. He had collected cereal cards just like the ones I found in my rolled oats in Krefeld. Pictures of birds and flowers printed on porous cardboard - each one identified in Latin and with the German common name. Günter had sent away to the company for the album, preprinted with the descriptions for each card. The set was complete, each space filled. A dusty smell clung to the pages. When we closed the book, I asked Tante Anni how old Günter would have been. She said he was one year older than my mother, so he would probably have a child my age by now. We looked into each other's eyes. Tears rose up in hers. I promised myself to be as much her grandchild as possible. I didn't know how many miles the future would thrust between us, but I would keep my promise as well as I could.

*****

I understood that old people like my grandparents and Tante Anni and Onkel Otto were too rooted in the East to leave. But Tante Isolde, my mother's sister, had stayed in East Germany because her husband didn't want to leave home. When she came to visit Eilenburg from Berlin, she'd fill the watering can and sweep into the living room singing German folk songs, while I trailed behind and joined in. The sun streamed in and lit a reddish glow in her dark brown hair. Her eyes smiled behind the thick glasses she wore. One day, I must have been five, my admiration just overflowed.

"You're so young and beautiful!" I called out to her as she paused for breath.

"Me?" she laughed. "I'm just an old bag!"

"No, you're not."

"See," she pointed to the corners of her eyes. "I'm getting wrinkles already."

I moved closer. If I really strained I could see the faintest beginnings of crow's feet.

"I still think you're beautiful," I said and walked out of the room before she could deny it.

Her husband, Onkel Horst was handsome. He was tall and slender with smooth dark hair and skin that tanned easily. His height made him seem remote as a god, and I got nervous when he tried to joke with me. He always tickled a tad too hard and his laugh rang a little too hearty. But from a distance I thought he looked like a movie star. He and Tante Isolde lived in East Berlin where they were students. She planned to become a nurse and he was studying veterinary medicine. My mother said they'd been sweethearts since Isolde was sixteen. I thought it was amazing that he was the son of Tante Anni's baker up on the hill - every time Tante Anni sent me for pastries, Onkel Horst's father, who looked like a worn, puffy version of his son, greeted me like a relative and gave me an extra *Berliner*. Not only that, one of my grandparents' sisters-in-law was Horst's aunt. Where I lived we had no connections to anyone. I wasn't sure I liked the idea of marrying someone I'd known as a kid or being related to the same person several different ways, but then it was unlikely to happen to me.

Just after Tante Isolde and Onkel Horst graduated and returned to Eilenburg, they had a son they named Matthias. I was six when he was born and teetered between being thrilled, since Matthias was my first close experience with a baby, and terrified of being displaced from my privileged position as the only grandchild. I knew Opa would adore having a grandson, and even worse, my rival lived close by year round. My mother advised me to love my little cousin, because if I gave in to jealousy it would make me look bad. As long as Matthias was still a baby, I could easily follow her advice. I begged to push the pram on walks and smothered his pudgy face with kisses when I could get away with it. It got harder once Matthias turned about four or so, and he and Opa went hand in hand everywhere, searching out new toys. Eilenburg had a toyshop, and Opa chatted up one of the workers until she notified him whenever an exciting new toy was delivered. I loved the little electric woodworking shop Opa bought for Matthias. It had a working band saw, a drill press, and would never be allowed by any toy safety organization today. One day, as we walked down the sidewalk on Leipzigerstrasse, Opa and Matthias leading the way hand in hand, my mother and I following behind, I complained.

"Why is Opa always buying him everything he wants?"

"He'd buy you things too if you asked for them." My mother answered. Opa and Matthias had stopped at the window of the *Haus der Geschenke* - house of presents - to watch a toy helicopter turning circles. Matthias stood, entranced, his eyes wide, his mouth open.

"Can I have one of those?" he whispered. I was aware suddenly of my ten years and my growing self-consciousness. I knew I couldn't see and desire anything that openly.

Opa said, "Let's see whether we can get one." Just because a store had a toy in the window didn't mean they had it. I scanned the display. There were a few hand puppets draped over a ledge, and a doll with ill-fitting clothes. Nothing I wanted, even if I could have overcome my reluctance to ask for it. My jealousy was tempered by the knowledge that I didn't have to rely on East German stores to fill my desires. I was lucky. How could I begrudge Matthias anything? Back in Krefeld, the stores had ten times as many toys, and you didn't have to use connections to get them. I could just save up my allowance and buy them. Matthias did eventually get his helicopter, but it took Opa months to procure.

When Isolde got pregnant again and had twin girls, Opa bought a house for her and Onkel Horst in Bad Düben, thirty kilometers away. The house was heaven as far as I was concerned. It sat on a big lot with a willow tree in front and a cherry tree in back. Its two stories and many rooms looked palatial to me. I especially admired the square fountain by the front patio. Onkel Horst put in a huge vegetable garden in the back. He planted apple, pear and plum trees, put in rows of strawberries plants, gooseberry bushes and raspberries. He grew tomatoes, cucumbers, green beans, and peas. The crowning achievement was an asparagus bed: first he excavated a rectangle, then layered it with manure and sandy soil and mounded the dirt over the plants so the growing stalks would remain white and delicate. I loved harvesting the asparagus. First, you found the top of a shoot just poking through the dirt, then, you loosened the soil around it gently with you fingertips until you could reach down to the bottom and cut it off with your knife. Each stalk was a treasure.

Now that Onkel Horst was a veterinarian, the family had a good supply of meat, too. The farmers whose cows and pigs he treated often gave him sausages or pork chops in return for a job well done. Once in a while, he was able to get his hands on a share of a pig. I was glad for Tante Isolde that she didn't have to rely on the scanty groceries from the HO. Within walking distance of their house, the government had put up rows of identical apartment blocks. In the center of this development sat a low building that looked like a modern self-service grocery store. Whenever I accompanied Tante Isolde there, I thought it was especially cruel that this store was just as empty as the old one in Eilenburg. The plate glass windows and rows of shelves only underlined the problem.

As Matthias and I both grew older, I saw the benefits of having another child in the family. We became buddies. I asked to visit him in Düben whenever possible, and spent long hours waiting for him to return from the preschool across the street, so we could play. One afternoon, when Onkel Horst came home from work, he caught Matthias in a fib, something along the lines of not admitting that he'd left the gate open or picked some buds off a cucumber plant.

"Did you do it?" Onkel Horst looked down at Matthias from his considerable height.

"No," Matthias said, but his face said yes. Onkel Horst grabbed Matthias by the shoulder and shoved him down the cellar step. He shut the door and turned the key. Matthias banged on the door, his sobs rising to a scream. I stood by the steps, unsure what I could do. Finally, I blurted, "But Onkel Horst, Matthias is terrified of the cellar."

"This should cure him." Onkel Horst said, and walked away.

I sat down on the cellar steps. As Matthias' sobs quieted down, I sang folksongs I had learned from my mother on the long train rides from Krefeld to Leipzig, hoping to soothe him.

Opa's Mercedes crunched around the corner into the yard. He saw me sitting by myself on the steps, my face as tragic as I could make it.

"Where's Matthias?" Opa was used to his grandson's immediate welcome. I told him. He stomped toward the back garden, shouting, "How can you do that to the boy? You know he's scared of the dark!"

They argued for a while, but before long, Opa marched Onkel Horst past the cellar stairs. He stepped back and let Onkel Horst unlock the door himself. Now I knew that Matthias needed Opa nearby more than I did. I hoped Onkel Horst had learned his lesson.

Most of the time my relatives tuned the TV to West German channels, with one notable exception: *Das Sandmännchen* - the sandman. Somehow this daily little goodnight vignette, acted out with puppets, escaped the didactic force of East German media. In later years, only the sandman survived the disappearance of East German TV. Every evening at seven the sandman rides onto his set (sometimes on a motorcycle, sometimes in an airplane) asking the children if they are in their pajamas and ready for their goodnight story. Matthias and I never missed an episode.

When I stayed overnight, I slept with Matthias upstairs in his room. We lay under the covers, a reading light Opa had bought for us clipped to a book, and read and told stories. We'd leave the door open, and once in a while a huge grown-up whoop of laughter filtered up from the living room where our mothers watched TV.

We spent long days in the yard, digging sand with Matthias' little sisters, chasing the family dog, and picking cherries. We imagined fairy groves hidden in the bushes and under the willow tree. Nature hid the ugliness that so bothered me in East Germany. In that yard, you could pretend to be anyplace, even somewhere normal.

Always, my feelings about East Germany bristled with conflicting emotions. The private spaces and the people I loved glinted like jewels set in barbed wire. Most of the time, I concentrated on the pleasant memories and ignored the fear and anxiety, the oppressive atmosphere. I tried to forget the guilt I carried, the flipside of luck. Why did I get to leave, while my cousins were trapped?

By the time I was twelve, we'd traveled all over Europe on summer vacations. If anyone had thought to ask, I could have told them that the places I cherished weren't remarkable. No one would include the sights of Krefeld, Eilenburg or Bad Düben on a tour of Germany. I treasured them because they were home.

But I had no reason to compare home to the rest of the world, because I had no idea how much my life was about to change.

*****

One afternoon in 1965, my father leaned against the kitchen doorframe, his hands stretched out, pleading with my mother, "I have to accept. Look at what happened to Bernd!" My mother concentrated on the dishes. From my place at the table, I saw only her back, but I could imagine her lips pressed tight, her chin jutting out, and two vertical lines furrowing the wide plane of her forehead. Her shoulders stayed stiff, and her dark, teased hair barely moved as she shifted plates from the sink to the dish drainer. My father's blue eyes implored her to react. He really wanted this. For weeks they'd been tossing arguments back and forth. Should my father accept his boss's offer to be vice president of sales at the American branch? The silverware clinked. My father kept going. "They sent him to the US, but Ruth hated it and made his life so miserable that he asked to come back. And now his career is finished. He won't get another chance at a promotion." I imagined Bernd locked in a supply closet, counting pencils.

Over her shoulder, my mother said, "He still has his job." My father threw up his hands and turned on his heel. His clipped brown hair stuck up in back, parrot-style. Once my mother heard the living room door shut, she slumped.

I knew better than to think he had lost. My father's career was a family project and my mother would never condemn him to oblivion. And she'd never want to be like Ruth. I heard my parents talk about her for years. The men in the department gossiped about her. She had embarrassed Bernd by making a scene to his boss when one of his business trips stretched to six weeks. And they said she made Bernd help with the housework! I pictured him dusting with an apron tied over his suit. My mother didn't think to ask why Ruth was so miserable in South Carolina. My father knew what he was doing when he brought her up.

My mother didn't get much help from her father either. When she asked Opa Gustav what she should do, he told her, "It will be horrible for us if you move that far away, but he's your husband. You have to support his career and go with him."

I watched my parents' arguments with growing irritation, knowing my father wouldn't give up and my mother would give in eventually. Why was she always afraid of adventure? Living in America would be exciting.

At school, I began to picture my presence as temporary. I doodled my new address in my English book's dust cover: "Claudia Poser, Clempson, USA." I hadn't learned to spell the name of the town, nor realized the importance of the South Carolina part of the address. One morning, my friend Sabine, who sat next to me, glimpsed what I'd done. She snorted, and then refused to talk to me for the rest of the day. I was embarrassed to be caught in my fantasies, but I had no idea what had upset her so.

I savored my unknown future. It marked me as different from the others in my class at the girls' *Gymnasium* – secondary school. The feeling that my life promised adventure carried me past my futile struggles with Latin grammar. My body was changing and no matter how hard I tried I couldn't concentrate on details, but Frau Dr. Porten wanted me to keep track of verb, noun and adjective endings for five different cases. Even the German *Gymnasium* tradition of cheating as much as you could get away with didn't help. There's only so much room for ink on your thigh. My Latin grade stayed mediocre, but my father had mentioned that American schools didn't require Latin. I liked hearing that, but I wasn't so sure about the rest of his information. He reported that American school lasted until three in the afternoon, so the kids had to eat lunch there. My longest school day was Tuesday when I didn't get home until one-thirty. I dragged home on those days certain I deserved a medal for concentrating so long.

What did I know about moving? The only move I remembered was the one from one side of Krefeld to the other just before I started school. We had traded the upstairs apartment in the Siemenstrasse row house for a newer, nicer apartment with a small patch of grass and lots of open space. I had missed my best friend for a while, but I made new friends. In fact, I was ignorant enough to shift easily from accepting the move we had already been contemplating - the move to a small town outside Krefeld where my parents had bought a lot and intended to build a house - to this move across the Atlantic.

And what did I know about America? On TV we watched dubbed versions of *Dragnet* and *Seventy-Seven Sunset Strip.* An America of cities, clean streets, and shiny cars. I never watched *Gunsmoke* or *Bonanza*, because I couldn't fathom Indians as bad guys. Like other German children, I'd lived inside the books of Karl May for several years of my childhood, identifying with his Apache heroes. It didn't matter to us that Karl May had never set foot in America, or that his geography was sloppy, and his Indian languages a mishmash from different tribes. We adored the noble Winnetou - played by a Frenchman in European movie adaptations - and his German cowboy sidekick Old

Shatterhand. I knew it as fiction, set in the 1800s. Even so, I secretly hoped to meet Winnetou, though where he would fit in a space-age land of skyscrapers and high technology I couldn't imagine.

After my mother's opposition collapsed, she told me one day that she felt betrayed by my collaboration. Oh, she didn't blame me, she said. She knew my father had been working on me. A wave of doubt assaulted me so suddenly it threatened to pull me under. Had he really tricked me into thinking this was a great idea? I struggled to find my balance. No way. I wanted to go. She was just mad because she wasn't getting her way.

My father left for America in late winter, with my mother scheduled to visit him there for two weeks in the spring. If she approved, we'd move in the fall. When my mother returned from her trip, she bore gifts and lots of baffling information about South Carolina. Three TV channels broadcast all day with constant ads, even right in the middle of news programs - they cut directly from images of wounded soldiers in Vietnam to deodorant jingles! Our two channels started in the afternoon, and ads ran in a twenty-minute clump before the news. In Clemson only students lived in apartments; most of the houses had little white columns in front. Women left their curlers in when they went shopping, but even old ladies wore make-up everywhere. In the summer the weather turned so hot that the grass turned brown and flowers couldn't survive. My mother strung these odd pieces of information together in a breathless rush. They flashed across my mind, creating disconnected pictures, but I didn't really know what they meant. I couldn't feel the details any more than I could imagine the South Carolina summer heat. My father later admitted he'd been sure to have my mother come when the dogwoods blossomed and before the heat took hold. I shook my head and trusted that if other people could live there, so could I.

I loved my present from America. My mother had bought a battery-operated record player for me, along with a single 45 to get me started. It didn't matter that I didn't like the song - *Eight Miles High* by 'The Byrds' - I couldn't believe I struck it that rich. I played it over and over just because I could. A record player was such a luxury I hadn't even dared to put one on my Christmas list. It was such a clever design, too. With the tone arm fastened into place, you could slip the speaker over the player, snap it into place, and use the plastic handle for carrying. Except for this marvel, once my mother returned, life slipped back to normal.

Well, not quite normal. My father's absence didn't bother me for a few months; he traveled so often that I could pretend he was just on one of his sales trips to France. It was my grandfather, Opa Gustav, whose odd behavior first forced me to take this move seriously. When my mother and I arrived for a visit in East Germany that summer, he acted like he never expected to see me again. Not in a maudlin way. No, he announced it was time for me to learn local history and took a week off from work. I knew my grandparents occasionally took vacations, but I had never seen my grandfather separate from his factory. I was disturbed he was willing to leave for a week, and embarrassed he was making all this fuss - after all we would only be gone for a few years.

Opa had suffered a mild stroke the year before, and didn't trust himself to drive. So he hired a driver for his Moskwitsch (a Russian car that took patience and connections to acquire in East Germany) and off we went on day trips to do the grand tour of Saxony. Opa sat in front and I wedged into the back between my mother and grandmother. We hit all the high points: Wittenberg, where Luther nailed his 95 theses to the church door; Weimar, where Goethe and Schiller created the core of German literature; Dresden which the East German government was trying to restore to its architectural splendor; and finally, just outside Leipzig, the site of the Battle of Nations where the Prussians, Russians and English defeated Napoleon in 1813. Most of the week, the weather was lousy, I particularly remember taking a boat ride from Dresden down the Elbe in a drizzle, and I had to keep reminding myself that Opa was trying to do me a favor so I wouldn't fall into a twelve-year-old sulk. Luther captured my imagination. He was a man so full of life that he burst the seams of four hundred-year-old stories. I could picture him ranting against indulgences, marrying an ex-nun, and presiding over his growing family.

What I most noticed about the trip was how different tourism felt in the East. My parents and I had traveled all over Western Europe, to Holland and Italy, Denmark and Yugoslavia. Everywhere the rituals had been the same. Not here. Even though we were visiting tourist attractions, there were no gift shops, no racks of colorful postcards and souvenirs. I did find some black-and-white postcards in a bookstore in Wittenberg. The usual socialist slogans hung from the house fronts, especially in the town squares.

When lunchtime approached, you couldn't wander through a town, reading menus, deciding which place looked most appetizing and had good prices. Instead, we were lucky to find a restaurant with manageable lines. The surroundings were functional: rows of tables, dusty curtains, and bare walls. The service was always indifferent, if not downright rude. After a long wait, a grumbling waitress slammed our plates down in front of us. A small piece of pork, a pile of potatoes, a dab of cabbage, all dumped onto the plate with no regard to looks.

Thank goodness the cooks couldn't seem to help making savory gravies, the way their mothers had taught them.

As we rode in the back of the Moskwitsch, I noticed that my grandfather's head nodded and tipped forward onto his chest. "Old men," my grandmother whispered next to me, "old men and dogs. All they do is sleep." I didn't want to hear it. My grandfather wasn't old, and he certainly had no reason to act like he'd never see me again. I refused to even think it.

*****

What was life in Krefeld like for me in the last few months before we left? Did I have enough awareness to say goodbye to the places I knew? The last few years of my childhood, I'd been drawing ever-larger independent loops through the city. Once a week, I took the tram to the public swimming pool with its old fashioned tiled halls and the separate women's and men's pools. When my friends and I first went on these outings, we thought we had achieved the height of independence, because we not only went swimming by ourselves but discovered we could use our fifty pfennig spending money to buy a large slab of *Butterkuchen* - a buttery yeast cake - at the bakery near the tram stop. In the winter, we skated at the public ice rink; I'd saved my allowance for a year to buy figure skates.

Every Tuesday, I took a bus to my guitar teacher's apartment, where for several years I tortured him with halting renditions of classical sonatas. I wanted to sound like the Beatles, not play Bach. Just before I left, we'd reached a compromise: folk songs.

When I turned twelve, my mother and her best friend Gudrun bought season tickets to the youth symphony for Gudrun's daughters and me. They sewed elegant dresses for us using slight variations on the same pattern. Mine was burgundy with a pleated, stand-up collar. We even got little black clutch purses and were allowed to wear new nylons. We focused on this rite of passage and didn't even think about what kind of music we might hear. The intensity of live orchestral music took me by surprise. In that darkened theater, wedged between Ulli and Bine, I first discovered the power of Bartok and saw a hint of what had moved Hindemith. My father had early introduced me to the romantic composers, but he had no interest in anything more modern.

The spring before our move, my best friend, Sabine, first suggested we meet in town to go shopping. How grown up I felt, waiting for her in front of the *Kaufhof*, clutching my shoulder bag. We wandered into record stores and gave each other the courage to ask to listen to the

Rolling Stones song in the sound booth. Then we discovered magic in the discount bins at Woolworth's. We took three hours to each spend a few marks, and capped our afternoon with an ice cream cone on our way back to the central tram stop.

Did I go to these places aware it was the last time? I doubt it. I briefly and sporadically kept a diary starting that September. In it I chattered about homework, what we called *Beat-musik*, an old coat I no longer wanted to wear because it wasn't fashionable, losing some change and not being able to go swimming. I sound like a typical twelve-year-old pouting about my mother, although I apparently had enough self-awareness to attribute some of the tension between us to missing my father who'd been in South Carolina for months. Yet there are signs that I was nervous. "At night in bed, I feel so lonely. I don't know why. Is it longing (for my father) or fear? What is going to happen?" In the next entry I try to understand why I can't seem to concentrate on schoolwork and am suddenly making costly mistakes on tests, not just in Latin, but in Math and English too. And finally, late in September, after a portion of our belongings had been shipped off, "Everything I happen to need is already gone. Since Karin has been acting so distant lately, I wanted to take my stamp collection to school. Gone! Then I wanted to look up the northernmost city in Russia in my Atlas. Gone! This is getting serious!" And then in English, "Terrible!"

I do remember getting tired of waiting. My father was supposed to return for us in September, then in October. The date kept getting pushed back and we were in limbo. On the phone, my father explained the delays away in a mysterious manner. He was busy, he'd had a little accident, but it wasn't much, just a scratch. So we were shocked, when he got off the plane, several pounds lighter, his face ashen with purple bruises under his eyes, his arm encased in plaster. He hadn't wanted to worry us. My mother grilled him until we thought we had the full story: he'd been driving back to Clemson from Greenville late at night, at the end of a busy week at the Greenville Textile Show, and had fallen asleep. The car drifted into the median and flipped over. His arm shattered into a compound fracture gushing blood all over the upholstery. Lucky for him, his boss was following him in the other company car. My mother and I handled most of the packing while he sat in one of the remaining living room chairs watching, an eagle with a broken wing.

On the last day of school, I felt an odd mixture of nostalgia, dread, and excitement. When I arrived, I memorized the stately four-story building with its copper-roofed dormers. I dawdled on my way to my classroom and sat between Sabine and Karin wanting to hold on but feeling myself drift away, a ghost in the making. In the end, I just wanted to get out of there because being there was too painful. As the last bell rang, I slid my books into my satchel, said another goodbye to my friends - not looking at them, because I didn't want to be a crybaby - and climbed down the broad main staircase to the entrance. My parents waited there to take me to our meeting with the principal. I'd never been in Frau Dr. Porten's office before. I sat on the edge of a chair, intimidated into silence by the combination of her dignity and the scholarly aura of her sanctum. She presided at her desk, her silver hair in perfect waves, wearing a tweed suit with a silk blouse, a few simple pieces of jewelry glinting as she moved. Her voice was always measured. I knew that, because I'd had her for Latin the past year. Her unbending posture and earnest delivery in class conveyed a gentle distance. My performance in Latin had been so inadequate by my standards that I assumed she'd be glad to get rid of me. She surprised me by smiling into my eyes as she handed me my final report card. I tried to listen to her wishing me luck, but really my heart was in a quick scan of my grades. She'd given me a 3! I knew I deserved nothing higher than a 4. I looked up, smiling back at her with my heart in it. We all shook hands, and I led the way out of the building. A bell drilled the air. I leapt down the steps, two at a time, feeling like a leaf fluttering from a tree.

TERRA INCOGNITA

I had not expected anything like this.

This was where I was supposed to go to school? I hunched in the back of my father's car, appalled. Margaret Morrison Junior High School sat on a huge, scruffy piece of land, next to Highway 123. Flat concrete roofs topped a single story. The building crouched off-balance on its lot; later I would learn a fire had consumed the other half. An awning with dented aluminum supports covered a walkway from the curb. Two temporary classrooms squatted to the right. Tufts of weeds spotted the red clay between the buildings.

I swallowed. My father turned his head to look at me and reached over the seat back to pat my hand. Next to him, my mother reached for her purse. With shaking fingers, I tugged on my favorite jacket, navy blue with knit cuffs, all the rage in Krefeld, and picked up my satchel to get out of the car. I eyed the double-doors shaded by the awning. What would I find in there?

Our shoes clacked on scuffed gray linoleum as we followed the signs to the office. The trail led past the kitchen and lunchroom, along a pale green cinderblock hallway, past a small library partitioned off with plywood, to another plywood wall around the corner. It looked like a good strong wind could bring it down. The office door stood open.

A stout woman with twinkling eyes peered at us over the tops of her reading glasses. Stacks of paper littered her gray metal desk. A fine net covered her thinning white hair. A baggy sweater draped over her dark blouse. When she pushed herself up off her chair to greet us, I noticed she also wore a peasant skirt and stood only a few centimeters taller than me. Her lips burned bright red and rouge spotted her wrinkled cheeks. I had never seen such obvious make-up in anyone over twenty-five before. The color bled into her wrinkles and highlighted them.

She introduced herself as Mrs. Whitney. This was supposed to be the principal? The way she was dressed, she should have been at home fluffing up pillows for her grandson's nap. She pointed to the padded metal chairs across from her desk and sat herself down with a puff.

I worked extra hard on my English the last six months, but in the two weeks since we arrived in the US, I realized that the Oxford accent Frau Tümmler modeled in Krefeld had little in common with Southern American English. Mrs. Whitney's drawl confirmed my trouble. After the first few phrases, I let my father handle the discussion. I handed over my final report card, which she barely glanced at. If my muscles hadn't been so tense, I'd have sagged. I had been so proud. My grades didn't matter here. My mother and I settled into attitudes of polite attention, even though we could only grasp at islands in the river of talk.

Eventually, my father stopped to translate. Mrs. Whitney had told him that they divided their grades into four tracks. She thought, since my English was limited, it would be best to start me out in one of the easier tracks, so I could have a chance to learn the language and they could find out what I knew. Mrs. Whitney gave me a typed schedule, levered herself out of her chair, and I understood her saying "Goodbye" to my parents. They turned toward me, hesitating. My mother touched my shoulder and wished me luck, then my father squeezed my hand and they disappeared through the door.

This was it, then. I tried to look like I didn't mind. Mrs. Whitney bent over to pick up and move some papers. I saw the tops of her knee-high nylons. Her shoes were worn flat. How I longed for Frau Dr. Porten in her English tweed suit with the discreet lapel pin, her feet elegant in gleaming pumps. This principal shuffled off in front of me to lead me to my classroom. I gulped some air, told myself to stop shaking and followed her.

The first week of school rushed past me in a kaleidoscope of bizarre impressions. Isolated desks, instead of rows of benches. Kids carrying loose books. Groups of girls quizzing me at recess – I understood them if they fed me one word at a time – about conditions in Germany. Did we have enough to eat? Did we have bathrooms, TV's and refrigerators? Little and big shocks jumbled together.

School prayer. The first time, I didn't have a clue what was happening when Mrs. Edwards asked the students to rise. They closed their eyes, folded their hands, and recited the Lord's Prayer along with Mrs. Edwards. Could they really mean it? They looked so theatrical, as if they were imitating pious pictures, competing to see who could appear most holy. I had never encountered prayer outside of church before. Besides, after a flurry of attending regular Wednesday morning services and trying to act mild and meek sometime in the fifth grade, I became an agnostic. I decided it was lucky everyone else was so fervent they closed their eyes. That way, they couldn't see me mumble along with a grimace.

Pledging allegiance. I thought this even stranger than prayer. I'd never seen anyone adulate a flag before, except in grainy film clips from the thirties. The first time, when everyone put their right hand on their chest I followed suit. I decided imitation promised the safest way to pass through the day. When they recited the Our Father, I could make out the meaning from the rhythm of the familiar prayer. But I couldn't understand the words aimed at the flag on the wall. After a few days of bungling the words and feeling increasingly weird in that dramatic pose, hand on chest, I asked my parents what they thought. My mother suggested I stand to show respect, but keep my hands at my side and my mouth shut. It wasn't my flag, after all.

Lunch. Three black women cooked all morning, everything from scratch. The food may have been strange to me, but their skill converted me to Southern cuisine. All morning, the smells of meat and fruit pies teased my stomach. The other kids rolled their eyes, and only cleaned their plates on hamburger day. Otherwise, they shoved their trays through the line, then scowled at their vegetables and picked the fruit out of the pastry crust. I loved chicken potpie, banana pudding, and peach or cherry pie, especially the crunchy edge. So I cleaned my plate, and puzzled over the garbage bins full of food at the exit. I couldn't overcome my post-war training to imitate the local ways. My mother's admonitions - never take more than you can eat, food is precious - amplified by epic tales of hunger, knocked against each other inside my head.

By the end of the first week, I knew that my navy wool tights, my composition books, and my leather satchel didn't fit in. I dragged my parents to the drugstore to buy spiral notebooks, and convinced my mother I needed to wear nylons every day instead of only on special occasions. She shook her head, but didn't argue. She didn't want to make it harder for me to adapt. I left my satchel at home and dug out the purse I'd begged my parents to buy on our vacation in Italy. It was *mod* - black and white check with black trim - and I had been sure when strolling through Sirmione that it made me look so grown up that no one would know I was with my parents if I just hung back a bit. Now, I stuffed it with my school supplies. It was a purse, even if it didn't resemble the brown leather ones my classmates carried.

I knew my clothes didn't fit in either, but I didn't want to wear the cotton smocks and matching skirt and sweater sets I'd seen on all the others, even if it had occurred to me to ask for a whole new wardrobe. I was certain my clothes were fashionable and theirs dowdy. I piled my books on top of the notebooks, hung my purse over my shoulder, slammed the screen door (another new concept!) of the house my father had rented for us and waited for the school bus at the bottom of Grace Street.

By the end of the day, I was exhausted. My mind sizzled from all the detail it had to master. I returned from school, nerves rubbed raw from unaccustomed experiences, ears exhausted from jagged syllables. My brain was rubbery from trying to stretch around a new language. My body drooped after hours of staying on guard. No move was natural. At the *Gymnasium*, my classmates were girls only. Here boys sat at the next desks. One day, I dropped my purse and spilled its guts along the aisle. Bobby Cook, a blond boy who looked fully-grown at thirteen, with a deep voice and manly muscles, picked up my pencils and handed them across. Why did that make me flush until I couldn't breathe?

At home, we had watched civil rights marches on the news. We saw dark-skinned people, in suits and impeccable dresses, sprayed with fire hoses and attacked by dogs. I was outraged that people would treat each other that way. The schools of Clemson had been integrated the year before I arrived, and I was determined not to act prejudiced. There were a few black students in my classes, but when I tried to smile at them, they lowered their eyes as if I threatened them. I noticed that they looked down at their shoes when talking to the teachers. The other white students didn't seem to see them at all. I could tell I would upset a delicate balance if I weren't careful.

I felt like my tongue was lead and my body angled. I bumped into everything - desks, lunch tables, and rules. On the first cold day, the principal stopped by my desk during homeroom. She was very gentle. She bent forward and whispered into my ear, "You probably didn't realize this, but our dress code doesn't allow girls to wear pants." She didn't send me home to change. All day long my black ski pants glowed on my legs. I alternated between humiliation and fury. What's a dress code? What kind of a place was this? It was supposed to be the land of freedom!

Every afternoon, when I came back on the school bus, I got off on Skyview drive, never raising my eyes to scan the horizon for the promised Blue Ridge Mountains, trudging up the Grace Street hill with my eyes trained on the pebbly blacktop. I barely grunted to my mother, who was hungry for conversation but observant enough to give me some recuperation time. I collapsed on my bed and wished myself home. I'd call up my German life: riding my bike to the indoor pool, taking the tram to meet Sabine for a stroll through Krefeld's shopping area, or walking to the corner bakery to buy pastries. I liked to bring myself to the edge of tears by indulging the piercing tugs of nostalgia I could conjure at will. After an hour or so, my headache subsided.

I emerged and tried to make sense out of all I was learning by telling my mother about it. My feelings of bewilderment turned into wailing and whining in her presence. Why couldn't everything be the way it was at home? When you're feeling displaced, the first impulse is to catalogue why everything was better there. Whenever I slipped too far into condemning this new place, my mother vacillated between sympathy and worry. She hated it too, but I mustn't criticize. I was a guest in this country. And I was German. Especially as a German, I had no right to act superior. She was right, of course. But that didn't help me figure out what to do with my misery.

Mostly, I crawled back into my room. I tried my AM radio, but the South Carolina stations played twangy music I didn't recognize and lots of Elvis. Elvis was fifties music as far as I was concerned. I listened to the records from home: the Beatles, the Rolling Stones, Herman's Hermits, and Cilla Black; read and reread my German books, wrote letters to Karin and Sabine, drew and designed houses totally different from the one on Grace Street. No three-bedroom ranch houses with brick exterior for me. Even the three-quarter bath that connected to my bedroom - I was thrilled when I first saw it: my own private bathroom! - couldn't console me. The houses I drew were modern, with seas of plate glass, roofs extended at futuristic angles. Sometimes I experimented with odd shapes. Series of circles strung together. The challenge was how to fit everything a house needed into the space I created.

In December, one of our teachers taught us how to make "stained glass" out of wax paper and crayon shavings. My mother and I picked up some crayons and wax paper at the Winn-Dixie and I covered over every single windowpane in my room. The panels softened the light, filtered and subdued it. I could no longer see the screens that cast an alien haze. I could dream without having to confront the unfamiliar trees, the stretch of Bermuda grass and the oversized, washed-out squirrels outside my window.

By February, my exhaustion began to subside. I ventured outside my cave. Across the street, the tangle of uncleared scrub sloped down toward a creek. At first, I explored there with a girl who lived around the corner. Kay's father was in the army and they had just moved to Clemson from Arkansas. She delighted in educating me in civilized ways. She taught me that you're supposed to wear underpants under your nightgown and read the Bible before bed. I chalked both of these up as more weird customs. Who'd ever heard of actually reading the Bible? And wearing underpants at night was just plain unhygienic. Didn't Kay know your body needs to air out? I never said a word though, just nodded and smiled. When I spent the night at her house (another new concept: the sleepover,) she introduced me to Johnny Carson and salted popcorn. I had only ever had it sweetened. In her company, I felt safe enough to venture into the woods and discovered that there weren't snakes under every bush, as I was certain there were.

After that, I wandered on my own. Kay's constant instruction tired me. My brown leather shoes became clotted with rusty dirt. I loved the quartz flakes that sparkled in the mud after the rain. On our side of the street, within a few meters of my bedroom window, I found a pine that was perfect for climbing. Its branches were just strong enough to support me and spaced perfectly, so I could pull myself up, bracing my foot on a stub. I sat in the tree, my back leaning against its rough trunk, and faced away from the house into the woods. Pine trees and kudzu, wild dogwoods and trees I hadn't learned to recognize faded into a vague haze of brown and green against the dried-blood color of the ground.

In early spring, the air in South Carolina is misty and gentle. I can't remember what I thought about while I sat there. I may not have thought at all. I was trying to get a feel for the land, find some way to absorb this new place. I watched the big gray squirrels and no longer compared them to the little red ones that lived in the Krefeld city parks. I listened to the bird song, not discriminating or identifying, just trying to tune my ear to their sounds. A deep melancholy settled into my thirteen-year-old bones. Did it well up from my displacement? From the inevitable shifts of adolescence? I will never know. My life was a drama whose scenery had changed. My awareness had split. I felt a step outside myself, narrating, watching myself act in certain ways knowing that other ways were possible. I couldn't be impulsive, because I had to find the right behavior for this culture, not that one. Instinct wasn't good enough any more. I'd always check the mist in the air, the color of the dirt first. There would always be a screen of thought, a haze of deliberation between me and the world.

*****

How could I measure the distance between Krefeld and Clemson? If I could have scuttled crabwise across the globe, I would have covered 4,400 miles between them. But the wild waters of the

Atlantic take up most of that distance. Icy swells, sharks. Somewhere between Northern Europe and the Southern United States, I passed through a culture warp, and entered a parallel universe. The English language melted like Dali's clocks, space expanded between houses and towns, colors intensified under the Southern sun. The distance could not be measured in miles. It was the distance between urban and rural, humanist and fundamentalist, North and South. No wonder I felt lost.

As I inched my way out of the paralysis of shock, what I missed most at first was my independence. In Clemson, I couldn't go anywhere by myself, and even if I could have, there was no place to go. I had known Clemson was small. My father had told me there were 8000 people not counting the college students. When we had studied local history and geography in elementary school, I learned that Krefeld had 300,000 inhabitants and was considered part of the Rhein-Ruhr industrial area, one of the most densely populated spots in Europe.

When I tried to imagine Clemson, I pictured what I knew: a tidy European village with a market square, sidewalk café, and public transportation that would get me to the nearest city in less than half an hour. I couldn't have conceived of the way Clemson rambled loosely over the Blue Ridge foothills surrounded by a scatter of other small towns. There was a main street, College Avenue, with two drug stores, a hardware store, a movie theater, a dress store, a bar and the Winn Dixie. At one end of the street, the Clemson University Campus with its dorms and married student housing simulated a real town, but in 1966 it was still mostly a boys' school and off-limits to young girls. A mile or so away, the A&P and Mack's Variety store anchored the Clemson Shopping Center. Wooded roads led to subdivisions with single story houses dotting expansive stretches of Bermuda grass. When we wanted to shop for anything other than basic necessities, we had to drive the twenty-five minutes to Anderson which did not qualify as a city either along a smooth ribbon of four-lane highway that curved through pine forests and meadows with barely a house in sight. In Germany, a twenty-five minute drive would have taken us from Krefeld to Düsseldorf on roads that sliced through dense fields of apartment buildings and houses.

Except in the three blocks that constituted the business district, Clemson's roads faded into grass at the edges. There were no sidewalks, no pedestrians and no bicycles. My father laughed about the time he'd decided to take a walk in the neighborhood. Three drivers had stopped their cars to check whether he needed a ride.

There was no doubt about it. I felt stuck in a wasteland. When I complained, my father strung me along with promises that I would find compensations once I adjusted.

*****

Within six months, my sentences lengthened. My Oxford accent's stiff edges and throaty German undertone smoothed and opened into the sounds of Upstate South Carolina. I could converse on any subject without searching for phrases and halting the flow to translate a thought. Even so, I frequently ran up against a gap I could not bridge.

My new friend Kay asked me right away, "Are you from the good part of Germany or the bad part?"

I had never thought of it that way. "East Germany is the communist part. I'm from West Germany." Behind my simple answer, complex memories crowded in. "My relatives all live in East Germany."

Kay's eyebrows rose. "Really?"

Maybe I could explain what it was like. "My parents escaped to West Germany, but my mother and I used to go to the East several times a year for visits."

"How did you do that?"

What was she asking? Had she never crossed any border at all?

"You have to apply for a permit, and then you get on a train and they let you across. You have to exchange money for every day you'll be there." I wanted to keep talking, but Kay's empty eyes told me I'd lost her. When I stopped, she tried once more.

"How can they make you exchange money?" She asked.

I had to think about that for a minute. Following rules in East Germany was so automatic, that I had never wondered how enforcement worked. There were forms and stamps and certificates. Oh, yes.

"When you leave, you have to have papers proving that you've exchanged the money. Otherwise, they don't let you out." As I spoke I pictured myself sitting on the train at the border crossing, a border guard standing over me, frowning at my passport. Outside the train window would be barracks, attack dogs, mine strips, and guard towers. How could I describe the pervasive fear?

Before I could try, Kay asked: "Do they still have Nazis there?"

She had knocked the wind out of me. Nazis? In 1966, Nazis and the war were history; they had nothing to do with me. I managed to sputter out a "No," but I was silenced. Kay's question provided my first hint that living outside Germany would force me to confront history in a whole new light.

As long as I lived in Germany, I could regard Hitler and his war as a human problem, a calamity that held a universal warning. I wouldn't wrestle with the question whether Nazism grew out of a German cultural character flaw until much later.

Over time I would learn that 'German' and 'Nazi' were intertwined enough in Americans' minds that I would have to learn to answer for German history in a way that had never occurred to me before. At first I thought it was enough that I was born eight years after Hitler's suicide, but later I had to confront the reality that many people believed my nationality made me more likely to commit organized mass murder. And now I had to adjust to the reality that for the girls that became my friends in junior high, Nazis daily roamed the TV screen and West and East Germany might as well have been on another planet.

*****

The first year in South Carolina, my mother and I grew closer than ever, even though I was thirteen. The girls at school acted like they hated their mothers. The way they talked, their mothers were stupid, embarrassing, and knew nothing about their daughters. While we were still in Germany, I felt myself wanting to hide when my mother questioned a price in a store or checked with a stranger at the tram stop whether the tram was just late or we had missed it. I was twelve; I wanted to be invisible. Now that I was in South Carolina, the opportunities to feel mortified multiplied, but I couldn't afford to treat my mother as the enemy. My mother was the only ally I had. We didn't exactly make a pact to stick together; we stumbled along in this alien country joined by confusion.

Because I spent hours every day at school, I felt like an emissary sent out into the world to bring home news of the culture. I collected new words and observations like treasures. When I arrived home in the afternoons, my mouth aching because Americans smiled so much more than Germans, I collapsed for an hour or so while my mother finished watching the soap operas that were supposed to expand her vocabulary. As the sands came drifting down through the hourglass at the end of 'Days of Our Lives,' my mother turned off the TV. We talked. I spread the day's nuggets and observations before her. What did it mean that girls constantly used the word *cute*? We spent weeks trying to gauge its timbre. The word applied to boys and puppies, purses and dresses. Mostly, *cute* circulated all day in a daily exchange of compliments. The girls bounced it around like a Ping-Pong ball. In Germany, remarks about new clothes or shoes were considered intimate conversation reserved for close relatives or best friends. Over several months my mother and I decided that the constant trade of *cute* meant you were always watched and appearance was critical.

Another word that stumped us was *popular*. We'd both grown up having one or two best friends. The rest of our classes at school had operated more or less as a unit. When I first started hearing the words *in crowd* and *popular*, I asked my classmates to explain them. They couldn't. The best they could do was tell me which girls belonged. My mother and I spent weeks trying to figure this one out.

"Are they pretty?" my mother asked.

"Some are. But no, I don't think that's it. The one they all say is in charge has kind of a horsy face." I thought some more. "Maybe it's the clothes they wear?"

"What's special about their clothes?"

"They all wear the same thing. Those Bobbie Brooks outfits with the matching skirts and sweaters. Plus they all wear loafers with pennies." But how could clothes set you up to be different? "No, wait. That can't be it. Jackie wears the same kind of clothes, except when she has Girl Scouts on Thursdays, and she doesn't seem to belong."

"Are they smart?"

"Sort of. They're in the smart class. But they aren't *brains.*" By now we'd detected the derogatory undertone in the word brain. By the time I advanced to the first track at the end of seventh grade, I was considered a *brain,* but it didn't bother me because I was simultaneously considered *cute.* We never did figure out the mystery of *popularity.* When the *popular* crowd started being friendly to me and invited me to a boy-girl party, I hesitated. Being invited felt oddly like being knighted, but I'd heard rumors that their parties involved games like *spin-the-bottle* in darkened rooms. When I discovered that there would be no parents at the party, I worried out loud to my mother. She suggested that I refuse the invitation on the grounds that my parents wouldn't let me go, and I leapt at that suggestion with immense relief. Thus ended my flirt with *popularity.*

My mother had her own cultural mysteries to ponder. One day someone at church took my father aside and said, "I saw your wife over at the liquor store yesterday." My father nodded, wondering why this remark required a confidential whisper. The man continued, "I know ya'll are new here. Thought I'd let you know that it just isn't done." When my father still looked confused, he added, "Ladies going to the liquor store."

Even my father admitted to being stumped. How odd. My mother fumed. Not go to the liquor store? It was an easy stop for her on the way back from the Winn-Dixie. For several days we discussed her options. I got righteously indignant on her behalf. Just ignore the comment, and show them. My mother wasn't so sure. The liquor store parking lot was behind the building, so passers-by couldn't see who was shopping there from the highway. If even the locals didn't want to be seen buying alcohol, this must really be a big deal. In the end, my mother grumbled but she had my father stop to buy their Bourbon on his way home from work.

We got in the habit of working as a team on issues that were divisive for my classmates and their mothers. We didn't fight over how soon and how far up I could shave my legs. My mother had just realized she too would have to shave if she didn't want to offend. Our big problem was overcoming what we'd always been taught: "If you shave your body hair, it will grow back coarser and darker, so never, ever shave."

Finally, we bought two bottles of Nair and retreated into separate showers. When we were done, we sneaked glances at each other's naked legs. My mother looked exposed, I thought. The hair had hidden her psoriasis and the scar from her broken kneecap. My own legs looked childish without the hair, but at least no one would think we were unclean.

We also didn't argue over when I could wear a bra. I didn't actually want one, but even the most flat-chested girl in my class had one.

"You're sure?" my mother asked, when I told her we needed to go shopping.

"I know it seems silly," I answered. She shrugged. By now we both knew that I was the authority on American teen customs.

Stores didn't carry undershirts for girls, but they did have something called 'training bras'. We had a good laugh over that. Why would you need training for wearing bras? When you needed one, surely your body could deal with this new article of clothing without first having to practice? Or was that little white piece of cloth with elastic straps supposed to train your body to make breasts? I couldn't imagine wanting that. To me, my budding breasts came as a surprise. They explained why my chest ached whenever I tried to sleep on my stomach.

Most of the time, my mother and I felt equally confused as we felt our way through the maze of social nuance. There was one area where I quickly took the lead: communication. Since I was immersed in English six hours a day from the very first week, my English rapidly improved. My afternoon reports became more of a mishmash of German and English every day. My father got so concerned about my drift into exclusive English that he instituted a rule: no English on weekends. Whenever I told stories from school, I cheated, justifying my inability to articulate my school life in my mother tongue by saying, "I can't tell it in German, because it happened in English."

My mother, on the other hand, spent few hours with native speakers. Her sources of vocabulary and daily idiom were the soap operas she watched and the words I brought home from school. Her accent remained formidable, as if her scaffolding of sounds was poured in concrete. In German, she was witty, her speech spiced with metaphor. In English she plodded, formulating her sentences deliberately and stumbling over the same letters predictably. Whenever she attempted to make phone calls, she composed her words on paper first. She practiced sentences she needed to ask sales clerks. Her preparation did not pay off. Few immigrants lived in Upstate South Carolina in the sixties. Foreign students and professors were rare in Clemson until the seventies. The sales clerks and receptionists my mother had to deal with had no experience with accents different from their own. When my mother talked, they panicked. They identified her as 'strange' and knew they could never understand. My mother began to dread their glazed eyes and distressed faces. How embarrassing to end up with the entire sales staff clustered around, repeating the same questions at louder volume as she worked harder to get the right emphasis into a word she knew was correct. She recruited me to become her voice.

I made the phone calls. When she wanted to go anywhere other than the grocery store, she waited until afternoon, so I could come along to translate. At first I enjoyed being needed and demonstrating competence. With time though, I grew resentful that my mother wouldn't try harder to overcome her own embarrassment. I simply would not believe that she couldn't remember not to pronounce a j like a y, no matter how many times I reminded her. My protests did no good. I had to go shopping with her, and she kept me in front of her like a shield.

Even when I resented having to speak for my mother, I never equaled my classmates' animosity. I flirted with pouts at times - I'll never forget the trip we took to Charleston over Easter Weekend; not because of Charleston's charming architecture, but because my mother forced me to wear white ankle socks with my black pumps, so I wouldn't get blisters. I refused to speak to her that whole day. But to say, "I hate my mother?" If I said such a thing wouldn't lightning strike me dead? Wouldn't she know it in her heart, even if she were miles away? I could just as easily pick up a knife and stab her.

But American teens appeared to think it was okay to talk like this. Parents, in their view, were inconveniences, providers of material goods, people who could never understand one's feelings and should therefore be deceived. My mother and I puzzled over this, too. Where did such an attitude come from? We talked about everything, daily, even before we had a culture to decipher. My German friends too, talked with their mothers. Sometimes, if you had done something you felt guilty about, you might omit it and hope to get away with it, but you certainly never hid your problems.

Every time I got caught up in the anti-parent attitude my classmates modeled at school, my mother complained about me becoming 'Americanized.' All she had to do was tell me to remember that she was a person too, and that I was hurting her feelings when I acted like she was stupid, and guilt stopped me. Especially since I already felt sorry for her. My mother clearly suffered extreme homesickness. She'd lost her best friend, Gudrun, though they wrote every few weeks. Making new friends was a daunting task, especially with the culture difference. She was thrown back on the wives of the handful of Germans in the area; most of them people she would never have sought out at home. English fit her tongue like a straitjacket. Krefeld figured as paradise in her conversations. Her longing for the shopping streets and trams, the smooth walking paths in the parks and the smells and tastes of home weakened her. I couldn't hurt her. Instead we nurtured our homesickness together.

*****

Homesickness, I would later learn, is a form of grief and comes in stages. The feelings of loss and bewilderment baffled me, but I was totally unprepared for what came next: red-hot seething anger. Like an exile, I felt I had nothing to gain from this move, yet I could not declare it a mistake and go home. If only I could convince my father of my suffering. The acute powerlessness of early adolescence stoked my rage and confusion. And then there was the matter of golf.

My father was now an American manager, and American managers play golf. I had never seen my father swing anything other than a croquet mallet and that rarely, with little finesse. However, golf, along with a large American car, was a prerequisite for being taken seriously by his customers. Besides, during the six months my father had lived alone in Clemson, before my mother and I arrived, he had nothing to do on weekends. He acquired a set of clubs and spent Saturdays and Sundays at the Boscobel Country Club.

In spring, my father purchased a set of Ladies' Clubs for my mother. I'm not sure what possessed him to think she would like golf, or what stopped her from asserting her resistance. Maybe he convinced her that playing golf would replace the Sunday afternoon strolls we took in Krefeld. He was a salesman, and my mother was off-balance. The only physical activity other than walking my mother ever engaged in was swimming, and she did that with her neck stretched out of the water, so her hair wouldn't get wet.

My mother returned from the first few trips to the golf course fuming. She muttered to herself that golf was a stupid game and she'd never learn it. My father followed her into the house, lecturing about relaxing and watching the ball. My mother rolled her eyes as she walked out of the room.

I ducked, determined to stay out of the way, glad I didn't have to go along. After three or four of these outings, during which my mother did not discover a passion for golf, the weather heated up and my mother learned she was pregnant. She couldn't possibly keep playing under these conditions. The clubs sat in the carport, attracting spiders for a few weeks. Then both my parents decided that I should accompany my father.

I was furious. I was coping by directing my rage at everything unfamiliar. Golf was just one more American thing. Ever since we arrived in Clemson, my father had been working harder than ever. He wasn't gone for weeks at a time, but he went to the office on Saturdays and talked and breathed nothing but work. Maybe he decided to take me golfing to recreate our Sunday morning walks, to try to rebuild the closeness we always had. What he wasn't counting on was that I held him responsible for my misery. I would be at home in Krefeld if it weren't for him.

Since my father is a planner, he announced his intent to play golf over Saturday breakfast. To avoid the worst summer heat, we played late in the afternoon. That gave me all day to pout. I scowled at him every chance I got. As four o'clock approached, I disappeared into the far corners of the house. I wasn't rebellious enough to refuse when he found me and announced, in a cheerful tone that made me want to scream: "Time to go golfing!" I dragged my feet, took extra long to put on my shorts, went to the bathroom even though I didn't have to pee, all the while aware that my father stood next to the car, golf bags already in the trunk, his foot tapping, his keys jangling.

Although golf is an American sport, my father approached it in a German way. We would not use a golf cart - that was stupid. Why go outdoors for exercise and then drive? Neither would we hire a caddy. The purpose was to get exercise, not spend money. We pulled our bags on two-wheeled carts, creeping along so slowly we constantly had to let others "play through." I watched with envy and humiliation, as well as superiority as groups of middle-aged men zoomed past us in their electric carts. In a rare display of cultural criticism my father joked that Americas used their legs so little that it was a wonder they hadn't atrophied into stumps.

I don't know if my father ever had a golf lesson - I know I didn't. We hacked our way from hole to hole, leaving divots in our wake and golf balls in the rough pine forests and water hazards. The pond that bred armies of mosquitoes along the third hole swallowed my balls. I never dared retrieve them, even when I could spot them near the water's edge, because the muddy banks looked like a haven for snakes. The humidity condensed on my hair and my face, mingled with the sweat under my arms and between my thighs, and weighed down my already resentful disposition until I felt my limbs were too heavy to drag another centimeter. If my father imagined us having father-daughter talks he suffered disappointment. I was hot and crabby and that gave me the courage to deluge him with my grievances.

"I hate it here," I'd start. We were walking down the fairway, headed toward a stand of pine that had swallowed his drive.

"Give it some time," he'd soothe and pretend to be absorbed in his search.

"There's nothing to do!" I heard the whine creep into my voice. Yuck. But maybe it would puncture his composure. It didn't. He bent his head to search, as he poked his driver into the underbrush. I felt my free hand tighten into a fist.

"None of the girls read real books, they think modern art is stupid - they've never even heard of Mondrian, or Klee or anybody..." I sputtered, staring at my father's back, trying to come up with an insult vile enough to force him to turn around. What would it take?

"The only place to go swimming is that muddy hole behind the clubhouse, and it's so hot you can hardly move all day, and people talk about you if your skirt's too short." How could I take my enormous disgust and throw it at him? Broken down like this, even I feared that my criticisms sounded trivial.

"Aha!" My father had found his ball. He emerged onto the fairway with a look of triumph. Had he been listening at all?

"I want to leave this dump and go home!" I felt my foot jerk to stomp the ground.

He looked at me then and said in his most patient voice, "We can't just leave. You know that."

Of course, I knew. But that didn't help at all. I couldn't speak; I'd choke on my frustration. I turned away, slouching toward the sand trap, looking for a ball to whack.

The only thing I looked forward to was the air-conditioning in my father's company car on the ride home. I'd lean forward into the stale, cool air, relieved that another golf game was over, and plotting excuses why I couldn't go next week. I can't imagine why my father didn't go by himself. I couldn't have been very good company. Was it penance for the hard time he knew he was causing? Or was it just his stubbornness? *We are going to have family time now whether you like it or not.* I could hang on to my stubborn dislike of golf just as long as he could hang on to the hope that I'd get over it. Especially since I wanted to make him pay.

My mother too was miserable. She hated everything; she longed for Krefeld. Together, on weekday afternoons, we created fantasy shopping trips. We imagined the fabric stores, with their imported French buttons, the *Markthalle* - the indoor farmer's market - with the fish booth wreathed in tendrils of *Schillerlocken* - strips of smoked mackerel - and the tank where carps blew bubbles. We strolled down the Hochstrasse in the *Fussgängerzone* - pedestrian zone - admiring the elaborate window displays installed by trained professional window decorators. We picked up a cheap bouquet of Dutch gerbera, my mother's favorite. We rushed toward the tram stop on the Rheinstrasse and waited for a tram marked 5. It glided to a stop and we climbed in and plopped down cradling our shopping nets, bulging with paper-wrapped packages. The tram rocked us gently as it edged around the traffic circle at Friedrichsplatz. By the time we got off at Kapuzinerkloster, our feet were rested enough for the ten-minute walk home.

Whenever we indulged in these reveries they led to a hangover of anger. My mother had days where nothing suited her. She greeted my father with a long list of complaints: she couldn't find proper basting thread, nylons were wimpy and ran more easily than the German ones, there were no undershirts for women, they didn't even make them. We all knew the bread was a lost cause, but when my mother was in such a mood, she muttered under her breath at the ever-present taste of salt spoiling the butter. Cucumbers were seedier and watery; they made her burp. At the dinner table, she and I ganged up on my father, offering our hoarded criticisms like handfuls of thistles. *See here, you're making us sleep on these. You're forcing us to live with this.*

Most of the time, my father infuriated us by reacting as little as possible. My mother said, "I know what you're thinking. *Ja, ja*, let them talk; they'll get over it eventually. Well, it won't work."

She didn't say what would happen, though. I felt her words shoot toward him, he flinched, but I saw no apparent damage. Once in a while, we pushed him hard enough to puncture his pose.

"Stop it," he ordered, "you're exaggerating." Then he reminded my mother that she never felt at home in Krefeld either, and, his voice getting sharper, accused her of poisoning me against him. This stung me more than her. I rose to the defense of my independent anger.

"I can't stand this place," I sobbed.

My father's lips pressed together - maybe he felt sorry for me, more likely he was disgusted - I couldn't tell. I would have loved to fling my napkin on the table and flee, but I was still hungry. I knew if I left, I couldn't come back. I subsided, while my mother's eyes locked with his. The tension between them zinged.

Trapped. That's how I felt. I couldn't go home, and the very people who forced me to live here were the only ones who understood who I was. My mother's suffering rivaled my own. She was too weak to stand up for herself and for me. Before my sense of betrayal could even flare up, it transformed into pity. And the habit of adoration for my father remained just strong enough to prevent me from going for the throat. I had dreams in which I screamed and screamed but couldn't make a sound.

I found it easier to blame Clemson.

*****

What broke my parents' tension was the baby. When my mother first discovered her pregnancy none of us dared to believe that a baby would result. I had wanted a sibling as long as I could remember. But both times my mother had been pregnant after my birth she'd had a miscarriage during her fifth month. So we held our breath, and tried to shield our hearts from hope.

Later, my mother attributed success to American medicine. I watched from the sidelines, wishing her well, but refusing to share her faith. Every other week, she drove to Anderson, clutching the steering wheel, knees locked to maintain the correct speed in the right lane. Everything Dr. Hand told her, she repeated with devoted fervor. She weighed herself daily and forced down glasses of milk at every meal. As our first Southern summer slid beyond its infernal peak, she passed through the danger zone and the whole family relaxed. By her seventh month, my mother finally looked pregnant.

She decided it was safe to discuss baby names. What German names worked in English? We savored syllables in both languages, tossed ideas around as we drove from store to store, seeking a crib. They teetered between 'Nicola' and 'Nicole' for a girl, so they let me decide. I rolled the sounds around my mouth. 'Nicola' flowed better, I announced. The low knell at the end of 'Nicole' gonged like a sad bell. It didn't occur to me that 'Nicola' with a Southern accent rhymes with Cola. I enjoyed this conversation, not just because I gloried in the power of such an important decision. Choosing a German name implied that this child would someday go home with us.

Since Dr. Hand guided my mother through the worst of her fears and brought her out the other side, safe and bulging, she gave up any thought of questioning the American way of birth. When Dr. Hand suggested inducing labor a few weeks early so my father would be sure to be in the country for the event, she chalked it up to American progress. I felt a bit queasy about scheduling a birth around a business trip – why couldn't my father postpone his trip? - but who was I to question authority in the matter of birth?

The first few weeks, I hovered around my mother and Nica, fascinated. I learned how to change diapers and dress her in tiny undershirts and sleepers while supporting her head with the cup of my free hand. My mother let me hold Nica in my lap while she drank from her bottle, and showed me how to drape her over my shoulder and pat her fragile back to elicit a burp. Nica's crib stood in the bedroom that connected to the other side of my bathroom. One night, I even woke to her cries of hunger and got up to feed her so my mother could sleep. I settled in the rocking chair, with my sister propped in the curve of my arm. A surge of love swept from the center of my chest through my whole body, framing us in the bright room, the dark night. Not many nights later, I got used to my sister's intermittent crying and slept right through it.

Once the spark of learning baby care sputtered to a dull glow, I began to count my losses. When I returned home from school, Nica lay asleep in her crib. No more turning the Beatles up loud in my room. My mother, if she was awake, listened to me with a distracted air, as if there were more important concerns than who said what to whom in the lunch line. We couldn't take off for Anderson to shop for a new blouse on a weekday, because there wasn't enough time between the baby's nap and dinner. I had heard of big siblings being jealous of a new baby. Surely that wouldn't happen to me. I was practically grown up. I loved my new sister. I had wanted her for so many years. How could I possibly be petty enough to get jealous?

I was not jealous. I was just having trouble with the never-ending consideration I had to show. My needs, my wants took second place. I understood why. I could see that you couldn't explain to a month-old-baby that it needed to show some consideration for its big sister, too. Then why did I find myself in my room, sobbing, pounding the mattress with hard fists? My universe had shifted again, this time internally. I knew I was still near the center somewhere, but it was no longer exclusively mine. A little baby had torpedoed its way right to the heart.

My mother still chimed in when I indulged in the criticisms that grew out of homesickness, but most of the time, her eyes were either glazed from lack of sleep, or locked in bliss with the baby's. For the moment, at least, unhappiness had little room in her heart. If I wanted to cling to my anger, I was on my own.

*****

While my mother found distraction from her homesickness in baby care, I found consolation in my newfound effect on boys. At first, the presence of boys in my school life was just one part of what made America alien. While I struggled with language and manners, clothes, and culture, boys were the least of my worries. When, after a few months, several boys sent messages via friends that they 'liked' me, my mother who as usual was my first confidante, shook her head. "Just say thank you." she counseled. I took her advice. Jimmy, a skinny kid with a bony face who lived just across my backyard wasn't satisfied with that answer. "But do you like Jerry?" Jerry was my next-door neighbor. I had barely noticed him. He was a quiet boy who said little in class and never talked to me. "I don't know," I blurted and turned away to hide my confusion.

When I tried to quiz Kay on the bus, I bumped into a new level of language mystery. "Do you like him as a friend?" she asked. I still didn't know how you could like someone you never talked to. She tried to explain the difference between liking, which seemed to mean tolerating, and *Liking,* which was romantic. I sneaked a look at Jerry who was at that moment horsing around with Jimmy in the back row. Jerry's blond hair was bristly; a lot of boys had military haircuts that appeared bald to my European eyes. He had that gangly look of a thirteen-year-old whose energy was being consumed by growth. How mysterious. What made him think he *Liked* me?

I'm sure budding boy-girl relationships are confusing to every thirteen-year-old. But here I was transferred from a girls-only school where we had channeled our romantic longings exclusively toward movie stars and rock musicians, dropped into a cauldron seething with boy-girl tension, trying to decipher customs and code in mid-development. I vacillated between trying to appear indifferent and giving in to my growing curiosity. Curiosity won out.

The first time I heard the girls at lunch talking about the 'canteen,' it was just another word that didn't translate. When I asked, they told me it was a dance. There would be a seventh grade dance in the school cafeteria on Friday night. We were years away from the *Tanzschulalter* – dancing school age. Every German child whose family had enough money knew that at seventeen they would sign up for ballroom dance classes. For those who attended the gender-segregated *Gymnasiums*, dance classes were the first formal contact with the opposite sex. Apparently in America you didn't need dancing school, you just danced. And at thirteen. How deliciously frightening. But I didn't know how to dance, I didn't know what to wear, and I couldn't picture this event, so I thought I should just stay home. Kay urged me to come. There'd be square dancing for part of the evening. I had seen square dances on TV; they looked like fun. Kay asked if she could ride with me. I agreed to go.

In the car, Kay confided that she didn't think anyone would ask her to dance. "It's only the popular kids and the kids who are going together who dance much," she said. "Except for the square dance part. Everyone dances those." She didn't have to explain *going together* - we had covered that a few weeks before. I wondered what you did the whole evening if no one asked you to dance, but I didn't expect the canteen to go any differently for me than for her. I felt so out of place in Clemson, a watcher rather than a participant, that I imagined I was invisible.

Bright lights and a Beach Boys tune greeted us as we walked through the lunchroom doors. The linoleum tile floor gleamed empty over a vast expanse. Kids hugged the walls in clots separated by gender. The boys were cuffing each other, shoving each other into the vast open space in the center. Shrieking girls' voices competed with the music. A group of girls absorbed Kay and me. I noticed that my voice shook when I tried to yell a greeting into someone's ear. Yes, my hands were icy again.

The Square Dances took care of my icy hands. Most of the kids rolled their eyes as the caller, decked out in a string tie and cowboy boots, announced the first dance, but everyone lined up just as he asked, 'ladies' on one side and 'gents' on the other. I listened and watched as he and his wife, who wore a petticoat and flouncy checked skirt, demonstrated dance moves I had never heard of: *allemandes* and *do-si-do's* and *promenades*. When the dance finally started, my body adjusted to the rhythms and I began to feel the music. A changing array of boys twirled toward me to become partners for a while, but I didn't have time to get nervous. By the time the music stopped, I was breathing deeply and flushed. I had learned something: I liked to square dance. The girls I knew from my classes regrouped on the chairs against the walls. Kay's face had flushed bright red and she was wiping sweat off her forehead. When I told her that that was fun, she said: "Yeah, it was okay."

A new song started with a rush of violins. Kay whispered in my ear, "It's a slow dance," and settled back to look indifferent as a large group of boys detached themselves from their wall and drifted across the dance floor in the girls' direction. The first few couples moved to the music. I saw that slow dancing meant getting into dance position and barely moving your feet to the music. Before I could observe more, Jerry stood in front of me, mumbling an invitation. I rose out of our tight girl cluster, feeling Kay's eyes on my back as I followed Jerry to the far edge of the crowd. I was glad he was tall enough so I didn't have to look at him while we danced. All I saw was a plaid-shirted shoulder and a patch of white t-shirt at his neck. I wondered if we were supposed to converse while dancing. In the movies people talked. But what about?

By the time I returned to my chair, my knees were shaking and I collapsed. Kay said, "I told you he had a crush on you," as if I'd been arguing with her. A fast song – the boys seemed to avoid these – gave me time to rest. When the next slow dance started a different boy appeared in front of me. I felt giddy. Two dances! That was more than I had expected. Kay looked at me sideways as I got up again. I wondered why they were asking me, and not the girls who'd befriended me. It never occurred to me that they might have found me exciting with my odd accent and my strange clothes. I was trying so hard to blend in as I staggered through the school day I imagined everyone saw me as awkward, since that's how I felt.

The rest of the evening spun by. I danced every slow dance and tried to tell myself it wasn't bothering Kay, who sat in her chair, hands wrapped around each other, face frozen. When the music stopped, I walked away from my last partner, dazzled and drained. I would need to go home to think about what had happened here. Kay and I emerged into the cool night. My father's car idled at the curb, at the far end of the sidewalk. We walked past a group of boys that clustered around Jerry. They egged each other on to shout goodnight, as we climbed into the backseat of the Plymouth. When my father asked whether we had a good time, Kay didn't make a sound. I told him yes and leaned back, closing my eyes. What could I say? I'm sorry nobody asked you to dance? I didn't think that would help, even though I felt that way. I couldn't wait to get home so I could be alone with my surprise. Boys liked me enough to want to dance with me. For the first time in months, I didn't feel awkward or stupid.

After that night, I looked at the world differently. It wasn't just that I noticed boys and thought for the first time about which ones I found attractive. I felt suddenly powerful. The excitement of boys didn't compensate for my homesickness, but the distraction helped. I didn't know I was walking into a trap. Eventually, it would be American boys grown into men that would keep me here and bind me to this country.

*****

How could my parents make friends in South Carolina? My father examined the lay of the land and concluded we needed to join a church. Go to church? To meet people? I was outraged. In my thirteen-year-old moral universe, his idea smacked of hypocrisy. The only time my parents had set foot in a church in my lifetime was my mother's cousin's wedding. Okay, there was also the Müller's daughter's wedding and a baptism or two.

I had spent more time in churches than they had. When I was eleven, my friends Ulli and Bine and I experimented with going to children's services. I got up while my parents still lazed around in bed, put on my best dress and my Sunday shoes and waited for Ulli and Bine to ring our doorbell. Together we walked, our footsteps echoing in the still morning, to the tram stop we usually used to go to school. When the tram squeaked to a stop, we climbed in, flashed our monthly passes, and stood, our feet braced, near the exit door. We were too grown up to sit, and besides we were only going three stops.

The St. Johannes Protestant Church's towers were not yet repaired from their World War II bomb damage. In Krefeld, Protestants were the minority religion. During the reformation, way before Germany had become a nation, each German state had either adopted Protestantism or remained Catholic depending on the decision of its duke or prince. Krefeld was in a Catholic state, but had a history of tolerance. We met inside the intact front part of the church; barricades partitioned off the rear. Children sat in the pews in clumps, divided up by age, a few rows apart. Each group, led by a teacher, discussed the same Bible story. Then, the pastor arrived at the altar and conducted a short service.

I'm still not sure what motivated these outings. Part of it was the excitement of going somewhere other than school without parents. Part of it was that Sunday was family day, and we wouldn't be able to play with each other that afternoon. Probably most of it was that our parents showed no interest in church, so we had to try it out for ourselves. We went regularly for about a year, before we got bored.

Going to church felt optional to me, a personal matter I controlled. I certainly didn't expect my parents to suddenly want to go to church, and to insist on going as a family. I fumed while my parents considered how to convert their traditional German Protestant roots to a church from the American religious supermarket. They heard that the Methodists and Baptists frowned on alcohol and tobacco. A glass of wine or beer with dinner was just plain civilized. Both of my parents smoked. An easy elimination. The Episcopal Church clearly had English roots; the Catholic Church was out anyway. Martin Luther founded the German Protestant Church, so my parents decided that the Lutheran Church was the obvious choice. Over my ineffective protests, we got dressed up in our best clothes and went to church on Sundays.

The Lutheran Church was tiny by Clemson's standards - it held about forty people and crouched on a backstreet in the shadow of the town's real churches - Baptist, Methodist and Presbyterian. When we joined, Kay, a Baptist herself, was scandalized.

"Did you know the Lutheran pastor smokes?" she asked me, her blue eyes and her mouth in the shape of o's.

"So what," I answered, warming to my parents' choice.

But Kay wasn't done. "They use real wine in communion too!" she added with that 'I know you're going to hell look' I was starting to recognize. I still protested when I had to peel myself out of my featherbed on Sunday mornings, but at least I felt like we weren't being total conformists.

At least the Lutheran church felt familiar, not like another form of religion I was about to encounter. Angelica, who sat behind me in eighth grade Math, introduced me.

"Your birthday is November seventh?"

I nodded.

"So is mine." Angelica's voice somersaulted. "And it's Billy Graham's birthday too!"

Billy Graham? I recalled my parents and their friends discussing his 'crusade' through Europe. A phenomenon they considered baffling.

"Oh, really?" I turned back to my math text.

On the page, groups of circles intersected. We were supposed to figure out which areas they held in common. I pictured myself marooned in one of the white crescent slivers near the edge.

Angelica tapped me on the shoulder. I looked around to see her lips compress into a smile, while she fingered the gold cross she wore on a chain. "I'm a Christian," she said.

Why was she so proud of that? Weren't most people in the Western World? Just to be friendly, I smiled back.

"I've been saved," she said.

"Saved from what?"

"The devil."

"How?"

"I've accepted Jesus Christ as my personal savior."

"How do you do that?"

"The feeling just comes over you." Angelica looked up, smiling with her mouth slightly parted.

I wanted to understand, but no matter how I tried to rephrase my questions, I got no closer to an answer. Her certainty left me feeling dense, like my brain was deficient.

The other girls avoided Angelica. They giggled at her clothes, and tried to provoke her by saying "darn." Angelica smiled her tight little smile, flipped her hair over her shoulder, and tried for a look of patient forbearance. I could almost hear her whispering "Lord forgive them for they know not what they do."

In October, Angelica invited several girls to a hayride. Had there been any other social venues in Clemson, SC, she would have had no takers. However, we were all starved for a destination. A group of girls from my class decided to go and I joined them. Angelica gave us directions that led us out into the country until we reached some fields at the edge of a stand of trees. Our parents dropped us off next to a bus parked on the grass. The bus said "Tabernacle Baptist Church" on its side. We moved in a bunch to eat hot dogs from the smoking grills, and later lined up to take a ride on the back of a tractor piled with bales of hay. As the dark soaked into the field, a bonfire flared up near the edge of the trees.

A young man I hadn't noticed before stood by the fire and called out to everyone to gather around in a circle. We stood, talking and giggling, and I asked what was about to happen. A few feet away, Angelica leaned into the circle and whispered, "We're just going to pray a little before we leave." Strange, I thought. Why would you pray when you're having a party? The young preacher began to read from his Bible.

I expected a few verses and then maybe the Lord's Prayer, but he didn't intend to let us off that easily.

The preacher's voice grew louder and louder. He asked question after question. Are you willing to give your life to the Lord? Are you ready to receive Him into your life? He sounded urgent and when he shouted that we were unworthy, that we couldn't save ourselves without the Lord's help, I wanted to agree to whatever would please him. The bonfire warmed my face. No, no, I didn't believe I was damned.

Never in my life had I been harangued like this. The preacher's voice beat against my spirit, begging and pleading, then shouting and demanding. My head bowed down under the weight of his voice. Everyone else was looking down too; I could feel it more than see it. The preacher cried out, the sound a desperate need welling up from deep inside him, "Come forward now! Accept the Lord and let Him into your heart!" I looked down lower. I feared the preacher's eyes, was sure that one glance would pull me forward against my will into something I didn't even understand. I was a good girl. I followed instructions. I had been trying my hardest to adapt to local customs. How could I resist this man shouting at me to step toward him?

A few kids stepped out of the circle, moved toward the preacher with halting steps. I glanced up to make sure I didn't know any of them. I didn't need saving, did I? The preacher sounded so sure I did. His heart was breaking for me and my stubborn resistance. But I didn't understand what he wanted, and I could not agree to something I didn't understand. I'd be lying and that was wrong. No, I had to stand there, unmoving, even if he didn't like it. Martin Luther knew that. *"Hier stehe ich, ich kann nicht anders"* - I stand here because I can do no other. That's what he said when he was tried for heresy at Worms. I saw the woman pastor who had been my religion teacher in fifth grade, standing in front of us, acting out Luther's resolve. The preacher's spell broke. He had no right to pressure me. I glanced to my left, at the girls who looked pale. Were they miserable too? The preacher's voice rose in praise of those who had come forward. He implored us to join them, one final time. No.

As the circle broke up, the kids around me moved as if emerging from a trance. We took a tentative step or two and broke the silence with giggles and whispers. I was furious, but I didn't dare discuss it with the others. I didn't know what they thought. Maybe they hadn't stepped forward because they already considered themselves 'saved'? I stewed all the way home. How could Angelica trick us like this? And what gave that preacher the right to shame and manipulate us?

Underneath my anger, I glimpsed a new idea. I didn't have to adapt to every new custom I encountered. I would have to learn to pick and choose.

*****

The lease on the Grace Street house was by the month. In the spring of '67 my parents hired a realtor and toured the town. After the first few times, I chose to stay home, reading or watching TV rather than trail the realtor and my parents through another columned brick on a patch of open lawn. Besides, I grumbled, why bother finding the perfect place when we were only staying a few years? Neither of my parents reacted to my grousing. Instead they tossed around words like split-level and ranch. Eventually they decided to build and found a stretch of wild property that edged Lake Hartwell.

A 3/4 acre lake lot! All their lives, my parents had dreamed of home ownership. In Germany, where the ground is sold not by the acre but by the square meter, we scouted the small towns around Krefeld for years, before buying a handkerchief sized lot in the farm town of Neersen. My parents were concerned about the long bus ride I'd have to school. It would have taken almost an hour each way. Before they could save up enough to begin building in this former cabbage field, we moved to the US. A lot this large on water wasn't even a dream in Germany. We weren't millionaires.

Buying a lot and building a house carried that mixture of thrill and anxiety that was growing too familiar. Catalogues filled with plans and architectural magazines piled up on the coffee table. I leafed through them daydreaming, imagining glamorous contemporary exteriors and lavish layouts, while squeezing my eyes shut to the permanence house building implied. What to build? After discussions with local builders revealed that they knew how to design any kind of house as long as it had columns, sash windows and bricks, my parents ordered an architects' plan for a contemporary split-level with copious sliding glass doors and a cathedral ceiling in the living room. The house sprawled twice as big as a normal German single-family home. The first builder they approached with this plan shook his head. "Sorry. I don't rightly know how to build something like that." They did finally locate one who was willing to try. I chose the bedroom facing the lake; my sister, who was only three months old, got the street view. We moved in the spring of 1968, into the first and only house my parents would ever call 'ours.'

Later that year, when I started ninth grade, my accent was gone, my clothes, though a bit eccentric, were American, and I was the only one in Clemson who remembered I was German. Ninth grade was the first year of high school, and the local high school drew kids from three different towns: Clemson, Six Mile, and Central. We were all nervous about starting at the big school and being mixed in with a bunch of new kids. I was a part of the Clemson crowd, a known quantity, familiar. I had a steady group of girlfriends: good studious girls, whose parents taught at the university. We had overnight parties, passed notes between classes, ate lunch together, and sat around gossiping and giggling on the grass at recess. I looked like any other high school freshman.

I still felt different. It showed in the mock presidential election held in homeroom one morning. None of us were supposed to look up as we cast our votes for Nixon, Wallace, or Humphrey by raising our hands. *Can I vote? I'm not a citizen!* I felt a storm of hands shooting in the air for Nixon. *It's not a real election. Maybe I should.* Another wave of hands rose at Wallace's name. *How can they vote for that racist!* The teacher saved Humphrey for last. I raised my hand and sneaked a peek. *I can't be the only one!* I wasn't. When the principal read the results over the intercom, there were eight votes for Humphrey. Eight votes out of four hundred.

I studied high school culture like an anthropologist. In some of the novels I had checked out at the Junior High Library, I read about the social customs of American High Schools - football games, pep rallies, cheerleaders and Homecoming Dances. In Germany, school, sports, and social life were separate activities. Even though others forgot I didn't belong, I wandered wide-eyed through the first few months of high school, alert for cues on how to behave, trying to sort out which activities I could afford to reject and which were necessary for survival. Pep rallies were not optional; they were scheduled to replace a portion of last period on Fridays before home games. What was the point of yelling cheers from the bleachers in the gym, while the cheerleaders jumped up and down? What was the point of cheerleaders? I did go to a few football games. My friends and I sat in the bleachers, shivering on cool October nights while they tried to explain the game to me. To me, football looked messy and disorganized. It happened in fits and starts, the ball was rarely visible, and the action constantly stopped, which only lengthened the game. After three or four games, I decided football games were optional.

My alien roots appeared too in the way my family had to improvise when I first began to date. A date was an odd idea. Girls and boys in Germany usually socialized in groups and if they did pair up, they used public transportation, since the driving age was eighteen. My mother had never had a curfew either, so we had to put our heads together to settle on a time that made sense.

Years later, when I saw the first of the Conehead skits on Saturday Night Live, I squirmed in recognition. Here was a family of three space aliens trying to negotiate American culture without a clue. Every new experience from ordering pizza to the daughter's first date threw the family into a turmoil of rapid conferences and improvised solutions. The aliens had huge cone-shaped heads, which the natives never seemed to notice. I couldn't laugh when I watched those scenes. The best I could manage was a pained snicker. The Coneheads' struggle to figure out how to pass mirrored my family's experience too closely to be purely funny.

Even though I went on a few actual dates, ninth grade was a year of friendships with girls. Our new house had a basement family room with a fireplace, perfect for spend-the-night parties. I have gobs of photos of myself in a cotton nightgown with matching robe surrounded by a group of girls posing in goofy ways. We tried to see how many marshmallows we could stick in our mouths, or posed as if we were using the fireplace tongs to drag each other across the sea of sleeping bags. We toasted the New Year with Sprite and listened to The Monkees on my parents new 'stereo console.' We covered pieces of paper with notes expressing our opinions of teachers and guessing at each other's crushes.

My new room had wall-to-wall carpeting and a phone. Like any American teenager, I spent hours in there, talking to friends, while pretending to do homework. Unlike the teenagers on TV, I also spent a lot of time in mourning. My flare-ups of anger now alternated with periods of intense sadness. Late in the evening, I lit candles, turned off the lights, and set up my portable record player on the floor. Choosing deliberate melancholy, I pulled out a record I bought in East Germany on our last trip there. Even the cover was somber: A photo of the Russian violinist David Oistrach and a German harpsichordist. The jacket designer had altered the photo using an olive wash. A brown stripe announced the composer: Johann Sebastian Bach. The first movement of Sonata no.2 in A major is an adagio. At the first strains of the violin, I felt a deep ache in my chest from my sternum down to my waist. Each bow stroke vibrated that middle region until I was sure my heart strained to shatter. I reveled in that ache. Couldn't get enough of that sweet pain. I lay on the carpet next to the turntable, and closed my eyes to feel it better. Tears crept down my cheeks.

I didn't know why I longed for this pain. I only knew I wished to hide in its moist cave, draw its velvet black around me, merge with it. I endured the sprightlier allegro, so I could get to the andante that follows and dip once again into the strains of heartache. When my mother knocked, I wiped the drying tear tracks with the back of my hand and answered as brightly as I could. She said she only wanted to ask me if I'd like some ice cream before bed, but I knew she wanted to pry me out into the light. Some evenings, I agreed to emerge, and sit, still mute, but strangely sated in the basement with my parents, spooning cool vanilla while watching the 11 o'clock news. Most of the time I preferred to change into my nightgown without turning on the lights. I braved the bathroom light to brush my teeth, but in my room, I blew out the candles one by one, and slid under my feather comforter. Curled around my still vibrating middle, I cried myself to sleep.

FIRST RETURN

The summer I was fifteen we went home for the first time. I strained forward in my plane seat, drinking in the forests, the neighborhoods and the strip of Autobahn near the Frankfurt airport. My longing for home leapt ahead of me, out of the window and merged with the steep tiled roofs and white stucco walls that defined my primal sense of house. My soul expanded and spread itself in a single layer across the ground, then sank and attached. I reminded myself to breathe. For three years, I waited for this moment. The plane's wheels clunked on the runway and tears pooled in my eyes. I was shocked by the intensity of my emotions. This was home, even if we landed in Frankfurt, a place I had never visited before. We were arriving here because it was close to my father's sister's house; we'd recover from jet lag there. My mother's eyes met mine. They were shiny.

A month of Germany stretched ahead of us. I tried to feel an expanse of time, even though I already knew it wouldn't be enough.

Around us, travelers stretched and retrieved luggage, overhead compartments snapped, coats rustled. I slipped my book into my carry-on and offered to take my little sister's diaper bag. My mother handed Nica, who fought waking up, to my father to carry off the plane. My legs shook as I inched down the aisle and climbed down the steps. My foot touched the ground. If I hadn't been too self-conscious, I'd have thrown down my bags, fallen to my knees and kissed the ground. But that would have been ridiculous. How could I be such a sentimental slob? Instead I imagined a flow of energy from the soil through the concrete through my shoe soles into my heart.

Inside the airport, I thrilled to the German announcements that flowed over the PA system, delighted in the German signs, and smiled at the *Grenzkontrollbeamten* - passport inspection officers - as I handed over my German passport. Even though I had not slept a second on the plane, I pulsed with life. While my parents dealt with the logistics of distributing baggage for carrying to the car, I stood in the Frankfurt arrival hall scanning the shops. I wanted it all. I wanted to run into the magazine stand and buy copies of *Brigitte* and *Bravo*. I wanted to rush into the sandwich shop for *Schinkenbrötchen* - hard rolls stuffed with ham -and *Sinalco* - orange soda. The *Lotto* - lottery - signs startled me; how could I have forgotten them?

My mother was exhausted, Nica's eyes were glazed with the need to be awake in the middle of the night, and my father ushered us out to our rental car. We glided into traffic. From the car window, I observed every detail down to the exact shape of traffic barricades. It all fit! Each object slotted into the archetype reserved for itself in my brain. Traffic signals, cross walks, Autobahn entrance signs, trees, rest areas. Two and a half years of absence brought them into sharp-edged focus. *So this is what they really look like.*

We exited near Pforzheim. Wheat fields edged with poppies! Villages with towering steeples! It was all real and I was here. My mother stared out her window transfixed, just like me. Students and shoppers waited at the bus stops in Mühlacker's market square. A waiter, dressed in black and white, wiped a table at a sidewalk café. When we stopped for a light, a group of school kids with satchels rolled past on bicycles. A new shopping complex disoriented me for the moment, but then I recognized the steep downhill toward the river Enz, the narrow bridge at the bottom, the half-timbered butcher shop where we turned up the hill to Tante Nanne's house.

When we lived in Krefeld in our apartment, I envied my cousin Ulrike this house. How small it looked now. Even so, I would have traded our new American house on Lake Hartwell for it in an instant. This house had white-lacquered doors, and solid door handles, not knobs. Wooden roll shutters protected the windows. The clay roof tiles glowed in a satisfying shade of brick red. You could open the windows inward or, with a twist of the handle, switch them so they tilted. It was a proper German house.

Tante Nanne waited with *Kaffee und Kuchen* - coffee and cake - for we arrived at *Kaffeeklatsch* time. A few strands of gray glinted from Tante Nanne's short perm, and she'd put on a few pounds. She hugged me tight, so tight I could feel her breasts flatten against my chest. That's when I realized I'd grown to her height. Over her shoulder, I spotted Ulrike, slim and boyish, her blonde hair cut short as always. Her new frames, square and black, weighed down her face. Ulrike and I were shy with each other; it had been so long. We followed the grown-ups into the dining room and sat down next to each other, grinning. I was only dimly aware of Ulrike's little sister and brother, climbing on my father, whom they adored.

I felt like a time traveler as I sat at the dining room table and consumed torte with whipped cream. How I had dreamed of doing this! Tante Nanne accepted my effusive compliments on the cake with a puzzled air. I realized she thought it quite ordinary. She asked us what kinds of cold cuts she should pick up at the butchers. I could barely remember the choices beyond what I'd most longed for: *rohen Schinken, gekochten Schinken* - raw smoked ham and boiled smoked ham. When she tossed out other varieties, *Bierwurst, Gelbwurst, Blutwurst, Fleischwurst,* I wanted them all, but I knew that wasn't polite. She saw my hesitation and invited me to come along. The walk would do me good after sitting so long on the plane and in the car.

Exhaustion struck me as I trotted down the hill behind Nanne and Ulrike. Even the aching thrill I felt at walking on a sidewalk paved with hexagonal concrete pavers could barely keep me on my feet. I applied willpower. My father said it was better to stay up until after dinner. That way, I'd get over the jet lag sooner. The spicy smell of cold meats at the butcher shop revived me. I inhaled deeply. I didn't know enough yet to break the smell into its components of smoke, marjoram and thyme. The glass case displayed fanned slices of hams, salamis, and bolognas, next to whole liverwursts, three or four kinds, and several kinds of *Würstchen* - sausages. They beckoned from their lace doilies, their top slices bedecked with sprigs of parsley, and promised juicy, intense flavor, so unlike the plastic bubbles of cooked ham and bologna in the lunchmeat cooler at the Winn-Dixie. A wave of jealousy knocked me in the gut. On the way here, Tante Nanne had apologized for the meager selection. The butcher she usually visited closed an hour earlier and was on the other side of town. Would Tante Nanne and my uncle take me in, if I begged?

That evening, I slept under a thick feather comforter with the window open. Every hour, I jerked awake as the church bell tolled the time. The pleasure of hearing a real church bell almost compensated for the interruptions. In Clemson, none of the churches sounded bells. Already I sensed my precious four weeks beginning to pass.

I moved through the next two days with my awareness turned up, tuned to the tiniest detail. The most mundane rituals of German life excited me. Even breakfast grabbed my attention. Crisp hard rolls and sweet butter. The way my aunt asked "hard or soft" as if there were no other choice in the world but boiled egg for breakfast. She served them in their eggcups, each topped by a crocheted warming hat.

If I had still been living in Krefeld, I would have dismissed Mühlacker as a provincial backwater that could offer nothing of interest, but the view from my exile in South Carolina turned both places into just "Germany." I loved the way pealing bells broke the Sunday stillness, and adored it that we all got dressed up in our best shoes and stockings to take a Sunday stroll up to the ruined castle on the hill. On the way we encountered families - parents with their children, joined by an Opa or Oma who puffed hiking up the smooth but steep path. The boys wore suits; the girls white socks and starched dresses. A few years ago, I had been one of them, running off the path in full Sunday regalia brandishing sticks I found under the trees. The ruins dated from the twelfth century. The castle was too insignificant and in too much disrepair to warrant more than a small marker. The children climbed on the broken walls. We stood up there and looked into the valley, then headed back down, walking slowly, working up an appetite for torte.

Later, with our bellies full of whipped cream, Ulrike and I retreated to her room. Her satchel lay half open, exercise books spilling out. I savored the scent of ink from her fountain pen mingled with the raw satchel leather and lingering odors from *Wurstbrote* - cold cut sandwiches. As I inhaled and wished myself back at my old school in Krefeld, Ulrike longed to know what it was like going to school in America.

I hated to remember how lost I felt the first six months as I stumbled through unfamiliar rituals. How much I despised Clemson for being too small, too uncultured, too different, too much not home. By now, I had learned how to hide my broken heart under a layer of imitation Southern manners. My friends had forgotten I wasn't American. Even I had days and weeks during which my homesickness lay buried under slumber parties, homework, and crushes. How could I explain what had happened to me in almost three years of living in an alien land?

I tried. I demonstrated what a Southern accent sounded like. I described my daily schedule. I could talk all day about the details of my life, but I didn't know how to explain how sweet her satchel smelled and how much I envied her schedule anchored by *Deutsch, Mathe,* and *Englisch.* We moved on. She showed me her records and books. We sat on her bed and sang "Mellow Yellow" along with Donovan and our awkwardness dissolved. By suppertime, we were so deep in conversation Tante Nanne had to call us twice.

When I noticed my mother over supper, I saw that she looked radiant. The two furrows above her nose were almost gone. Words tumbled from her mouth as she and Tante Nanne compared notes on their lives. She was drunk on being able to soar in her language and could hardly stop talking.

At night I fell into bed exhausted, my senses saturated from sucking in every detail all day, my jaw sore from so many hours of speaking German. My mouth, at least, had gone native in South Carolina. I refused to dwell on what that might mean. Just like I refused to worry about the border crossing that loomed between us and the next leg of our trip. Instead, I burrowed under the feather comforter determined to savor the joy of my homecoming and ignore the nagging undercurrent of loss.

*****

One morning a few days after our arrival, we packed up our rental car and headed for the East German border. Even Nica, eighteen months old, caught a case of nerves from the rest of us. She fretted in the backseat, barely distracted by my attempts to entertain her with songs and finger rhymes. I always tensed at the approaching border, but this time I was terrified: my father had decided to risk going home to Gera. For twenty years he stayed away, afraid the East German police still wanted him for breaking parole. He wasn't really sure twenty years was enough, but he decided to gamble that his residency in the US added protection.

Months ago, we learned that we needed a special document from the US government in order to travel to a communist country. US immigration required a 're-entry' visa, otherwise we couldn't come back into the States. After we applied, FBI agents visited our neighbors to question them about our attitudes toward communism. When the re-entry visas arrived, they looked exactly like a US passport. A gold eagle spread his wings on the cover; a passport picture with a description and stamps filled the inside. The only difference was the white cover instead of blue. My father hoped that this document would intimidate the East German border guards. Up until that morning, my mother and I thought he might back out. But there he was, driving, pretending to be calm.

The border post looked temporary. One lane was marked *Transit West Berlin.* A long line of cars idled, waiting to be processed and pay their fees for using the East German Autobahn on their way to West Berlin. The other lane, simply marked *DDR,* lay empty. *DDR,* short for *Deutsche Demokratische Republik* – German Democratic Republic, was what the East German state called itself. My father slowed down to exactly the 10 km/hr the sign demanded. He coasted to a stop in front of the wooden shack that served as a guard post. My mother inhaled sharply; the same sound she made when she thought my father was about to wreck the car. Her hands clamped down on the pile of visas and passports she held ready. I felt my lungs contract. Nica waited for me to start singing again. Her hand burned mine when I moved to hold it. *Shshsh.*

A guard crossed toward my father's side. My father cranked down the window and said *"Guten Tag"* in a jovial voice.

The guard spit out, *"Ihre Papiere!"*

My mother passed the pile of documents across to my father, who handed them to the guard with the bright re-entry visas on top. I couldn't see the guard's face, but his body stiffened with surprise. Slowly, he walked away, paging through our stack and entered a barrack a few hundred yards beyond the crossing. Through a window, we saw him conferring with another guard. My mother sat with her back straight and her hands clasped on her knees. My father shifted around, unable to settle. He tapped his palm on the steering wheel. Nica whined and I shook myself, then fished for a toy in her bag. The guards looked like they were consulting a huge manual of some kind. A list of escaped criminals? I squeezed my eyes shut against an image of guards dragging my shackled father away. When I opened them again, I saw one of the guards dialing the phone. I wondered if we could just back up and drive away. My father said, *"Mensch, was macht der denn?"* - Oh man, what's he doing now?

My fingers hurt. I must have locked them around each other without noticing. I didn't dare move them now; the way I didn't dare move when I woke up at night with my heart pounding from a nightmare.

The guard emerged, carrying our papers. When he reached us, he shoved the gleaming white visas toward my father with an annoyed, "These aren't passports. These have nothing to do with us."

He stamped East German visas into our West German passports and handed them back. "You can go now."

My father started the engine and nudged into East Germany. I watched for the mine strip and the line of guard towers. My mother and I competed to point out the landmarks to my father. For years, we'd carried intimate knowledge of the country's scars inside us, and we were eager to point out the physical realities. He had heard about the long-legged guard towers that perched at the edges of communal fields like parasitic bugs, he had seen the raw wound of earth with its hidden explosives on television, but this was the first time he felt the border closing around him. His eyes followed our extended fingers, but he could not speak. My mother and I fell silent, too. It was absurd to be pointing out East Germany's deadly fortifications with the excitement of children sharing a special secret.

The intensity of the crossing wore off slowly. We didn't know whether the US Visas had distracted the guards, or had only worked to make the crossing more difficult. My father later told us he was still worried they'd get him on the way out. But he didn't want to make us nervous, so he kept his fears to himself.

I noticed how different East Germany looked from the Autobahn. When my mother and I came by train, the tracks ran through the middle of every city, through districts crammed with apartment buildings close enough so we could see inside their windows. The highway stayed firmly in the countryside. The huge fields looked less alien to me on this trip; American farms were so large that they too covered the earth in monochromatic spreads. My father marveled at stooping women, the horse carts, and the mud-colored barns.

"Looks just like it did in the thirties," my father said, "except for that." He pointed at one of the roadside signs. They shone bright white like the houses in West Germany and blared their slogans in red letters. *Alles für den Frieden!* - Everything for peace! *Lang Lebe Deutsch-Sowjetische Freundschaft!* - Long Live German-Soviet Friendship! The phrases hadn't changed since I first read them on banners in Eilenburg. Even then the exclamation marks that followed had struck me as an attempt to prop up hollow sentiments and clunky phrases. Some of the signs along the Autobahn simply paraded the red, black, and gold hammer and sickle of the East German flag. Most of the cars on the highway bore West German license plates and appeared headed for Berlin, so they must have been the targets of this roadside education.

As we approached Gera, my father grew excited. He pointed out castle ruins and villages he remembered, and warmed to the rolling, wooded landscape he had sought to rediscover on our vacations to the Black Forest and Bavaria. He smiled now, and breathed more deeply.

The Gera exit sign. My mother and I had moved through Gera as a backdrop for my father's relatives, a place we had to go for a week every year, so I would know my aunts and uncles who couldn't visit us in the West. As we drove toward town, my father's accent grew more and more "*Gersch.*" He pointed out the landmarks of his childhood: the theater in its formal gardens, wildly overgrown, the *Sommerbad* - the outdoor swimming pool where he learned to swim. I had never seen Gera through his eyes before. A whole new city opened before me. Gera as the stage for my father's childhood - I had never thought of it before.

We skirted the center of town, disfigured by a tall concrete apartment tower, and reached the *Ostviertel,* the decayed eastern quarter where my father grew up. The car rattled on the cobbled, potholed streets, past rows and rows of old apartment buildings, every one of them untouched by stucco or paint since the war. My father navigated through the medieval maze of streets by twenty-year-old memory.

He turned the corner into Calvinstrasse. "Boy, does it look awful here," he whispered. To me, the street looked the same as ever. A layer of worn cobblestones bucked in the center of the street. Here and there, huge pits of gravel interrupted the rough surface the cobbles provided. Our heads bobbed as my father guided the car between craters as slowly as the gas pedal allowed. The houses lining the street were stained near black by pollution. A few boxy East German made Trabants and several battered trucks parked along the sidewalk's edge. I noticed my father's face still frozen in shock. Maybe now he'd understand why coming here had always been hard for me.

I liked it when Omi Hedwig and Opa Willy visited us in Krefeld. (They were retired, so the state allowed them to travel to the West.) Omi Hedwig spent hours sitting at our kitchen table surrounded by fabric, thread and pins, telling me stories while she sewed. She didn't tell conventional stories, she fashioned drama from the details of her life. With her, I relived the rococo gown she tailored for a special ball in her teens. She recreated her agony trying to decide which of her suitors to marry. Despite her permed white hair and soft, expansive bosom, I believed that she had been irresistible. I was grateful she chose my grandfather. In the afternoons, Opa Willy slipped into his overcoat, picked up his walking stick and invited me for a ramble through the neighboring fields. In his youth, he sailed with the merchant marine. He picked up a smattering of languages and a store of sea shanties. On our walks, we made up rhymes and bellowed *What Do You Do With a Drunken Sailor,* though I barely understood the words.

But each year, at the end of one our trips to Eilenburg, when my mother told me it was time to go to Gera, I resisted. If Eilenburg looked dowdy and unkempt, the neighborhood where Omi Hedwig and Opa Willy lived was depressing. At least in Eilenburg, a few scraggly trees and nearby greenery broke up the gray. And unlike my mother's parents, my father's family didn't have money to cushion East German reality.

Now, my father saw the desolation for himself. My grandparents' apartment house resembled the others in the neighborhood: four stories of grayed and crumbling stucco that dated from the thirties and a wooden door stained and faded from its long exposure to the elements. My father pulled the car to a stop right in front. As he opened the car door and stepped out, the shock gave way to a grin. He hadn't wanted to worry his family, so he hadn't told them he might be coming. Now, he could surprise them. He walked up to the front door, rang the bell marked "Willy Poser" just underneath his brother's "Klaus Poser", and stepped back to wait. The kitchen window above the door opened. A white-haired head poked out.

"*Es ist der Sieger!*" Omi Hedwig shrieked - It's Sieger. She only called him that when she was really excited. Otherwise it was Siggi. "What are you doing here? *Mein Gott.*" Her voice trailed off. She was beaming at her oldest son from behind the hand she'd clasped over her mouth.

"So come on down and open the door, *Mutti,*" he called from below. His smile had spread, down to his toes.

The shouting alerted Opa Willy that something was going on. He stuck his head out. "Siggi! Where did you come from? I'll be right down with the key."

I felt like I was bearing a Christmas present. My father's sisters and brother hadn't seen him since the late fifties when the government stopped issuing visas to the West for anyone below retirement age. They had all been at Sunday afternoon *Kaffeeklatsch*, waiting for my mother to arrive with Nica and me. One head after another popped out the window to see that he was really there. Klaus with his thick glasses, Bärbel's beehive (she clung to this style because it made her feel taller,) Gina, whose hair was blond this year, and finally Alice, the oldest, but least pushy.   Then the front door opened and they all spilled out: Bärbel, Klaus, Gina and Alice following Omi and Opa, surging around my father, squealing and talking, laughing, and crying, hugging and kissing. I watched from the curb.   After the first hugs, Omi stood back, panting, waving a hand in front of her face to cool herself.

"I don't believe it," she repeated over and over. "After all these years."

I followed my father up the stairs. He exclaimed at the old doorbells that sat smack in the center of each door, the slim iron railing that curved along the staircase, and the gravity toilets in the hall. When he reached the door into my grandparents' apartment, a throng of in-laws and children greeted him: his sisters' husbands, two of whom he never met before, and Klaus's wife who had visited us years ago in Krefeld. The little ones hung back from this new uncle, but the in-laws crowded around for hugs, handshakes and shouted introductions. We couldn't squeeze into the hall, so we surged into the living room, filling it to the brim. Several of the men hauled in chairs from the kitchen. My father came to rest on the couch, at the table still set for coffee. He pointed at the grandfather clock through the bodies. It dominated the corner, just as he remembered. His wrinkles smoothed and his shoulders moved easily. I pictured him bouncing off the couch to run into the courtyard for a game of tag. Omi rushed to bring more plates and cups. Everyone fussed over little Nica, and told me how much I was growing up. But at the center of it all sat my father, looking like a pea that had rolled back into its pod.

My father's homecoming signaled a shift for me as well. Before we moved to America, Gera had been a duty stop on my way elsewhere. The center of East German family revolved around my mother and leisurely stays in Eilenburg. But now that we had to cross the Atlantic, we would fall into the habit of allocating equal time to both places. Gera grew in importance. Later, when East Germany collapsed and my mother's family connections self-destructed, I would learn to cling to Gera as my link to the East.

*****

The morning after we arrived, we had to wait for hours in stuffy waiting rooms at the police station as always, until a surly official summoned us to his office, slammed a series of stamps onto our visas and passports to prove that we had registered. He presided under the eternal portrait of Walter Ulbricht, the head of the East German state ever since I could remember. Ulbricht's smirk called up his voice, combative like a small dog's yipping.

The next step was frantic shopping to spend the East German currency we had been forced to buy at the border. On all our trips, we struggled to dispose of wads of money we didn't need. We had no expenses, after all we stayed with relatives, and desirable goods were scarce. My mother and I had come to favor handicrafts, classical records, and sometimes books, if we could find any that were classics instead of socialist tracts. We swooped into stores, took anything that looked likely, and rushed off to our next stop.

This time with four of us, the amount of money we needed to consume seemed impossible. Of all East German rituals, I liked this one best. Usually my mother budgeted carefully, but here I could have anything I desired. My pleasure had diminished only slightly when I noticed that the average East German stood by with resentment. The goods we grabbed without reflection represented luxuries to them. Store clerks shook their heads as we snapped up Bach recordings without even giving them a listen in the sound booth. I wished I could explain that we were neither rich nor rubes; we were just short of time. At the end of our visit, we slipped a still substantial amount of money to Omi Hedwig to supplement her pension.

As we whirled through the shopping district, my father marveled at the empty grocery stores - the butcher's cases empty except for a few sausages, the greengrocer's display of a few cans of mixed peas and carrots stacked in a pyramid. Most stock vanished as soon as it arrived; either set aside for barter with special friends or sold to a crowd that materialized by word of mouth. How many times had one of my aunts arrived with a few pork chops or a pound of green beans and a tale of how long she had stood in line for them?

We didn't talk about the harried look of the pedestrians, nor the way they growled if someone accidentally jostled them. I believed people here had a right to be grumpy, especially while trying to procure what they needed to survive.

The East German government officials couldn't have foreseen how their hunger for Western Currency, the reason they forced us to exchange money on these trips, would sow the seeds of discord between East and West. There was no doubt that East Germans resented us for sweeping into their country and throwing their money around like the play money they often joked it was. If the Socialist Unity Party wanted to plant seedlings of resentment that could blossom after reunification they couldn't have devised a better plan.

Most of our stay took place in the private sphere, firmly separate from East German public life. My aunts lived either in dilapidated apartment houses built before the war or in sterile apartment blocks made from prefab concrete slabs. But once you left public space you entered lavishly feathered nests. Inside, the apartments brimmed with the latest furniture provided by socialist factories. Glossy storage systems, bulky sofas and chairs crowded into tiny living rooms. Lovingly placed knickknacks - Romanian pottery, Russian carvings, crocheted doilies, Vietnamese grass mats - decorated every available surface. I felt as if I was entering a cozy bubble, wild with color and texture. We were passed from apartment to apartment, eating dumplings, sourdough rye with cold cuts, or cakes from tables pushed against sofas and upholstered chairs, while our relatives let off steam. The rooms echoed with passionate complaints about the idiots in the Party, fed by the West German news that issued every night from their exorbitantly expensive TV sets. A haze of blue smoke from Egyptian tobacco settled over the tables after supper. The uncles consumed beer after beer, while I sipped barely carbonated East German pop. Voices rose as injustices were aired and embalmed in commiseration.

I hadn't exactly missed any of this, hadn't really thought about it since my last visit three years ago. But the familiarity made my rediscovery thrilling. I recognized too the peculiar mix of emotions that welled up as a response. Pity, guilt, relief. These private spaces that bordered on the claustrophobic would describe the limits of my life too, if it hadn't been for a twist of fate.

After a few days in Gera, it was time to move on. This didn't bother me. I had never spent more than a few days at a time there. But the next leg of the trip was completely out of phase with my expectations. I wanted to brace myself against the flow of time. How could I spend only a week in Eilenburg? Layers of visits, each one weeks long, had engraved my expectations.

Instead of staying in Eilenburg, at my grandparents' apartment, we slept at Tante Isolde's house in Bad Düben. There were four of us now, and we just didn't fit into the *Kinderzimmer* – children's room – my mother and I had shared before. I longed to recreate days of lazing in the garden, but there was no time for that. Matthias and I had a hard time trying to bridge the gap between his nine years and my fifteen. I spent my time with the grown-ups, chatting with Tante Isolde in the kitchen while we did dishes, or sitting around the dining room table after we finished the pork roast Onkel Horst had procured from one of the farms.

Opa Gustav acted like a faded copy of himself: softer, grayer, as if his spine had weakened and his color was going. Tears welled up in his eyes when he saw us, and he fished for his handkerchief after hugging us hello. He wandered off into the garden while the rest of us chattered. He never did like competitive conversation. Tante Isolde whispered that he had grown emotional since his most recent stroke.

One afternoon, we went to Eilenburg for a visit. Omi Paula fussed with the two combs that held back her gray hair as she ushered us into the living room. There was Opa's chair and his ashtray; I don't know how many times I had watched him read the newspaper there. But what I really wanted was to sit in the kitchen while Omi prepared the main meal, the way I had on countless mornings. I used to beg her for chicken soup with homemade noodles. Her hair would whip in wisps over her forehead as she kneaded the dough on the kitchen table. Then she rolled it out in sheets and sliced off noodles with a shiny knife. It looked like magic to me, to take a pile of flour and a few eggs and produce thin threads of golden dough.

But I wouldn't get to taste Omi's noodles this time. We were only here for a few hours, sitting like Sunday visitors at the coffee table, while Omi served us cake. Even though time was short, when we finished our streusel cake, I asked Opa Gustav if I could see the factory. Together we walked through the empty rooms. We didn't turn on the lights. In the dusk that filtered through dusty windows, the giant cloth cutting machines loomed before us. Beyond, rows of worktables rested quietly. Aprons draped on chair backs. Nothing had changed.

"Does Liesel still sit here?" I asked. I pictured myself, working by her side, gluing scrap velvet on rejected jewelry case pre-forms.

Opa nodded. "Of course."

I was fifteen now. I couldn't have played in the factory, even if it had been a workday and I had all the time in the world. The factory felt like a museum. I could peer into the past, but no matter what I did, I couldn't reach back there. I hurried through the echoing rooms trying to outrun the cold loss settling in my stomach.

I wished I could spend a whole day at the farm with Tante Anni and Onkel Otto, but that wasn't possible either. On this trip, when Tante Anni invited us to the farm for supper, I made the mistake of wearing a ruffly mini-dress and low-heeled sandals. I must have known there'd be no time to climb into the haylofts. Instead, I let Nica pull me along to the rabbit stalls and watched Onkel Otto capture a soft brown fur ball for my little sister to pet. Then Tante Anni carved smoked ham for our sandwiches and served us in the living room at the table covered with a white cloth. Every familiar picture on the wall and each Meissen figurine on the sideboard resonated within me, but I felt myself count the minutes until I'd be gone again. After Tante Anni finished eating, she rested her hand at the side of her plate. I anchored myself by wrapping my own around it. Her fingers felt rough inside my palm.

Had I lost touch with Eilenburg because I was no longer a child? Or could I have reconnected if I had more time? I couldn't tell. I felt immobilized, graduated from a participant to a watcher. On later visits, I no longer expected to be readmitted to the magic world of childhood. This first time, I buried my sadness under growing anticipation. I couldn't wait to get to Krefeld.

*****

Even though I promised myself I'd savor every day of my stay in Germany, the week in Krefeld beckoned to me in colors of paradise. I longed to immerse myself in the familiar, to test my fantasies and see if they would prove colorfast. My father tried to warn me that reality might not live up to my dreams. I pretended to shrug him off, but I worried too. Could Krefeld really be everything I remembered?

We stayed at a hotel near the zoo. The morning after we arrived, it hit me: I could get around in this city. All I needed was a few marks and the nearest tram stop, and I could go anywhere I remembered, and by myself! I knew what to do first. Sabine and I had made plans by letter. I said goodbye to my parents and sister, and walked to the tram stop. I wore a raincoat and carried an umbrella. Wet leaves dotted the sidewalk. The air - moist and rich with the smell of humus - surprised me. I didn't know I missed that smell until my body relaxed with sudden recognition. Out of the corner of my eye I noticed that my hair curled, just the way it always had. I stopped on the sidewalk and ran my fingers over a frizzy halo I hadn't missed until that moment. Next to me, a hedge bloomed profusely - tiny white flowers whose sharp green smell had accompanied me on my walks to kindergarten. I breathed more deeply, drinking the air, filling myself up and up. Slowly, I began moving my feet again glorying in the half-forgotten way I swung the umbrella in rhythm to my steps. I was walking to catch a tram on a damp summer day in Krefeld. Joy threatened to break my heart.

Every detail throbbed in Technicolor: yellow tram cars, the blue stamp the tram conductor landed on my ticket, the concrete tubs of red and white pansies in front of the train station. I looked until my eyes ached, and still I couldn't stop. I got off with a bunch of girls carrying satchels at Moerserstrasse, at the same stop where I once waited to go home after school. The rows of trees stood unaltered, as if they'd been holding their breath for my return. Around the corner stood the Ricarda-Huch-Schule, its broad steps seething with girls arriving for their classes. As a student there, I hardly noticed the stately building with its majestic window bays and slate roof. Now, it seemed as dear as a family photograph. For a moment, I tried to forget. Forget everything I learned since I last emerged from this school, clutching the final report card that hadn't impressed anybody. Turn myself back into a girl who lived in Krefeld, attended this school, and had never heard of South Carolina except for a brief mention in geography. Couldn't I just turn the clock back? Was it too late?

I searched the crowd for Sabine. Relief swept through me when I recognized her instantly. Her auburn hair was longer, but it still curled around her round face in that way that put me in mind of a baroque angel. Our first reaction was to hug each other, but then we stepped back to size each other up, trying to judge the unknown that lay between us. We were shy, but just for a second. She led me inside where her teachers expected me. She settled me in at her bench with an extra chair - her new friends moved over to make room for me. The class was familiar and strange at the same time. The room was the same, and so were the furniture and the raised platform with the teacher's desk and the blackboard. I knew about half the girls: they looked at me sideways, trying to guess how much I'd changed. The ones nearby peppered me with questions that took me aback. I, too, had once thought of America the way they did: a shining beacon of skyscrapered cities filled with the clean streets and the sparkling cars that drifted through Hollywood movies.

During English, the young teacher who replaced Frau Tümmler upon her retirement had me stand up and read a passage as an example of an American accent. I read twice. Once in my best newscaster voice, then a second time with a twangy Southern accent. When everyone howled at the latter version, I felt a tiny twinge. *Was this betrayal? Oh, why not.*

The morning burst with half-forgotten sensations. Smooth marble floors, wooden benches with ink well holders that hadn't been used for years, the rustle of girls rising to greet each teacher with "*Guten Morgen.*" At recess, the older girls gathered in corners formed by the irregular building foundation, while the young ones raced around tagging each other, or grouped under the chestnut trees to hop through complicated Chinese jump rope patterns. When I left, we were right on the edge, alternating between conversation and games. Now, we were too old to run. Sabine's friends pulled me into their group conversation without hesitation.

During art, we sat in a small room next to the airy studio. The teacher pulled down the shades and turned on a slide projector. Abstract paintings appeared on the wall, as she lectured the class about an aspect of nonrepresentational art in the early part of the twentieth century. I sat in the dim light, filled with the longing to belong. These girls would take me back. One girl, who'd been my friend in elementary school, sat in my line of view. I studied her mod haircut: short on one side, bobbed on the other. No hairdresser in Clemson would even consider such a style. Here they sat, taking for granted their lesson in abstract art, not even imagining a school where the teachers and students would laugh at those paintings, if anyone ever thought to show them such images at all. That's what I had been missing. A place where art mattered, where classical music might not be what you listened to as a teenager, but where you knew it was important and waiting for you later. Where culture was not suspect or ridiculous. Where I could feed my interests and be me.

When the last bell rang, I hated to leave. Sabine and I walked to her new house, just a few blocks from school. After lunch, we spent the afternoon cocooned in her room on the third floor, playing snatches of her favorite records, comparing European and American fashions, and talking about the differences in our lives. I asked detailed questions, because I wanted to be able to blend in when I came back. By the time my father picked me up, late in the afternoon, I knew we were still friends.

We had *Kaffeeklatsch* and *Abendbrot* - supper - with our old neighbors, Gudrun and her daughters Ulli and Bine. Although we had been in Germany for weeks, the food at Gudrun's ambushed me with renewed nostalgia. She served pastries from Hanten's bakery, the bakery right at the corner. I knew I had to have a piece of the *Grillage* torte: the layers of meringue coated with dark chocolate and filled with half-frozen whipped cream figured prominently in my dreams of Krefeld. Normally, one piece of pastry would have been enough, but there were glazed puff pastry treats, a Napoleon, a piece of *Bienenstich*. I ate until I could barely move. A few hours later, she surprised me again, with dark rye bread and pickled herring in cream sauce, along with Westphalian ham I couldn't refuse. How could I say no to any of these flavors, when I had hungered for them for almost three years, and didn't know when I might taste them again?

Ulli and Bine chattered non-stop, all at once. For an evening, we could get along without a fight, instead of dissolving into a pair and an odd-one-out, the way we always had as neighbors. Ulli, who never liked school, had finished at fourteen and entered a business management apprenticeship. She attended classes part-time and worked part-time and made a little money. Bine went to the *Gymnasium* and talked about becoming a gym teacher. They asked endless questions and couldn't understand why I envied them. This boring food, this unexciting town, the unvarying routine of their lives. At least I was having an adventure.

My mother and I spent several afternoons shopping. Shopping was a delirious process on this trip, because the currency exchange rate was still four marks to the dollar. Clothes in Krefeld hadn't changed in price much, but because we arrived with dollars, they appeared cheaper. We considered shopping at stores we only used for inspiration before. My mother bought herself a new raincoat at Greve. On two separate trips I ogled a pair of blue sandals with red platforms at an expensive shoe store, before I succumbed. Through it all, Nica sat in her stroller, munching on a raisin bun, which she liked as much as I had. After I bought those extravagant shoes, I studied the sale racks at the discount store, because I wanted to use the money I had to reclaim as large a portion of my wardrobe as possible. I'd return to high school looking European again.

Sabine and I met a few more times. One morning on the phone, she suggested we meet at Café Bortolot for afternoon coffee. I flashed back to the days of my childhood, when my mother and I walked past the cafes, where ladies ladled whipped cream into their china cups. Was I really old enough to meet a friend at a café? That afternoon, my mother and I parted in the city where we had been shopping. I walked the length of the Hochstrasse, watching myself in the shop windows, wondering if I looked like I did this everyday. Sabine waited at a marble-topped table by the window. She stirred cream into her coffee. I felt like I was posing as a grown-up, a German grown-up, as I slid into my chair. Sabine said she loved to come here for strawberries when they were in season, which they were, right now. She ordered some. I had been fantasizing about a *Krokantbecher* - a fluted glass filled with hazelnut ice cream and crunchy sugared nuts - but her certainty that one must eat strawberries in June diverted me. When the waitress returned, she brought big bowls of berries with whipped cream for both of us.

As I realized the time to pay drew near, I grew nervous. I had never paid for my own food at a café or anywhere else, either in Germany or the US. What would I do about a tip? I didn't want to ask Sabine. Even though we were talking about how different my life was in the US, I didn't want her to know I had never done this before. She'd think I was stupid. From my father, I knew that German tabs included a service charge, and I had observed that he usually rounded up the bill and told the waitress to give him change for that amount. How could I do this fast enough? The waitress approached, handed us our totals, and pulled her big black moneybag out from under her apron in anticipation. My brain raced at a frantic pace, watching Sabine for clues with one eye, the other eye on my own bill, calculating whether I needed to round up to the next whole mark or whether that would be too cheap, until I felt the pressure of the waitress staring at me, waiting, wondering, I was certain, why I was paralyzed by such a trivial transaction. I dug in my wallet for a five-mark piece, handed it over, and said, "*Es ist gut so.*" - It's fine like that. The words sprang from a well of childhood memory; that's what my father says when he doesn't expect change. I must have done all right, because neither the waitress nor Sabine interrupted their practiced motions.

A few days later, on my last Krefeld afternoon, Sabine and I met downtown once more, to stroll and shop. We fulfilled my fantasies:

poking around in record stores, sorting through hair care novelties at the *Kaufhalle*, window-shopping at tiny boutiques. Together we leafed through modern art reprints at a tiny bookstore until I found the perfect reproduction for my room: a painting by Paul Klee in earth colors, greens and reddish browns; softened patches that add up to a village with a red house glowing at its heart. Home at the center.

When we finally parted at the central tram stop on the Rheinstrasse, we stood, facing each other, holding hands. I was surprised that the corners of Sabine's eyes filled up, as we said goodbye. I was afraid to cry, because I wasn't sure I could stop. I dropped her hands abruptly and turned to cross the rows of tracks to wait on the other side. I waved once more, before her tram slid across my line of sight. I stood in the summer sunshine, tightening the muscles in my face, blinking.

I did let myself cry when the plane took off the next day. Next to me sat an American G.I. who was stationed in Germany. "It's my first trip home," he confided, as soon as he sat down. He exuded joy, like a puppy who knows he's going for a walk, and I sat next to him, staring out the window with tears streaming down my cheeks, as paradise faded to gray below, as I tried to reel my soul back in, tried to detach it from the ground that was dropping away.

CONTINENTAL DRIFT

How could I be so sad to leave Germany behind and, at the same time, look forward to sleeping in my own bed? I was exhausted. That's how I justified the relief I felt walking into my room. When my friend Marilyn called to welcome me back, I argued with the rush of pleasure her voice gave me. I couldn't be glad to be back in Clemson. I might treasure my familiar mattress, my room with its view through tall pines down to the glinting lake, and Marilyn's companionship in longing to live elsewhere. She had moved to Clemson from North Carolina the year before, and didn't like it any more than I did. But I refused to feel like I was home.

For weeks, I dreamed in German again. By the end of the summer the only evidence of my trip were my new platform shoes and the clothes I bought in Krefeld. When I returned to high school, I teetered between trying to emphasize my difference and blending back in. I couldn't seem to remember how to act like my German self inside Southern culture. I zigged and zagged. Who was I? Maybe the best method was to just go along? I made one more serious stab at fitting in that culminated in my participation in a beauty contest.

"I got nominated for Miss Summit today."

My mother's head popped up. The knife in her hand hung suspended over a partly chopped onion. "Do you want to do it?"

I sat down at the kitchen table and fiddled with a placemat. I was flattered that anyone thought I should be in the high school beauty pageant. A group of boys in my homeroom had jumped up to nominate me as soon as Mrs. Skelton made the announcement. She sent me and the two other nominees out into the hall while the class voted. We stood next to the row of lockers, chattering. It never occurred to me they'd really pick me.

"It's kind of stupid." I said. I knew my mother wouldn't argue with that. "But, yeah, I think I want to."

The only beauty contest I ever heard of as a child in Germany was "Miss Universe." I saw a newspaper one day at the stationery shop where I bought the replacement tips for the fountain pens the school required. It wasn't a serious newspaper, not like the *NRZ* we had delivered to our doorstep daily. That one rarely had pictures. No, this was a *"Bild."* My mother considered it tacky, and not just because of the huge headlines and pictures of semi-nude women that took up half the front page. It wasn't a real newspaper because it didn't have serious news, just gossip about Princess Margaret or the heirs of the Hohenzollern. This particular time, the *Bild* front page blared "Germany wins Miss Universe." The picture showed a woman with permed blonde hair, wearing a bathing suit and the highest heels I had ever seen. When I got home, I asked my mother about it.

"Oh, that." she said. Her face looked like she'd just bitten into an unripe gooseberry. "It's disgusting." She went on to explain that some women - not smart ones, she made that clear - were so caught up in their looks that they went parading around mostly undressed for the entertainment of beauty contest judges and men. I could tell that even if by some miracle I turned into a bombshell, I would be expected to be above such behavior. Beauty contests were tawdry affairs. Choosing to compete in one was not for the serious woman.

At the very least, I expected my mother to think my being nominated for Miss Summit was funny. But she remained unsure of herself in this country. If other girls at school took beauty contests seriously, then she would help me do my best to participate. She said, "Well, if you're sure. Find out what we have to do."

Miss Summit commenced with a tea where the contestants met the judges and continued that same evening with the girls parading across the high school auditorium stage in evening gowns. My mother drove me to Greenville to search for the perfect formal, bought me little white gloves and matching satin shoes, and found me a new blouse to go with the wool suit I already owned.

Even though I had my doubts about this enterprise, once I agreed to do it, my competitive nature joined with my performance anxiety. For the tea, a Clemson lady volunteered her living room. The girls were invited in small groups at precise intervals of fifteen minutes. When I drove up in my mother's VW, Chevys and Buicks lined Riggs Drive for several blocks. I parked extra carefully, to compensate for my quavering insides. My heels clacked on the blacktop as I approached the columned entrance. A few girls were leaving, purses clutched in gloved hands.

Bright pink splotches glowed on their cheeks. They must be the ones who went to Merle Norman to get their make-up done. They greeted me with too bright smiles as they passed. The door stood ajar. Inside, more girls sat at the edges of chairs and sofas. Their brittle chatter bounced off the knick-knacks and curio cabinets. I found a place to perch between my friend Marilyn and another girl I knew. Marilyn wore a plaid wool suit and a white blouse with a ruffled placket. Her blonde curled hair barely moved under its load of hairspray as she turned her face toward me. Bright blue eye shadow topped her eyelids and pink blush circles burned on her cheeks. She whispered the drill: every fifteen minutes, the judges summoned a new batch of five to the study off the dining room. What did they do in there? Just then, a batch emerged, giggling, from the sanctum. When we asked them they reported, "Oh, they asked us questions, like 'what's the smallest state in the US,' stuff like that."

I panicked. I thought they were going to chat with us, "assess our poise" whatever that meant and here they were asking geography questions. American geography, which I didn't know very well at all. I whispered to the other girl next to me. "What's the answer?"

"Rhode Island, I think." Rhode Island. Okay. I tugged on my little white gloves. I was as nervous as I always got just before a test. When they finally ushered us into the judges' room, I sat down stiffly, at the edge of my seat, ready to spit out answers to difficult questions. My voice shook when I gave my name. Across from us sat two middle-aged ladies and a man. They made small talk for a while. Then the woman nearest me asked, "What's the biggest state?"

"Rhode Island." It shot out of my mouth before I had a chance to stop it.

The lady laughed gently and said, "That's very flattering to hear. I was born in Rhode Island. But I was actually asking about the biggest state, not the smallest."

I was so mortified I barely made another peep. On the way out, Marilyn was kind enough not to mention my faux pas. She just smiled and winked and said, "See you tonight."

Well, there was still hope, I thought as I turned the ignition key. Maybe the judges would be so stunned by my graceful walk across the stage that I would at least be a semi-finalist? As soon as my conscious mind detected those thoughts flashing across my brain, it slapped them down and replaced them with: Why should I care about some stupid beauty contest? I took a deep breath, shifted into first, and drove home.

That evening, the contestants assembled in the school's music room behind the auditorium. I wore a simple orange formal with purple piping, very 1970s. Everyone else was in red or green velvet or baby shades of satin, with generous bows and ruffles. I recycled my little white gloves from the afternoon, but most others wore theirs elbow length. I did make it across the stage without stumbling. When I wasn't chosen to advance beyond the pack, I reminded myself how ridiculous beauty pageants were. I'd never do that again.

The week after the pageant, I stomped around consumed by anger. Anger at living in a place where anyone would even consider having a high school beauty contest, renewed anger at my father for bringing us here, but most intense of all was my anger at myself for giving in to the temptation to participate. I had known better. I didn't want to be the kind of girl who fussed over her looks and competed with other girls. I was sick of trying to do it the local way.

Even before Miss Summit, my resolve to adapt to high school was weakening. I tried out for the basketball team - I suppose I thought I could make up for my five foot two inches by moving fast - and met with failure. I briefly dated a football player, so I could wear an oversize letter jacket to geometry class and fiddle with a clunky ring that hung on a chain around my neck. I broke off that experiment quickly, because this boy approached romance with the same energy he used to tackle opponents. Ever since I had arrived in Clemson, I had been trying to figure out how to adapt to local expectations, and when I couldn't, I kept my mouth shut and my profile low. Enough. From now on I was going to do it my way, even if it cost me.

*****

Once my decision was firm and my anger subsided, I backtracked a little. In the harsh daylight of high school, I didn't have the guts to totally flaunt the rules. The difference was internal. I stopped straining to fit in, and cobbled together a world of my own. When I couldn't hide the unconventionality of my choices, I tried to eke out territory along the rules' edges.

I felt safest dealing with my discontent by withdrawing into books. My parents had imported a substantial library that lined the basement 'office'. On Saturday mornings, my father worked there, behind the desk that had dominated the living room in our Krefeld apartment, paying bills, catching up on paperwork he brought home. Down there, the world literature that Sabine swooned over in her still frequent letters crowded each other on the shelves. I read mostly in German, because that's what we had. Sometime during tenth grade, I discovered the Clemson University library, but because I wasn't yet a student, I couldn't check out books and bring them home. I'd sit on the floor between the stacks, reading until my feet fell asleep. My parents' library was short on English literature, so it was at the Clemson library I first discovered William Blake. At home I read Camus and Brecht, Zola and Gide. My mother pushed me to read books by classic German authors, reminding me that when I went back to Germany, I'd need a firm grounding in the German classics. So I read Goethe and Lessing, too. In between, I read the cult books from the early seventies: the Lord of the Rings, and anything by Hermann Hesse. I read about eastern religions, and even borrowed a translation of the Upanishads from our Lutheran church library. I slogged through its antique prose by sheer will power.

I never discussed any of these books with the girls whose phone calls interrupted me. I switched into a different gear to giggle over a teacher's ill-fitting wig or elaborate on a rumor about who smiled at whom at the Y and what did *that* mean, or listen to them complain how many pages of *Wuthering Heights* they still had to read before Friday. I usually finished the books our English teacher assigned within the first few days; I couldn't stand the suspense of not knowing how the story turned out for weeks. I didn't let on though. I clucked sympathetically when others groaned about these "boring" books, and changed the subject by exaggerating how much algebra homework I had been assigned that day.

The girls I knew, all good students bound for college, didn't seem interested in politics either, despite the turmoil that was 1970. I watched protest marches on TV; I knew there were people trying to stop the war, young men growing out their hair, women questioning their roles. Excitement was in the air, but so far away that you could barely catch a whiff of it in Clemson if you strained. None of my girlfriends ever said a word.

Mrs. Olson, our world history teacher, tried to encourage us to wake from our lethargy by asking us to debate the issues we saw played out on the evening news. The first few times, I said little. I was in the habit of observing so I wouldn't accidentally offend. It took time for my new resolve to be myself to break through. I slowly lost my fear of sticking out, and jumped into the world history arguments. There were only a few of us who were critical of government policy and the military. The rest of the kids either quietly shook their heads when we spoke or yelled at us that we were commies and traitors. I was infuriated. These ignorant kids didn't even know what a commie was. I did. I spent my childhood in fear of them. Me, a commie! I hated them more than they could ever know.

*****

Just before we had moved to the US, after our last long stay in Eilenburg, we packed for our return trip to Krefeld. My mother piled contraband on her childhood bed - a gilded Meissen coffeepot, a mink collar, an etching from 1772, two antique pewter tankards, and finally four sets of size twelve girls' underwear and two nightgowns for me. Her old feather comforter flattened under the weight. I chewed my cuticles, as I watched her fold the forbidden items into her underwear and stash them in the suitcases. Every trip, I pleaded with her to take only one or two things, but she was reckless. This was her last chance to smuggle out every valuable she could. And, she reminded me; we never got caught. Over the years, we carried home the entire Meissen coffee service, cup by cup.

After my mother emptied the bed, she picked up the red leather jewelry case that waited on the nightstand. Should we roll it into my socks? I asked for another look inside. The brand-new ring glittered, and it was mine. Three weeks before, Opa had held out his cupped hand. In his palm sparkled a pile of cut stones: aquamarines, amethysts, and tourmalines, a few as tiny as diamond solitaires, some as large as robin's eggs.

"Pick one," he said, "I'll have it made into a ring for your confirmation present." My confirmation was almost two years away. Would I really not see him before then? Nothing else anyone had said had made the move this real for me. I shoved that thought away and focused instead on the thrill of such a fairytale present. He spread the stones out on his desk. I touched first one, then another.

"Where did you get these?" I asked. He told me he traded goods from his factory for them, during the time of inflation, in the thirties. I knew about that time; I had postage stamps in my collection in denominations of billions and trillions of marks. The stones glinted on the desktop. I picked an oval aquamarine, a medium-sized stone that threatened to dwarf my ring finger.

At the jeweler's I sat on an old wooden chair, flipping through a thick catalogue of photographs. The gold contrasted with the surroundings. Herr Breuer's jewelry studio was upstairs in an old office building in the city of Leipzig. His furniture was shabby, and the tall windows filtered light through layers of grit, but his designs flowed on the page, poised to spring to life. I chose a band that swooped upward to support the stone.

I hadn't thought about getting the ring through East German customs. My mother decided she would simply wear it, since that would seem most natural.

Our suitcases were heavy, so we checked them onto the luggage car. The train was jammed. Carrying our hand luggage, we pushed through the crowded cars until we found two seats in the same compartment. They were middle seats, across from each other. I settled in facing my mother, who adjusted the skirt of her light gray suit and pushed a few strands of her hair off her forehead.

The other passengers were old, since the government allowed only pensioners to leave East Germany to keep from losing workers. Most of the travelers were women, widows from the war. One old man slept in one corner of our compartment, while the three grandmothers around us peeled hard-boiled eggs and drank peppermint tea from their thermoses, chatting comfortably. They were going to the west to see their children, escapees like my mother.

As we approached the border, my stomach knotted up, as usual. The train screamed to a stop, and a hush fell over the passengers. Papers rustled, passports appeared, eyes darted from suitcase to string bag. Outside lay a sea of concrete, broken by low barracks, their windows painted white. East German flags flapped in the breeze. A row of guards waited, trained German shepherds at attention next to their jackboots. Guard towers loomed above, soldiers with machine guns posted at the windows. At the far end of the train, doors crashed.

We sat in our compartment, frozen, waiting. Pounding boots, slamming doors and shouted commands broke the silence. Inspection was thorough despite the crowd. Twenty minutes, thirty, forty, an hour. The sounds moved closer. Finally our door banged open. Passport control. Stamps crashed down on our papers. Then customs. The customs officer stood in the door, silent. His eyes bored through the luggage crammed into the overhead racks. He barked at us to raise our legs, then bent down to check the floor. Then he scrutinized each of us. Eyes locked, then broke.

I forced myself to look straight at him, willing my fear to hide. My mother returned his penetrating stare with one of her own. His hand reached out to take her customs form. His eyes stopped.

"Where did you get that ring?"

My mother's body jerked. She clamped calm on her face. "My husband bought it on a business trip to Turkey," she said. Too late.

"Pick up your luggage and follow me!"

The bottom dropped out of my stomach. My mother's hands shook as she scrambled to remove our hand luggage from the overhead rack. The old man jumped up to help us steady the larger bag on its way down. None of the grandmothers moved, but they looked on us with pity. The customs officer breathed impatience. He turned on his heel, and marched us down the aisle and to the train car's door. I refused to believe I was the one stumbling down the metal steps.

A female customs official waited to conduct us into the barracks. She commanded us to wait in a room that reeked of linoleum wax. Bright overhead lights, a single wooden bench, several closed doors and the blind windows. The outside door crashed shut.

My mother bent forward to set her bag on the bench and hissed into my ear, "Don't say anything. They're listening." We stood, facing the blind glass, hands tight on our bag handles. Ten minutes later, our train's engine began to huff. Patches of light and dark fluttered across the white windowpane as the rhythm of the wheels gained speed. Our train was gone.

A young woman with badly bleached hair and violent red lipstick emerged from one of the doors. Her eyes jumped from my mother to me, then to our two travel bags. She snapped, "Is this all your luggage?"

"No," my mother said, "we checked our suitcases. They were in the luggage car."

I quaked at the note of defiance in my mother's voice. No, my mind screamed, don't make her mad! I aimed my eyes at my mother's, but couldn't catch hers.

The woman snorted. "You were to get off with all your luggage."

"Nobody told us."

"Come with me. Bring the bags."

We each took a step.

"No, just you. Not the girl."

We stopped. My mother nodded in my direction, her lips pressed tight, her eyes unreadable. I handed her my bag. She disappeared through the door.

My body stiffened. Muscles fluttered inside my belly. My chest constricted. I turned away from the door and faced the white glass. Over and over I saw my mother flinch, watched the moment that gave her away. What would happen to us? When they arrested you in East Germany, did they tell your relatives? Yes, they did. They told Onkel Ernst when they arrested Peter. Since Peter had gotten out of jail in '63, the adults whispered about him. He had changed. He couldn't finish university; he couldn't sleep. It had been three years, and still he drank too much.

I tried to stop thinking. Tried to breathe, close my eyes. I didn't dare move. A move might trigger disaster. A new train pulled in and flicked its shadows across my face. I sneaked a look at my watch. An hour gone.

The door opened. I twisted toward it. My mother swept into the room, blazing with anger, the bleached official in her wake. "We'll have to get on the next train, wherever it's going."

My insides shivered with relief.

"It's going to Kassel," said the customs woman, "If you hurry, you can make it." Her face softened as she held the door.

My mother said nothing. A strand of hair straggled into her eyes. She handed me a bag, then nodded toward the door. We galloped outside as the inspectors jumped off the train, the engine already starting to wheeze. The woman official shouted to them to let us on.

As the train gathered speed, I swayed behind my mother as she bumped down the cars' aisles, scanning compartments for empty seats. She pulled open the door to the first empty compartment she found, even though it was in the smoking section. The stale air and sooty drapes didn't matter this time. She stuffed her bag on the upper shelf and collapsed into her seat. I dropped mine on the floor as my knees buckled. My shoulders spasmed around my shivering rib cage. I tried to take a deep breath. Outside, the last of the guard towers slid by.

My mother's voice quaked and she gasped between sentences as she filled me in. The customs woman had led her into a room with an empty desk and two chairs. Then she directed my mother to hand over the bags for inspection. My mother held her breath. She carried the mink collar between her washcloths, wrapped in a hand towel. The woman rifled through that bag last, glimpsed the mink, covered it back up, and zipped the bag. Then she pointed my mother to a chair and told her to wait.

Twenty minutes crept by. A short, wide man in uniform barreled through the door. He seated himself behind the desk, and asked, "Now, where did you say you got that ring?"

My mother stuck to her story. "My husband bought it in Turkey."

The man scoffed. Any idiot could see the ring was brand new! He asked her to hand it over, and walked out with it.

When he returned, he carried a three-ring binder. He held the ring out to her. "Look at the stamp inside the band. The jeweler's stamp." He waited. "Here's a register of all the jewelers in the German Democratic Republic." He flipped a few pages, then showed her the stamp next to 'Breuer, Leipzig.' A lower-case b with a star at the top. It matched the stamp on the ring. "So you see, there's no point in lying."

He lectured her on her crime. Defrauding the socialist state, attempting to smuggle precious metal, lying to a customs official. He was confiscating the ring, of course. He smiled. She would have to pay a fine, too. One hundred forty West German marks. Let this be a lesson to you.

My mother's voice had steadied as she told the story, but now it tightened with fury. How dare they steal from us, and then force us to pay a fine! To top it off they made us miss our train. How were we going to get home? She checked her watch. We'd reach Kassel in an hour. We should be able to get a train to Krefeld before it got too late. She looked at me, struck by a new thought.

"I'm so sorry I lost your ring. I feel terrible about that."

The ring? All I cared about was being alive and free, far away from the East German police with their hard faces, guns, and dogs. I gazed out the window, where the West German countryside displayed its brilliant green meadows under an aquamarine sky. I barely heard my mother worry that Opa would be angry with her.

"He won't be," I said. I pictured him, his stern face transformed by pleasure, as he'd held out the stones. The ring wasn't what mattered to him, I was sure. He often said, "The only thing no one can take from you is what you carry inside."

My stomach relaxed, then growled. I dug in my bag for a sandwich. I was ravenous.

*****

When the high school kids threw the word commie around I wanted to take them by the scruff of their necks and drag them off to East Germany, show them the guards and the towers, the way people lived. But no one had time to listen to my stories, even if I had tried to tell them. Once I had a shouting match with a cheerleader who sobbed and screamed simultaneously when she couldn't get me to back down. She lost control and 'let it all hang out', but she spoke for the majority. In the class, there were a few girls from the group that had been my friends for the past few years. They weren't hysterical, but they were certain that questioning the government was wrong. Outside of class, they never mentioned my alien opinions, so I didn't either. I felt myself sliding away from them.

My search for kindred spirits drove me toward the hippies. They were the kids who came down on the same side with me in political arguments. In Clemson in 1970, it didn't take much to make you a hippie. If you were a girl, all you had to do was stop applying hairspray. For the boys, a string of beads or a pair of bellbottoms sufficed. At lunch, they hung out in the student smoking area, a ragged patch of lawn they shared with the tough boys who worked second shift at the textile mill. I found an occasional refuge there, even though I soon learned I couldn't fit into that group either.

At first I discounted the buzz around the school that the hippies smoked grass at their parties. When Jenny, a freshman girl who always wore a Mexican poncho, invited me to her house one Friday night, I fretted over the rumors of drug use with my mother. She raised my anxiety level by pointing out that I could be deported if I was even in the room with illegal substances. (I didn't yet know it, but she would learn to use this tactic every time I veered too close to risky behavior. Go to an anti-war rally? No, you could be arrested and then...). I wanted to go back to Germany, but not that way. Neither of us could believe that Jenny, who was in my Sunday school class, would have anything to do with marijuana. Her house was in walking distance, so we decided I could always come home if I got uncomfortable.

My mother and I spent the next afternoon shopping for my first pair of bellbottom jeans, so I would have something appropriate to wear. At the party the lights were low, the music was loud, and a strobe light disoriented me further. A senior named Bobby, who wore the school's first wire rim glasses, offered to get me a soda. There were a few kids smoking grass at the party, but they stayed outside, and I convinced myself that they didn't affect me. We shouted over the music's din for a few hours, and Bobby offered to walk me home. I accepted. He talked about his dreams of becoming a bass player in a rock band. Then he said he'd just finished reading *Siddhartha*, one of my favorite Hesse books. I kissed him goodnight with enthusiasm.

My new romance horrified my old friends, but they were curious enough to still invite me to their gatherings, perhaps to see whether I would act any different. I believed I was in love with Bobby, but I couldn't go to any of his friends' parties. I quickly learned that the rumors of drugs were true; they were mild even. I heard details of what I was missing when I hung out with the hippies at lunch. There were stories of heroin and bad acid trips. One of the seniors worked construction part-time and almost severed his leg with a chain saw because he was tripping at work. It took one hundred and eighty-seven stitches to reattach. I learned to recognize that far-away look, without being tempted to try it myself. It was only partly my mother's constant reminders that the immigration service could go after me. I didn't trust

Bobby and his friends to take care of me. Bobby and I were doomed. When the dust settled, only I knew that I didn't deserve the reputation for drug use I had gained. I managed to isolate myself from much of the social life of the school. I did have a few loyal friends, but I had blown the illusion that I belonged.

Toward spring of my sophomore year, I got an unexpected break. Mrs. Booker was D.W. Daniel High's guidance counselor. She was shorter than me, wrinkled and gray, and had a sparse mustache. To get to her office, you first negotiated a windowless broom closet. The office itself had a big window and was roomy, but appeared tiny because every surface bore stacks of papers and books. She presided over this mess with a distracted air that suggested her office mirrored her brain.

When it was time to register for the next year's classes, I approached her for suggestions. In looking over the registration materials, I discovered that if I took what I wanted during my junior year, I'd have no requirements left to fulfill but senior English. What was I going to do my final year? I couldn't just take English? I supposed I could add typing and advanced biology but that still only filled up half a day.

Mrs. Booker looked up from my forms and tossed out two options: I could be a part-time student my senior year and start taking college courses, or I could take junior English during the summer, and skip my junior year altogether.

I could skip a year of high school? Yes. I knew instantly that's what I wanted. Mrs. Booker stared at me, stunned by my enthusiasm. I didn't bother explaining. I didn't know whether she wanted to hear that high school felt like jail to me. I looked past her, out the window, where the spring sky sparkled suddenly more brightly.

*****

I arrived in America full of naïve certainty that I would never treat a black person differently. The first week of school had taught me that society had some ironclad systems in place that would interfere with my intentions. I had to figure out the strictures surrounding race bit by bit, just like other Southern customs. An early clue arrived when I outgrew my German dresses.

How did people in Clemson dispose of old clothes? My mother asked around. She was told to lay the clean, folded garments on top of the garbage can, where the garbage man could sort through them and distribute them to the needy. That the garbage man and the needy were colored went without saying. (We had learned that 'colored' was the polite term for Negroes by then). A few weeks later, Portia, a small girl with a boyish figure, and the only colored girl who wasn't too cowed to return my smiles in the halls, turned up wearing the gray linen. A few days later she wore the pink and green my mother had made from one of her old skirts. I looked at her out of the corner of my eye. Portia was smart. She always looked scrubbed and tidy, her hair carefully oiled and slicked into a ponytail, her shoes gleaming. I couldn't believe she was so poor she had to wear dresses rescued from the garbage. I always wondered if she knew they had been mine. She must have. The dresses stuck out like swans in a flock of ducks. Of course, I knew better than to comment on her new wardrobe, but after that I always felt a kinship with her, especially since she never outgrew my German clothes and wore them well into high school. The suspicion that poverty lay hidden just out of sight popped me out of my self-absorption (at least for a few minutes at a time.)

Where did the "colored" live? I hadn't seen any in the patches of redbrick houses of "Sunny Acres" and "Brookwood," where we occasionally took Sunday drives or visited other German immigrants for coffee, or near the older white columned houses on Strode Circle, where the old Clemson families lived. When I rode a different bus one day, on my way to a friend's house, the bus turned off the paved asphalt and bounced onto a rutted dirt road. A strip of red dirt wound through pine trees like a faded wound. To the right and left, partly hidden in the tangle of vegetation, sat weathered wooden shacks with tin roofs. The bus jerked along the potholed path and stopped. All the colored students, who rode in a tight knot at the back of the bus, got up and shuffled out the front. Once outside, they exploded into life. Their faces transformed from the unreadable masks they carried in school. They shouted at each other, and though I couldn't understand a word of it, I heard joy, maybe relief. We continued bouncing down the dirt road, past a few more shacks and emerged through a thicket of pine onto asphalt into the world of white trim and red brick.

There was never any reason to drive through the colored part of town. One edge of it rose along a hillside on Hwy. 123, so once I knew what to look for, I could spot two or three run down houses along there. Over the years the houses along the highway grew more prosperous looking. One of the owners didn't just paint his house, but added brick and white painted window frames and landscaped the patch of yard. Now, the houses look like average Southern homes. But I still don't know what it looks like behind that first row, because I'd have to go out of my way to look, and I'd feel like an intruder.

During that first year, we bought a lot of furniture. These purchases entered us in the Maynard's furniture monthly sweepstakes and, for the first and only time, we won. The grand prize was a flowery gilt-edged porcelain dinner service for twelve. We didn't need another set of porcelain; we had a set for everyday, a set of good china and the set of Meissen we had smuggled out of East Germany. My father offered the china to the colored janitor at his office. My father and I played badminton in the yard when Jim drove up in his sagging Chevy to pick up the china. Skinny and bent, Jim emerged from his car, took off his hat and fiddled with it in his hand. He didn't seem too sure about coming in the house, but my father held the door for him and urged him on. I couldn't make out his words. I attributed that to the pink gums bare of teeth that flashed when he smiled, but it could have been his colored accent. When my father held out a coffee cup to be sure that Jim approved of the pattern, Jim's eyes brightened, though his steps toward the dining table where the box of china waited remained diffident. On the way he bowed rhythmically, punctuating his moves with enthusiastic thank-yous.

My father finally succeeded in getting him to take one end of the box, while he picked up the other and I held the screen door. China stowed in the trunk, Jim stood next to the Chevy's open door, torn between wanting to leave and making sure his thanks were sufficiently convincing. I got worn out standing watching him. I wished I could just say, it's okay, we didn't want it, you can have it, and we can tell you're grateful. When he finally slid in behind the wheel, hollered out one last thanks and backed ever so slowly out of the driveway, turning his head this way and that so there was no chance of hitting either the mailbox or the pine tree on the other side, I exhaled with force. It was my first experience with the ambivalence that comes from such acts of charity. It's great to give someone else pleasure, to give them something that you know they could never afford and will treasure, but I felt the inadequacy of the gesture, the burden of injustice thrown into stark relief by the extravagance of Jim's thanks. Weeks later, whenever my father walked past Jim sweeping the floor in the shop, Jim would stop him to tell him how much his wife adored that china. What had I done to deserve being born into a family that could give away a whole set of china? And why did this man have too little money to see a dentist? And why was it hard for him to walk into our house, even when invited? I was lucky to be a recent immigrant. I was white, but I didn't feel responsible for this mess.

At least early on, I could assuage my guilt by discreet acts of friendliness. Lending Portia a pencil in math class, or simply not looking away when Harry who sat behind me in biology met my gaze. But by 1969 even in Clemson a few black boys yearned to assert their right to equality. One humid June Saturday night, my father had dropped my friend Marilyn and me off at the Teen Center in downtown Clemson. We paid our fifty cents and dove into the heat, noise and dark. It took a minute to even see the band. They were stationed under a weak light against the far wall: three tenth graders with a drum, an electric guitar, a bass and two amplifiers, all three staring at their hands with fierce concentration. The posters on the wall glowed in the black lights.

We bought cokes in paper cups at the drink counter and carried them to one of the tables, as far away from the band as we could get, which wasn't very far. The Teen Center had once been a laundromat. Marilyn leaned back in her chair and tapped the rhythm on the table with newly polished nails.

Suddenly, the atmosphere shifted. The dancers moved more stiffly, attentively. All heads turned toward the entrance. Harry stood there; flanked by Darnell and another dark-skinned boy I didn't know. Harry walked in with deliberate looseness, but his smile looked glued on. Darnell and the other boy followed him looking ready to fight and run at the same time. The three positioned themselves at the edge of the dance floor and scanned the crowd that gaped at them. No black kids had ever been brazen enough to come here.

I saw Harry spot me and knew what would come next. Harry pulled himself as straight as he could and walked toward me. Darnell reached out as if he wanted to grab him by the back of that white shirt that was glowing like a flag, and pull him to safety. I wished he would.

With every eye in the place on us, Harry took slow steps that gave me a few seconds to vacillate. I told myself it would be better to refuse. It would be him the redneck boys came looking for, not me. That's what happened when Moses and Annie went out on a date. Moses got beaten so badly, he couldn't come back to school for a week. But Harry knew he was taking that risk. Was I afraid for him or me? I suspected it was me. I rose up to meet him, followed him out there, and tried to find a rhythm in the noise. Harry's skin glistened like polished walnut in the dim light. He looked businesslike, but pleased. The music slowed and his determination held me there. We moved, touching as gingerly as porcelain figurines. He hadn't had enough, but my legs would no longer carry me. I shouted an excuse and escaped to my table. Marilyn looked baffled. She patted me on the arm and yelled, "You crazy girl!" A trembling started in my gut and ran down to my toes. I barely noticed Harry and his friends leaving, mission accomplished. I don't know if it's because we only danced for a little while, but if anyone beat up Harry, I never heard about it.

That night, when I told my mother, she gasped. "You have to be careful," she said. She didn't seem to know she was actually wagging her index finger in warning. "You can ruin your reputation just like that."

Even though I was terrified myself, I shot her a disgusted look. I hated it when she told me to watch my reputation. It was so unfair to have to worry about something stupid like that. I was just glad I wasn't attracted to Harry, so I wasn't tempted to overcome my fear and go further.

When Harry had asked me to dance, I assumed he did it because he knew I was least likely to refuse, which is the same reason Portia asked me to be her campaign manager for student council secretary the next year. Portia was the closest thing to a black friend I had, and that wasn't very close. Since she was a good student, we sat near each other in all the college bound classes and occasionally chatted about schoolwork. I knew nothing about her beyond the fact that she got some of her clothes from the garbage man. If anyone else had asked me to be her campaign manager I would have said, "Are you nuts?" But then, no one else would have asked me. I was not a social asset. When Portia brought it up, I agreed without knowing what I would have to do.

Portia invited me over so we could plan our strategy. She lived with her aunt in a small brick house along Highway 93. When she let me in, I could feel myself smiling too hard, trying to pretend this was normal. Portia invited me into the living room and offered me iced tea. I stood there wondering whether I was really supposed to sit down. The living room was so aggressively tidy it looked like a museum. The French Empire style couch and chairs balanced on curled wooden legs; shiny clear plastic protected the upholstery. I heard no sounds from anywhere else in the house. When Portia returned, she put our drinks on coasters on the coffee table and sat at the edge of the couch. I lowered myself next to her, braced for the cool plastic on my thighs. I don't remember the campaign slogans we developed; it's a stretch coming up with a reason to choose one candidate over another for school secretary.

As I was about to leave, Portia invited me into her room so she could show me the supplies she'd bought for making posters. The room was slightly larger than a phone booth with walls painted a breath-taking shade of bright pink.

I meant to say, "I like that color," but what came out instead was: "I like your room." Portia flinched. Her eyes widened.

"Really?" she asked, arching her eyebrows. What could I say?

"Really," I lied, even though we both knew that was wrong.

We met before school to draw balloon-shaped letters in rainbow colors on long strips of paper and taped them up in the halls. I labored over my campaign speech. How can you make "Vote for Portia" last for ten minutes? One of my friends took a picture of me at the podium. It was a breezy spring day. I'm standing on a platform in the middle of the athletic field. Behind me, on metal folding chairs, sit the rows of candidates with their campaign managers. My hair is parted in the middle and falls almost down to my elbows. I am wearing giant hoop earrings. I had to shout into the microphone, so the student body could hear me in the bleachers. Looking at the picture, you could believe that I was engaging in an act of political importance. What I said didn't make any difference. Portia lost the election by a wide margin. But when I look at the rows of students I see something now that wasn't so clear to me at the time. Everyone else there belonged. Portia had the guts to drag me where she was even less welcome than I was, and nudge me to say something, anything, out loud and in public. It was the most American thing I had ever done.

*****

During the summer of nineteen-seventy, my grandfather Gustav had another stroke. This one was massive. The news was dire enough that my mother paced back and forth in the kitchen, debating: should she go now and see him one more time, or should she wait and go to the funeral. I sat at the table, watching as my mother paced. My Opa was in the hospital. I had never been in an East German hospital, but I pictured him, in one of his nightshirts, lying in a narrow metal bed. I imagined dark, worn linoleum, bare walls, and a dirty windowpane. He was partly paralyzed, my mother said, so he'd lie flat on his back, covers up to his armpits, eyes closed. What if I walked into the room and touched my hand to his shoulder? Would he open his eyes and turn his head? Would he be glad to see me, or would he be frustrated by ungainly sounds that were the only ones he could now make? I had never seen anyone who was dying. How do you talk to one who's dying? What do you say? I wanted to be there, but I was afraid.

My mother decided to go sooner rather than later. My sister was going along, she said. She was two and a half, too little to be away from her mother for two weeks. Could I go too? My mother thought that would get too expensive. Then she added that she thought it would just be too sad for me. She always tried to protect me from dying and death. I had never been to a funeral. I didn't press the issue. Flying across the Atlantic was still exotic then, something I had only done once since we moved. I couldn't insist in my ambivalence.

A week later my father and I drove my mother and sister to the airport in Charlotte, NC. I longed to get on that plane, but I knew it was too late to ask.

Once my mother and sister were gone, I stopped thinking about Opa. Instead, I plunged into running the house. My mother did everything herself because it was easier and more efficient. She did let me bake, but she hated having anyone in the kitchen while she was cooking. My father and I had never used the washer and dryer. Together we experimented with household tasks, piecing together what we knew from observations with what we could deduce from recipes and written instructions. I learned the hard way that turning the burner on high under the frying pan while making scrambled eggs is a mistake. Even with mistakes, I enjoyed a sense of growing competence. Three weeks later we drove to Charlotte to meet my mother and sister.

My mother emerged from the plane looking spent. Her hair hung in strands and her clothes were rumpled. She carried my sister, who clung to her, her arms around my mother's neck. We didn't ask for news until we pulled out on I-85.

With my sister asleep in the backseat, my mother leaned forward so we could hear her. There was no hope. My mother's voice deepened and cracked. He struggled so to talk, it was terrible to see. And one day Onkel Ernst, Opa Gustav's younger brother and his doctor, took her aside in the hospital corridor. Whispered to her that it wasn't just the stroke. No he wouldn't recover, because cancer was consuming his organs. He didn't want to alarm Omi. There was nothing they could do.

A month later, the Western Union lady called us to spell out another message. She garbled the letters to the unfamiliar words, but my mother unscrambled them as she wrote them down. She spelled out: VATI AM 25 SEPTEMBER VERSTORBEN STOP GRUSS ISOLDE. Dad Died on September 25 stop Greetings Isolde. Tears spilled onto the paper.

My mother stood in a pool of yellow light, bent over the kitchen table staring at the words she had made. She looked shocked even though the phone call should have come as no surprise. I felt nothing. Except guilt that I didn't feel anything. I shouted to myself, inside my head, OPA GUSTAV IS DEAD. YOU'RE SUPPOSED TO BE SAD

OR UPSET OR SOMETHING! I almost pinched myself to make sure I could still feel. Instead I watched my mother cry.

I consoled myself with empathy for her loss. At the same time, it scared me that my mother, who was always there to help me through a million trivial daily troubles, was inconsolable. She would have wandered through her days in slow motion but for the undeniable needs of my two-year-old sister. How did I explain my lack of emotion? I thought that I was just mature enough to accept that grandparents get old and have to die.

I was puzzled when my mother's loss didn't diminish with time. Isolde sent her a photograph of Gustav just before the stroke. In the picture he stands in front of his black Moskwitsch, an overweight old man. His eyes are soft and his smile is tentative. I hated that picture. I didn't want to remember him like that. But my mother placed the photo in a frame and propped it on the secretary in the kitchen. For the first few weeks, tears sprang to her eyes every time she looked at it. I just looked away.

I wouldn't believe that he was dead until a year later, when I returned to Eilenburg. Didn't believe it until I walked into the apartment and saw his reading chair empty, his ashtray clean and cold, and his books on the shelf. In the bathroom, his toiletries were missing. His half of the bed remained untouched. The door to his office was permanently locked. In his absence, he became vividly present in my mind. His glinting gold tooth, the knife blade nose, the way his forehead smoothed when he saw me. The blue work coat straining over his belly. His blunt fingers with their ridged nicotine-stained nails. The way he slicked his hair down with *Birkenwasser,* so the comb left behind straight separate strands. I felt a swell of tears, but swallowed them easily in the crush of arrival. By evening, I sat on my grandmother's couch, next to Opa Gustav's absence and didn't know how to call the tears back. I asked Omi Paula to take me to his grave. Maybe that would release the dull ache in my chest.

The old cemetery lay down in the river valley, in a juicy willowed meadow. Across the river hulked the brick buildings of the Eilenburg Plastics Factory. I had to discipline my eyes to focus down, so I could be in the presence of the dead. About half the graves were well tended, bordered with edging stones, planted with low shrubs and blooming with fuchsias and impatiens. The other half were wild with unpruned plants. Those were the graves of old people whose children had left for the West.

I had been here before. My grandmother used to bring me when she made her weekly trip to care for her in-laws' plot. As always, she carried her tin watering can. On the grave stood a black marble pillar inscribed with *Familie Hermann Sieg* in gold leaf. Hermann was my great great-grandfather. A new pedestal with an ovoid urn sat slightly in front of the pillar. My grandmother pointed to it. In there were my grandfather's ashes. I stood still, folded my hands in front of me, and waited for something to stir. Nothing did.

My grandmother climbed toward the back of the grave taking care to step only on the edging stones and pulled out the rake she hid in the bushes. She bent to prune a few dead blossoms off a red and purple fuchsia, then handed me the watering can and pointed me toward the well. She knelt down to weed. When I returned, she sprinkled the clean dirt with water, raked the earth in perfect straight lines, and balanced on the edge once more to slip the rake back under the bush. I asked her why the urn had no inscription. "The city is planning to close this cemetery, so he'll have to be moved in a few years," she explained. I felt a small sadness then, but it was for this place I remembered from early childhood. We held hands as we climbed back up toward the street. This at least I could feel: the warmth of my grandmother's palm against mine.

*****

As my sister grew, my mother regained her energy and her anger at being stuck far from home returned. I know she couldn't have frowned and criticized and complained constantly, but that's how I remember her during my last years of high school. She cultivated our early complaints about Clemson until they grew into a well-rehearsed litany for two voices. She sang the lead, I automatically supplied the descant whenever she called for it. My father, who was the intended audience, seemed to hope that if he gave the appearance of listening the song would dissipate. I was too self-absorbed to notice that the misery had become central to my mother's life.

What happened to going home after five years? My mother tried to raise the subject. My father's stance came as no surprise. How could we want him to go back now? Recently promoted to president, he was a man in charge of his own realm far from the company bureaucracy. If he went back he'd have to fit himself into the hierarchy. I pictured his sunny, sprawling corner office and tried to superimpose it on the warren of square rooms, one to a window, at company headquarters in Krefeld. I didn't want to sympathize, but even I could sense the claustrophobia of that trade. Worse, he'd have to endure the confrontational tone that characterized German business life. Oh, it was so much better here.

People were polite at work, treated each other with respect. If there is one thing my father hated it was unpleasantness. I later realized how much the American South suited him. In the South, padding confrontational issues in layers of politeness is a fine art, and manners are so deeply drilled into every child that rudeness never has a chance. And it wasn't just work. He loved the house on the lake. My mother had to admit that they could never afford to live this well if they went back. She tried to tell him that she'd gladly trade the lakeshore and the spacious house for life in a German city, but he knew she was just nostalgic. This was better, for her too, and he knew it.

I had been reading "The Second Sex" and analyzed the situation in the light of my newfound awareness of power in male-female relationships. My father had the power because he had the job and the money. He didn't have to listen. My mother took the only path open to the powerless - she gave up insisting they move back, but nursed her anger and used it to season his dinner every night. I noticed the space on the couch between them widen. As for me, my anger was tempered by age; soon I would be a free agent. I promised myself that I'd have a lucrative career and stick to it so I'd never be at the mercy of any man's power. And I was getting old enough that I could move where I wanted to go. My mother's unhappiness and her fierce devotion to it got on my nerves.

One afternoon, my mother and I sat on the deck during my sister's naptime. I see her clearly. She is wearing a yellow sleeveless shirt, her head is bowed, and she's wrapped her arms around her knees. She's just finished telling me once again how much she wants to go home, how she hates it here, how my father will not listen.

"Leave him, then," I say. Her head jerks up. Her eyes are wide, and her mouth is open.

"How would I live?" She says, with a short intake of breath. She's thinking about it.

"If you pick up and move to Germany, he'll come after you." I'm sure of this all of a sudden. Certain that my father would not be able to live without his family. "Take Nica, and I'll come with you too."

My mother shakes her head. "But what if he doesn't. What would I live on?"

"He'd have to pay you alimony and child support. You could figure out how to get a job. You have training." I'm excited now. I'd get to go home and I'd liberate her from servitude.

She looks at me, the surprise fading from her eyes. That she could even think about it. Then she slumps. "I wouldn't know what to do without him. To live alone for the rest of my life."

I argue with her, but the moment is past. She won't consider it. I'm disappointed, mostly for myself.

Shortly after our conversation, my father's patience blew. "We can't go on like this," he shouted, "we've got to settle this once and for all."

He and my mother locked themselves in the bedroom for most of a Saturday, while I took Nica first downstairs, then outside, and later for a walk, all the while trying to imagine what was happening and wondering if the world was coming to an end. It was the first time I discovered the effect caring for a child can have in forcing you to push your concerns way back into the depths of your head. To slow down and pay attention to what's before you now, because if you let yourself worry, you end up with a worried whining child and your job is that much harder. The hours wound on. Several times, we passed the bedroom window. Shouting gave way to murmurs I could barely distinguish.

When they emerged, calmer and almost smiling, an armistice had been reached. My mother didn't exactly lay down her weapons, but she did moderate her attacks. The following semester, she signed up for her first extension class at the university. It was called "South Carolina History." Later she took classes in local botany and southern cooking. If I wanted to leave, I would have to find a way to go alone.

*****

When I told my parents I planned to skip a year of high school, they set conditions. Since I'd only be seventeen when I graduated, I would have to live at home and go to Clemson. Even though I still longed for Germany, I didn't argue. At seventeen, I wouldn't feel old enough to move a continent away, and I knew it. I was anxious enough about the transition to college, much as I wanted out of high school. But the biggest problem was the mismatch between a South Carolina graduation certificate and an *Abitur* - the formal set of written and oral exams in the final year of *Gymnasium* that determined a German student's university career. I was missing six years of Latin and four years of French. My knowledge of German literature was spotty, and thanks to Sabine's frequent corrections, I knew that my written grammar had deteriorated. Worse, I lacked confidence that I could do well in Germany. Ever since I grew fluent in English toward the end of seventh grade, I had been a star student. Rows of A's graced my report cards, and I rarely had trouble with any of the concepts presented at school. I assumed I did so well because South Carolina regularly vied with Mississippi and Alabama as the worst ranked state in America for quality of education.

In my German *Gymnasium*, I had been a middling to good performer. Math, which now was one of my best subjects, had frequently given me trouble, and the year before I left I struggled to stay afloat in my Latin class. Most likely I had trouble concentrating the year before we left because my changing body was diverting energy from my brain. But I was afraid that if I went back to Germany, I'd once again be average, and on top of being average, I'd have a lot of catching up to do. When I worried out loud to my mother, she only nodded and agreed, which made me even more nervous, since she usually tried to calm me and convince me I could overcome whatever obstacle I was obsessing about. At the time I didn't recognize this as a clever parenting strategy. My parents didn't want me to leave. So they tried to slow me down, by letting me stew in my anxieties, and by suggesting I should wait until I survived a few years of college, and then transfer. My father always added, "…if by then you still want to." I was sure I would.

That summer my cousin Ulrike arrived to spend six weeks with us. She wanted to see America and to apply the English she was studying at school. I couldn't imagine how Clemson looked to her. Mühlacker, where she lived, was a small town, so Clemson's size wouldn't shock her as much. Still, I was a reluctant tour guide. What was there to show off?

I drove my mother's VW Squareback down Hwy. 123, windows open, hair flying. Ulrike rode beside me, awed by my driver's license and my confidence. Driving was so much easier here. You didn't have to maneuver through narrow twisting streets, there were copious parking spots most places you wanted to go, and best of all, if you killed the motor at a stoplight, the guy behind you neither honked nor tapped his finger against his forehead to make sure you knew he thought you were an idiot woman driver.

What belonged on a tour of Clemson? A walk around campus, preferably early in the morning before the heat threatened to strangle you, when the curving paths and the dark-green pools of shade between buildings spread the illusion of coolness. A visit to the John C. Calhoun house, with kitchen house and slave quarters. Late evening dips in Lake Hartwell. The water lapped bathtub warm against your legs. A drive past 'Death Valley', the huge Football Stadium that baked deserted in the heat. The Ornamental Gardens, maintained by the Department of Horticulture, and a perennial family favorite. In 1971, we would have carried plastic bags of stale bread, so Nica could feed the ducks at the pond. Nothing blooms in Clemson in July. Then we went further afield. A drive up to the Blue Ridge Parkway, complete with picnic. Shopping at MacAlester Square in Greenville. The sights felt paltry to me. A handful of pretty views. I wished I had a city to offer, a city with museums, shopping, dancing and cafes. But Ulrike enjoyed herself. She was away from home and the boys in Clemson thought she was exotic with her short blonde hair and alluring accent.

I loved our incessant philosophical discussions. For the duration of Ulrike's stay, I moved downstairs to the guest room, where we shared the double sized hide-a-bed. At night, we talked in the dark, mostly about heavier subjects than our love lives. We discussed existentialism and feminism, Maoism, and the Vietnam War. Our talk circled around books we read, and whether we could ever imagine having a lesbian relationship. All the subjects I had been reading about poured out of me, thrilled at having finally found someone else who read the same books and wondered about everything. I assumed we could talk like this for hours into the deep night, because we shared a German upbringing. I never thought about us sharing fifty percent of our genetic material.

She reveled in Clemson as a place of liberation. The wide-open spaces that had struck me as a wasteland when I arrived at thirteen thrilled her. She raved about the intense aromas characteristic of the South: the perfume of Magnolias at night, smoking barbeques, the musky odors catalyzed by heat and humidity. She experienced freedom on another level too. It was from Ulrike I learned that my parents' liberal attitudes toward curfews were not quintessentially German, but peculiar to their upbringing. Ulrike's father insisted she be home at nine every night. My eleven o'clock curfew coupled with my driver's license and easy access to my mother's car struck her as paradise. Years later she still remembered her American summer as a thrilling adventure and a life-changing experience. She said it gave her the self-confidence to completely change her social persona at school the next year. I just remember being puzzled at her delight.

Most undergraduates at Clemson lived on campus. The few of us that didn't had limited options between classes. I discovered the Canteen, because I had to eat lunch somewhere. The Canteen was a large coffee shop. Along one length, old ladies in pale green smocks, their hair covered in spidery nets, stood behind a counter frying up short order sandwiches. Glass opened the view toward a courtyard on the opposite wall. In between sat rows of Formica-covered tables surrounded by wooden chairs. A jukebox filled the room with endless rounds of *The Night they Drove Old Dixie Down, Maggie May,* and *The Day the Music Died.* I'd sometimes startle those old southern women by ordering French fries with mayonnaise, though most days I had a fried ham and cheese sandwich. It came on white - in 1971 no one in Clemson had heard of other options. I had it with coffee, because I needed to stay awake. I'd carry my tray to a table near the window, extract a five-pound textbook from my shoulder bag, and settle in.

Gradually, I noticed the table of regulars near the jukebox. One of them was Gordon who graduated from Daniel two years ahead of me. I remembered him for two reasons: his Canadian accent and the erudition he flaunted. He vaguely remembered me, possibly because I hung out with the same crowd as his little brother. Gordon chatted me up and invited me to sit at his table, where he surrounded himself with an entourage of intelligent girls and a sprinkling of male foreign graduate students like Amin whose main occupation was trying to keep his student visa valid so he wouldn't have to return to Libya and serve in Qaddafi's army. As the fall settled in, Gordon took to wearing a forest green wool blazer with suede elbow patches and smoking a pipe as he provoked us into ever more intense political discussions. He was passionate about foreign policy. He always had a final statistic or quote up his sleeve that would leave his opponent stuttering. I loved the intellectual stimulation, even if I squirmed when Gordon settled back in his chair to smirk victoriously. It was through Gordon that I met Deborah.

I remember Deborah swirling into rooms, surrounded by wispy fabrics, her bright eyes ready to delight in every detail of the world. She appeared perpetually ready to admire. Her hair was long, wavy and brown. I loved telling her stories. She focused totally, reacted to it all. She too, had stories to tell. She had spent the year before in Holland with Gordon, and was filled with admiration for everything European. She had come back hating big American cars, sprawling towns without sidewalks, rednecks who weren't informed about world politics, and militarists. We spent hours reading Newsweek to each other, spitting with disgust at Nixon's arrogance. Another thing we had in common was our determination to study science and force our way into 'male' careers. She wanted to go to medical school, a long shot when the only one in South Carolina had a restrictive quota for women students. Her required courses were similar enough to mine that we could trade warnings and recommendations about professors, though we never had a class together. Deborah and Gordon absorbed me into their group and gave me a home.

After the claustrophobia of Daniel High, I loved the anonymity Clemson's size offered. The professors cared only about how well I did on my exams, and didn't know anything about me beyond that. Well, almost. Since my parents socialized with some of them, that wasn't quite true. My mother would come home from cocktail parties with stories of professors telling her what a good student I was. I loved hearing that, she loved hearing it; we were both happy. What was so much better about university was that nobody cared what I did between classes. I could staff a table in a student government election, spend hours smoking and arguing with my new friends in the Canteen, hang out at the Study Hall (our favorite beer joint downtown) every night, or visit my new boyfriend's dorm room during open dorm time, and nobody paid attention. I was so dizzy with goodwill that I started noticing some advantages to living in Clemson.

It was wonderful that I knew so many people, I decided. Whenever I went downtown, I could hardly walk from one end to the other without running into someone I knew. The southern habit of greeting people with extreme enthusiasm began to feel warm instead of hypocritical to me. I could keep up with the best of them. "How are you?" can express a world of pleasure if you put the emphasis on the *are*, draw it out into a long, delighted surprise, and bring your voice up to a near squeal at the end. It used to get on my nerves, but when I ran into my art teacher from Daniel, and she looked positively thrilled, I suddenly remembered that she was the first person ever to take my attempts at drawing seriously. I said, "How nice to see you" and meant it. From this distance, even the occasional Daniel student just looked like someone I happened to know, instead of someone who might judge and categorize me. The university's size allowed me to appreciate the pleasures of the town's smallness. Being known could be a treat, especially when you had an escape ready.

I still dreamed of returning home to Germany. Failing that, I wanted to move out of my parents' house. The spring of my freshman year, Deborah and I looked for an apartment together. I had a scholarship that paid for tuition and books. One of the advantages of majoring in Textile Chemistry was that there were more scholarships than students in that department. I assumed my parents would be willing to pay my living expenses. They were, but not quite yet. I hadn't remembered that German kids didn't move out of the house at eighteen. They usually didn't even finish *Gymnasium* until they were 19, or if they'd had to repeat a class, 20. My parents wanted me to stay home another year. The first time we discussed it, I stormed out of the house, crying and slamming doors. Of course I was mature enough to move out!

After a few weeks of tense negotiations, in which I threatened to just move and support myself by getting a job, my father offered me a deal: if I stayed at home one more year, at the end of that year he'd buy me a used car and find me a summer job in Germany. I could live with friends in Krefeld for three whole months and see whether it still felt like home.

EXPERIMENT

During the long night between New York and Frankfurt, I obsessively check my purse to see whether my passport and ticket are still in the proper compartment. The responsibility of flying alone hypes me into a state of extreme alert. On the aisle next to my window seat, a middle-aged Indian man on his way home tilts his seat back and folds himself into a deep sleep as soon as the stewardess clears the dinner trays. I fight down a wave of panic when I realize that I will not be able to get up until he wakes without climbing across his stretched out legs. It's all right, I soothe myself. If it's an emergency, I'll just risk waking him. After all, he's only been sleeping a few minutes and already his mouth is slack. Briefly, I envy him. What would it be like to be able to relax like that in public?

I pull out a book, Emile Zola in German translation, in hopes that reading a novel in German will help reset my language center and shorten the days of brain sludge on arrival. The first few days back in Germany, I feel like I'm trying to drag words out of a swamp. Every visit, I struggle longer. I collect a repertoire of simple phrases that buy time. I dangle the phrases in front of me like a curtain, so I can disguise the frantic work behind: dredging for half-forgotten expressions, double-checking cases and articles, racing ahead so my verb will match the beginning phrase I'm holding up to hide behind. I struggle to hold my face calm, because the last thing I want is for anyone to suspect how fast I'm scrambling behind the curtain. No one seems to notice how awkward I feel.

My vocabulary is frozen at age twelve. I am grateful that I had ventured into Dostoyevsky by then so my tools are more advanced than that sounds. What trips me up more is that the language changes while I'm gone. I get off the plane and meet with a new set of words, usually borrowed from English, but slightly twisted. *Twens* - young people in their twenties - wear *"jeanshosen"* with *"blazers"* and in the evening the girls might put *"Augen make-up"* on their eyes. The papers are filled with articles on the *"Watergateskandal"* and *"interviews."* *"Discjockeys"* fill *"Diskotheken"* with *"Nonstop Musik."* The women's magazines advertise exotic American foods like *"cottage cheese."*

All through the night, I smoke cigarettes and read. By morning, my eyes burn and my throat aches. My seatmate sits up just in time for breakfast and lets me pass so I can brush my teeth. In Frankfurt, I race through customs and passport control unable to slow down until I've found my connecting flight to Düsseldorf. I've got that jet-lag buzz that comes from staying up till the dead hours of night and emerging into a bright European morning. It propels me alert all the way into the arms of Traudl Ruff, a family friend I've not seen for six years, who waits for me in the arrival hall at Düsseldorf. She has not changed a bit. She is tall and slender with permed blonde hair, slightly protruding eyes, and a laugh that hiccups at the end. Next to her is Thomas, the nemesis of many childhood Sunday afternoons, now grown to eighteen years of age. He is handsome enough now to make me hope he's outgrown his childhood tendency to grab and hurt whenever things don't go his way. I shake his hand, and wish I hadn't. He still doesn't know his strength.

I collapse into the back of their VW beetle, relieved and proud that I've made it to my destination on my own. Traudl chauffeurs us through the city streets, crosses the Rhine and heads for Lank, a suburb just east of Krefeld. The sun plays on the meadows dotted with grazing cows. The Ruffs' new house sits in a row - red brick, one and a half stories, gray tile roof, patch of lawn with flower borders. A few houses down, the street dead-ends at the edge of a field. This is the kind of house my parents dreamed of when they contracted with a bank for a *Bausparvertrag* - a home construction savings plan. Compared to our house in Clemson, the rooms at the Ruffs' are tiny. The number of days to adapt to the scale of living is the same number it takes before the morass in my brain loses viscosity and begins to slide me words as fast as I need them. Three days, four, by the end of the week, I adjust.

Our parents have arranged an exchange. When Thomas leaves for Clemson in a few weeks, I will move into his room, but for now, I use the spare. I sleep on a cot and keep my suitcase on the floor, folding and refolding as I search for my personal care bag and a change of clothes. My two-month job in the quality control lab at *Verseidag* begins on Monday, so I have three days of freedom. That night, Traudl expects me to help set the table on the terrace for dinner. Erwin, who's arrived home from the office and greeted me with a jovial hello, excruciating handshake, followed by a crushing hug, sits in front of the TV with

Thomas. They're drinking beers served to them by Traudl. Traudl and I shake out the tablecloth and center it. I carry a tray of dishes and silverware out from the kitchen and later return for a load of cold cuts, cheese, and pickles. The bread slicer whirrs in the kitchen. I'm too tired that evening to question why Thomas is in there reclining on the sofa like the prince of the house, while I'm expected to do 'women's work.' The stunning recognition of familiar tastes that ambushes me on trips to Germany reconciles and quiets me for now. It is pleasant, and oh so German, to sit on the terrace as dusk deepens, shivering just a little in the cooling May evening, sipping a beer, savoring the aftertaste of sourdough rye, tangy butter, and smoky ham.

Saturday night, Thomas invites me to go to Düsseldorf with him and a few friends, to hang out in the *Altstadt* - the old city that has been converted into an entertainment district. He describes it as *"dufte."* The closest German word I know is *duftig*, which refers to a pleasant smell, but I infer that it has morphed into the German equivalent of cool while I was gone. I wonder what I should wear. Because I desperately want to look native, I usually try to scope out what current styles are before I venture out. Thomas appears to live in jeans, so I decide bellbottoms will blend in until I have more information. Erwin drops us off at the closest tram stop. Thomas's friends are clad in blue jeans too, so I have guessed right. As we climb into the express tram that runs between Krefeld and Düsseldorf, Thomas announces we're going to ride *"schwarz."* I vaguely recall what that means. Not paying the fare and hoping you don't get caught. The fare can't be that much. Anxiety heats up my ears, but I dare not protest. They are so certain it's the clever thing to do, and I have no way to gauge how dangerous this prank is. We stand in the center of the car, leaning against posts, only grabbing on when absolutely unavoidable, as they joke about teachers I don't know. For me, the ride is endless. At every stop, I expect an inspector to board the tram. In my imagination, his voice cuts like that of an East German border guard. When we get off, I'm giddy to feel my feet on the ground.

The *Altstadt* simmers. Vendors sell balloons and decorated gingerbread hearts. At every corner, musicians serenade the crowd as coins clink into beckoning instrument cases. Knots of people stroll past restaurants, reading the menus that seek to lure them inside. We've already eaten, but I enjoy admiring the abundance of choices. Thomas steers us deeper into the heart of the old town toward narrower streets and houses leaning with age. His friends favor a skinny bar with a door built in the days when everyone was as short as I am. They bend their heads as we step down into the haze of smoke and beer. Way in the back a middle-aged accordion player with a gravelly voice wails sea shanties, some in rumbling German and the rest in transfigured English. We drink a few glasses of *"Alt,"* the sweet dark beer that is the specialty of the region. How much richer the taste than the "Old Mil" I routinely sip at the Study Hall in Clemson. I'm shocked by a stab of longing. I can't be homesick for Clemson. I won't be. Just because here, I sit in the smoky bar, an add-on to Thomas's gang, staring into the crowd, expecting nothing. When I go to the Study Hall, which I do most nights around ten for a study break, I'm greeted by smiles and hellos. On an average evening I know more than half the patrons by sight and if some guy who doesn't know better makes a nuisance of himself all I have to do is whisper a word to Tommy the bartender. I'm determined to prefer this anonymous bar, epitomous of city life.

Later we emerge into darkness, wend our way past a drunk trying to earn another drink by singing next to his hat, and dip back into the thickening crowd. Everything I see strikes me as the ultimate in sophistication, including the tolerance shown to the drunk we've just passed. What I most love is the crush of people walking, people outside on a Saturday night, listening to music, talking, strolling, and sitting at café tables drinking their beer. This is what I most miss when I'm in Clemson. I miss the common space, the heart of town, public life. By the time we trudge back to the tram stop, my legs are tired, but I'm reluctant to leave.

On Monday morning, when Erwin drops me at the *Verseidag* gate, an apprentice in a white lab coat leads me across a cobblestoned courtyard to Frau Dr. Rück's office. This is my first real job. I've filed correspondence for my father and keypunched registration cards for thousands of Clemson students for the registrar's office, but I've never worked in a lab. Frau Dr. Rück is in her fifties, with graying red-blond hair, watery eyes and a neck so prominent she looks like she might have a goiter. A bulldog leaps to mind. She is brusque, as if she's afraid no one will take her seriously otherwise.

She introduces me to the QC Lab staff - they are all women, except for Timmy, the Nigerian exchange student. One of the women reacts to my name. "Poser, Poser..." then she asks, "you don't have a mother who worked in QC at Reika in the fifties?" When I admit that I do, she wants to hear all about my family, then tells me a bit about herself. I'm fascinated because I've always wondered how my mother might be different if she had continued her career. Frau Janssen remained single, though, and the clothes that peek out from under her lab coat suggest she uses her salary to indulge her excellent taste. The women assign me my own spot at the worktables, and explain the different QC test stations. *Verseidag* specializes in umbrella fabrics; my first job will be to assess the effectiveness of fabric treatments for water repellency. I will simply shred fabric, weigh it, stuff it into a glass tube, insert it into an apparatus that saturates it in moist air for a specified time, and then measure the weight again. I can do this. The lab benches are tidy, and clearly labeled drawers store the equipment I need.

At nine-thirty, the women announce it's time for a break. They brew rose hip tea and serve it in clean 250 ml beakers and pull out sandwiches wrapped in wax paper. Traudl fixed me two sandwiches this morning; I pull out half of one to be sociable. A slice of sourdough rye, a slice of *Schwarzbrot*, held together by a layer of butter and liverwurst. My mother sent me to school with sandwiches like this. I stir sugar into my tea - the red liquid gleams in the clean glass - and use it to wash down a bite of my sandwich. The tangy rose hip softens the bread and warms the cool slide of liverwurst.

There are two tables in the lab, one on each side of the outside entrance. Each overlooks a large window. I've settled at the table with the younger assistants. There's a fifteen year-old apprentice, who spends part of her days at school, a blonde woman a few years older than me, who talks about her fiancé and which *Discothek* they went to the night before, an older woman whose job is to keep the lab clean and do the lab's dishes so the technicians can concentrate on doing measurements, and Timmy, who is a student at the technical school and works here during his semester break. At the other table sit the seasoned lab techs, Frau Janssen and several other women my mother's age, who are fixtures in this lab and daily pick up threads of old conversations. Frau Dr. Rück stays in her glass-walled office with the door shut, talking on the phone, or bending over piles of papers. When she can't hear, they call her *die Rück* instead of *Frau Dr.* and drop all pretense of respect.

Frau Dr. Rück emerges and asks me to follow her into the factory so she can give me a tour. On the way, she tells me I'll be getting samples of the finishing solution from the line every day, and analyzing it to make sure it has the proper nitrogen content. I've been in textile factories before, once or twice, on field trips with my textile classes at Clemson. I expect to enter a dingy hall filled with clattering equipment staffed by scruffy guys. But the factory is large and airy, every surface spotless and gleaming with fresh paint. The workers wear gray lab coats over dark blue workpants, and move unhurriedly down the aisles to adjust equipment. Frau Dr. Rück leads me to the finishing range with its stacks of giant rollers looped with fabric. She hails a gray-haired man and introduces him as Herr Rosenberg, the supervisor. Herr Rosenberg shakes my hand, and, before I have to wonder whether he is my elementary school friend Jutta's father, he asks me whether I am that

Claudia Poser. His delight at finding me again warms me. Frau Dr. Rück clearly has little time for this social moment, so we return to business.

At lunchtime I follow Fräulein Pitz to the company cafeteria, another sunny room overlooking the cobbled yard. In the lunch line, stout women ladle portions of boiled potatoes and goulash out of giant pots onto our plates. It may be cafeteria food, but it resembles the midday dinners of my childhood the way no macaroni and cheese with a side of Jell-o salad served at Clemson University ever will. My new coworkers are amused by my pleasure.

In the coming days, I fall into the daily rhythms of the lab. I try to imagine a life here, among these German women who address each other by their last names, even in the case of the two older women who've worked together for at least a decade. The formality doesn't appear to affect their working relationship. It may even help to delineate the nature of the relationship - colleagues, not chums. They accept me with warmth, and true to German form, make blunt observations when they observe me acting 'different.' Fräulein Pitz asks me why I smile so much. I jerk the corners of my mouth down and confess that I must have picked that habit up in the US. One day, as I skirt around her in a narrow aisle, I murmur an "excuse me." She turns abruptly and grouses at me. "What are you apologizing for all the time? You didn't even run into me. " I'm too stunned to answer. It's only later, when I've had a little time to think, that I recognize she's spotted another cultural adaptation. Whether it's because Germans and Americans have a different concept of personal space, it is true that in America I've learned to apologize when I cross an invisible boundary. I lie awake at night pondering these changes in me. And what does it mean that some of my American friends tell me I don't look American? They say there's something about me that's different, but they can't describe what it is. Are there some residual ways of moving? Maybe I smile more than a German, but less than a South Carolina girl? My mission during this summer in Germany is to see whether I can fit in again. I'm trying to fill in the gaps six years of absence have left behind and at the same time trying to fit back into this way of moving and talking.

I try so hard to look like I know what I'm doing, that I don't even dare admit to the kind of confusion any German might experience the first time they commuted home using a new tram and bus route. That first day, I use my observational skills in hyper drive to deduce where the trams I need stop, and where I need to get off. Traudl has donated some multi-ride passes, so I don't have to buy individual tickets. I use these to take me to the center of town, where I feign confidence on my way to the public transportation office. Lucky for me, it's easy to find. If it hadn't been, I would have searched rather than ask and expose my ignorance. When I ask for a monthly pass, the man at the counter demands a passport photo. I'm humiliated. I didn't know I needed it. He is indifferent. He directs me to a photo booth, where I can get one of those strips of four hideous pictures made for five marks. When I return, he staples one of the pictures to a pass, slips it into a plastic sleeve and takes my money. I feel like I'm officially a resident of Krefeld again.

That first night, I'm too eager to see whether I've got Traudl's directions right, so I don't stay in the city to shop or just wander. As the summer progresses, I rarely go straight back to Lank because there is nothing there for me. I usually stop first at Fontanella's ice cream café where my mother used to buy me cones of whipped cream on the theory that cold foods are bad for the stomach, especially a small child's. I sit at one of the tiny marble-topped tables and drink either an espresso or an *Eiskaffee* - vanilla and chocolate ice cream with coffee and whipped cream. After that, I either stroll around the shopping district looking for bargains that will transform my wardrobe back to a distinctly German look, or to the library, where I've been checking out German classics missing from my father's collection. I acquire a Krefeld library card and a checking account for my *Verseidag* earnings.

One weekend before Thomas leaves, he invites me to join him on an overnight trip to the *Eifel,* a hilly vacation area near the Belgian border. His mountain climbing club owns a cabin there. Both Thomas and his father are serious about climbing. They plan vacations in the Alps around rock faces they want to tame. I know nothing about climbing, but Traudl says I can always take walks in the country while the others scale practice cliffs. The climbing club reminds me that there are German traditions I know nothing about. The members are all sturdy looking young people, outdoorsy and clean-cut. They favor rustic clothes - leather pants and green vests with horn buttons. I've dabbled in hiking with some back-to-nature hippies in South Carolina, but this is quite different. This is competitive and certainly not vegetarian. The *Hütte* is a simple two-story structure, and we spread our sleeping bags in the single upstairs room, boys and girls mixed together. These people are friendly, but quite preoccupied with getting their ropes and spikes in order. I'm happy to escape into a nearby meadow and commune with cows.

I climb a dirt path that hugs the boundaries between patches of grazing lands. The grasses are knee-high and dotted with the flowers of my childhood. Spindly buttercups, Queen Anne's Lace and a myriad of flowers I can name only in German: *grosser Wiesenknopf, Hahnenfuss,*

Zittergras. Fat bumblebees hover above the juicy plants and the rich odor of drying cow dung warms the air. I open my eyes wide, inhale deeply and attempt to memorize every sensation from the buzzing bees to the earthy tang with its grace notes of sweet pollen to the weight of sun warming the back of my neck. Up the hill, a cow shifts position and its bell clunks. I look for a place to lie down, to better merge with this land. Rusting electric fences edge the patches of meadow, but the plants spill out beyond in strips along the path. I find a length of green, cropped close by the passing herds, free of cow pies. I sink down and for a space am able to ignore the black flies that gather and the ants whose paths I'm blocking. Through a screen of grasses I search the sky for shades of blue, the clouds for whites and grays. The bright light blinds me, and I close my eyes. I had no idea I carried a blueprint for this meadow within me. I hadn't even missed it until I found this match. *I must find a way to stay in Germany.* The thought terrifies me. I don't know how. Yet, at this moment I am sure that I cannot live anywhere else on earth.

The night before Thomas leaves, the family gathers to take him out for a farewell dinner. The destination is a Chinese restaurant. I'm curious whether my memory serves me right that Chinese food in Germany tastes different from Chinese in the US. There is no chow mein, but always *kropoek* - a crispy puff made from shrimp-flavored rice flour - served as an appetizer. We don't go to the restaurant my family favored, though it still exists. The Ruffs whisper that a reporter detected dog food cans in that restaurants' garbage - is this a universal Chinese restaurant rumor? The restaurant the Ruffs prefer opened long after we moved. I'm pleased when the waiter brings us trays of *kropoek* with our menus. I order the almond chicken I loved once and find that it's taste nudges that memory. The almonds are scattered on top, whole and crunchy. I don't know exactly what the Chinese cooks do to make their food taste more German here and more American there, but the difference is as real as I thought it was that first time my taste buds drooped with disappointment at the Dragon Den in Anderson, SC.

Once Thomas is gone, I realize that I know hardly anyone in Krefeld. I visit Gudrun for *Kaffeeklatsch* and dinner once. Ulli has moved to Paris to work, and Bine is at the university in Munich. Herr Rosenberg arranges a reunion with his daughter Jutta when she visits from her university at Freiburg. Sabine, too, returns to Krefeld from Berlin where she is majoring in art history, and takes me out for supper and a few beers one evening. I consider my options. During the week, I fill my time with work, shopping, reading, and painting in my room at night. The weekends are empty.

*****

Germans are famous for taking lengthy vacations, but the generous number of their holidays is less known. Krefeld is in North Rhine Westphalia, a traditionally Catholic state, and especially rich in feast days that have transformed into long weekends. These holidays are mobile, because, like Easter, they depend on the church calendar. The first of these is the Feast of the Ascension, which generally falls in late May. Then there's Pentecost in early June, followed by Corpus Christi Day ten days later. The day I began work, I realized I would have three long weekends ahead in my three months. I decided to use the first of these to visit Ulrike and her family in Mühlacker, a four-hour train ride away.

What I had imagined as a dutiful visit to my relatives turns into my window on Ulrike's (and, dare I generalize?, German young people's) social life. I'm fascinated by the way her friends move in a mixed gender band, performing hip variations on German rituals. On a Sunday afternoon, we pile into Ulrike's friend Volker's two-cylinder Citroen and drive in search of a café in the country. Behind us, we trail a group of motor scooters - most young people can't afford cars. When we reach the café, we assemble inside a smoke-filled room vibrating with American pop music. Yet we order the same cakes and tortes our parents consumed on countless Sunday afternoons. We drink coffee, slowly, smoke and talk for hours. Afterwards, we find a patch of woods for our Sunday stroll. Ulrike's friends absorb me into their fold. They ask question after question. I'm struck by their knowledge of American politics and foreign policy (which they criticize passionately). At the same time, their questions reveal awed fascination with the country and its culture. They don't want to hear that I miss the dense villages that confine them. In the evenings, they gather at each other's houses to play cards and drink beer. Late one night, we trek down to the corner restaurant for a snack of turtle soup and escargot served with hard rolls.

Unlike my cousin and many of her friends, I have a driver's license. Ulrike is eager to take advantage of this fact. She'd like to recreate the mobility she loved when she was in Clemson the previous summer. She badgers her mother to let me borrow the car. Tante Nanne is not just nervous about me driving her car; she communicates anxiety about driving in general. Her attitude suggests that a single scratch will bring down my uncle's wrath. Her worry makes me wish she would just say no, but she doesn't. She hands me the key. Her list of last minute admonitions underscores her reluctance. I nod and look serious, mostly because now she has me terrified. I know German drivers not only go faster and have less patience for others' mistakes; they maneuver on narrow roads through streets designed for horse carts. Ulrike is so thrilled to be leaving the house in a car without a parent, that she doesn't want to notice my nerves.

I slide into Tante Nanne's tiny Fiat, affectionately known as Snow White, presumably because it's white and she loves it, and try to figure out the controls. Ulrike's friend lives in Lomersheim, about 3 km away. I make it down the hill to the bridge. An unfamiliar sign reminds me that the street feeding into the bridge from below has the right of way and I finally gather the courage to accelerate and cross. The road is barely wide enough for two cars, and a semi careens toward me. I manage to get out of his way by edging into a restaurant driveway. My heart is pounding already, and I haven't even made it into the main part of town. The next part of the drive is simple: a stoplight, a turn, and then straight ahead until I get into the village. In Lomersheim an ancient half-timbered house sticks out into the street. From its corner extends a square mirror, angled so I can see whether any cars are approaching the intersection behind it. I slow to a crawl and wonder whether I can really trust that mirror. While I hesitate, a hay-wagon drawn by a pair of workhorses lurches toward me. I edge as far to the other side of the street as I can and wait. Hay spilling from the edges of the wagon grazes my window as the cart rattles by. I take a deep breath, and inch down through the center of the village. Ulrike directs me to a level spot along a meadow, where I can park Snow White. I switch off the motor with a deep sigh of relief.

The easy companionship of Ulrike's friends envelops me and throws my isolation in Krefeld into stark relief. I notice, too, that one of Ulrike's male friends, with the marvelously German name of Albrecht, is very interested in everything I have to say. Just before I left for Germany, I broke off a stormy relationship that had absorbed me for a year and a half. I promised myself to take a break from love. I thought I should prove to myself that I didn't need a man in my life. I guess my resolve to resist romance is purely theoretical. Albrecht is everything I find irresistible: tall and slender with a mustache and a twinkle in his penetrating eyes. He listens as if everything I have to say is a revelation and uses words in precise and elegant ways, often to humorous effect. I fight my attraction for at least half a day. When he invites me along to buy cigarettes I find myself - despite my best intentions - kissing him next to the vending machine.

The rest of my Krefeld stay divides this way: during the weeks I work (sustained by letters from Albrecht) and rediscover every corner of the city alone; on as many weekends as possible I commute to Mühlacker. In the letters we write to each other while I am in Krefeld we complain what a cruel joke the world is playing on us, letting us indulge in this impractical flirtation. Albrecht invites me to meet his family, and we drink whisky in his room while listening to jazz. I toy with the possibility that I could love a German man. I'm thrilled when he calls me *Schatz* - literally 'treasure.' My mother called me that as long as I let her. I never thought to hear it from a boyfriend. I rediscover other German endearments that have lain dormant waiting to blossom. We have very little time alone, and much of that is spent talking, trying to get to know each other. I notice how much more opportunity there is in South Carolina for privacy.

The scenes I remember play like a Hollywood movie: me on the back of Albrecht's scooter, arms wrapped around his waist, the two of us clowning at the Mühlacker swimming pool, kisses in the moonlight. All this takes place in the space of four weekends. By the end of my stay, the German endearments have escalated to include love and my intention to return to Germany firms up. If Albrecht hadn't been working a summer job I might have given up my plan to cap the summer with a train and youth hostel tour of European cities. As it is, after I've done Amsterdam, Brussels, Antwerp, and Paris, I forgo Vienna so I can squeeze in one last trip to Mühlacker at the end, just before I leave for East Germany. On that last trip, I stay at Albrecht's house, in the attic guest room, because Ulrike and her family are away on vacation.

Such close proximity allows me to gain some new insights. Albrecht ironing his blue jeans until creased, and, at breakfast giving me a demonstration on how to pour hot water into the coffee filter to extract the maximum flavor from the coffee grounds. I file those observations away, refusing to examine whether I could live with that much attention to detail. I also register that his family adores him. They intimidate me sufficiently that I am too nervous to consummate our relationship right above their heads.

The morning is cool and still as Albrecht drives me to the station in the little Renault that belongs to his sister. We both cry as my train pulls in. Our promises to see each other 'next year' ring in my ear all the way to the East German border.

*****

My luggage was light. A big shoulder bag made of recycled upholstery fabric I bought at the flea market in Amsterdam. It functioned as purse and snack-carrier. A single small suitcase with a few changes of underwear, some spare t-shirts and a few souvenirs. My extra pair of jeans had been stolen at the youth hostel in Amsterdam, and my umbrella disappeared in Heidelberg. I didn't even carry presents for my relatives, because I was meeting up with my mother and sister who were already in Eilenburg. I left my heavy suitcase stuffed with a summer's worth of shopping in storage at the Frankfurt railway station. Still, I was nervous out of habit. I had bought myself a book for the trip and I feared the border guards would confiscate it. Who could predict how the border guards would behave this time? I read quickly, then backed up every so often because I was missing the point.

The train was fairly empty, probably because it was a weekday. The stations were unfamiliar because I was approaching from a different direction than usual. Instead of crossing at Bebra or Oebisfelde, those two border town names that echoed through my childhood, my ticket said I'd be crossing at Hof. It was the easiest crossing of my life. The guards were polite and efficient. They didn't even look at my book, just stamped my passport, took my money and filed past. We were off again in less than an hour.

The wasted adrenalin rushed through me, leaving me shaky and hungry. I dug in my bag for salami and bread. The train moved deeper into East Germany and grew crowded. Two African exchange students sat down across from me. One of them was quiet, but the other one was very friendly. He introduced himself as David. They were from Angola and full of questions about the US. I was curious about them too. I had never met any Africans from a country aligned with the Russians. I can't remember what we talked about, only that we passed a pleasant hour.

The train stopped again, I believe it was in Zwickau, and two Russian army officers staggered into our compartment. They took the two seats next to mine, and barged into the conversation. Their alcohol-loosened tongues impeded their rolling attempts at German. The Russian near me put his arm on the back of the seat behind me and leaned close. I stiffened in my seat. The fumes were almost enough to get me drunk, too. Then he told me what a pretty girl I was. I said thank you and inched away. Much too subtle for a drunk, though. He kept leaning closer until his head was on my shoulder. My brain was trying to sort alternatives. He was a Russian officer. I knew this even though I am ignorant of army insignia, simply because I knew that Russian privates were never allowed out of the barracks except on military maneuvers. This was East Germany. An occupied country. Maybe I could tell him where I was from? Would he understand? Or get angry? I sat there, thinking, paralyzed. The Russian tried to kiss me. David leaned forward and said: "Hey, leave my sister alone."

The Russian sat up. He leaned forward in disbelief. "She's your sister?" David nodded solemnly. The Russian rubbed his eyes and looked at me, sideways. I nodded. We were lucky the Russian was so drunk he thought his eyes were playing tricks on him. For emphasis, my rescuer added: "She's my sister and you better leave her alone." Then he gave me an almost imperceptible wink. He chattered about his father and his family until the Russian got so confused he gave up and began to talk to his fellow officer in their own language. They got up and left just before we reached Leipzig. David shook my hand warmly as I prepared to get off. I wished him the best possible life.

That evening I stood at the stove in my grandmother's kitchen. I was fixing myself a late dinner of eggs over easy to Tante Anni's amazement. She grinned and pointed, "That's how the American soldiers fixed their eggs!" What soldiers? Why the ones quartered in her house in '45. She closed her eyes to better remember the scene. "They didn't speak German, so they had to show me how to flip the eggs the way they liked." Then she looked me up and down. In Germany, eggs came either sunny-side-up or scrambled.

My grandmother and Tante Anni wanted to hear about my trip. Anni especially kept asking whether I hadn't had any trouble. The East German newspapers were full of Western European street crime. I had seen those articles myself. They were based in truth, reporting real incidents, but couched in inflammatory language that made it sound like walking down the street in Western capitals resembled running a gauntlet of criminals. My relatives should know better than to believe the propaganda in the paper. Apparently, years of repetition had worn down Tante Anni's guard. She was surprised that the only threat I could report had come from Russians on an East German train.

The summer ended with a bang. I met my family in Gera for Hedwig and Willy's golden wedding anniversary party. I dove into the swirl of relatives of all ages, some of whom, like my Omi Hedwig's brothers, I had never met before. My cousin Ulrich had grown his hair long, and went everywhere carrying his guitar. He drafted me to help him practice the song he planned to perform just before dinner. It was a West German protest song, a humorous commentary meant to skewer Western consumption by describing the stampede at a buffet. Ulrich had learned it from the radio and wanted to make sure he had the lyrics right. Since Ulrike and I had been singing *Das Kalte Buffet* to each other all summer, I was happy to oblige. I thought the song a bit out of place here in the East, but its satire was gentle enough to pass for good humor. Just before we started our performance, I noticed a distant great-aunt sliding pieces of cake into her purse. Maybe the song wasn't as inappropriate as

I thought.

Late in the night, a group of us cousins, uncles, and aunts walked home from the restaurant, crossing silent squares, our giggles echoing off shuttered windows. A policeman materialized out of the shadows and followed a few meters behind. "Shh," Tante Gina whispered, alerting those of us who were oblivious. "Shh." She glanced behind, rather than pointing. Our laughter thinned, then sputtered. We walked on in silence. After a few blocks our tail dropped off. Our conversation recovered, a bit jittery and a lot less boisterous. I looked forward to leaving East Germany with my usual sense of relief and guilt.

When I got on the plane to return to the US this time, I didn't even try to hold back my tears. I let them stream down my face and drip on my t-shirt. Next year or at most the year after, I intended to move back to Germany for good.

CONTINENTAL DRIFT II

"I'd rather you didn't go." My mother's eyes focused on the amethyst ring she was worrying with her left hand. When I didn't say anything, she glanced up at me through her lashes. "I'd hate for you to be so far away."

What? Didn't she know I was doing this for both of us? All these years, she was my partner in longing for home. I assumed she'd be pleased if I went back. It would prove my father wrong. I sat up straight and raised my voice. "I'm old enough."

I didn't add 'I don't need you' but I know she heard me think it. She flinched, then sighed, "I know."

Why was she so sad? It scared me. But not enough to make me change my mind.

My father's reaction was more predictable. He rolled his eyes. "You can't mean it?"

I knew I looked obstinate sitting on the couch sticking my chin out at him. "Of course I do. I've been telling you for years how homesick I am. I just feel at home in Germany. It's where I belong."

"It's Albrecht, isn't it?"

So that's what he thought. He watched every boy I brought home to see whether this was the one who would steal his daughter. I shook my head, but he scented a track.

"He's not even gone to the *Gymnasium*. What kind of future would you have with him?"

I choked back a shout. My father always maintained that if I raised my voice I automatically lost the argument – if my logic was good, I wouldn't need to scream. I shook myself.

"I don't need a man to support me." I snarled. "And who's talking about marriage?"

We argued off and on for a few weeks. During one of our battles, he let it slip that he only helped me go to Germany because he thought it would lay my homesickness to rest. I felt triumphant to have tripped him up in his overconfidence. I wasn't going to cooperate with his plans this time!

The tension between us dropped when I moved out in September to a house trailer I shared with two roommates. I became preoccupied with learning how to manage independent living. Besides, applying to transfer to German university could wait a few months - especially since I wasn't quite sure how to go about it.

When Albrecht and I had said our goodbyes, we hadn't talked about what we expected of each other during our separation. I couldn't imagine wanting to date, but I supposed it would be all right as long as it was casual. I had come back a changed woman - I even let my leg and underarm hair grow out. Nobody would notice, I thought. And if they did, tough. Some evenings, I took myself out to dinner at one of Clemson's pizza venues. After all, I had gone out to eat by myself all over Europe, why not in Clemson? My aberrant behavior drew stares, but I was determined to ignore them.

My third year at Clemson, I filled my schedule with Engineering and Physics classes. In most of them, I was either the only female or one of two or three. It was only a matter of time - I think it took six weeks - before someone asked me out. Bob was the only one of the physics majors whom I wouldn't instantly have turned down. Most of these guys were textbook geeks, down to the slide rule holster hanging from their belts. Bob had long curly hair, wore blue work shirts with his jeans, and thundered up to Kinard Hall on his dirt bike just before class. He barely made it to Optics most days, because he worked first shift at the textile mill on Highway 123. I agreed to go to the Physics Department Picnic with him, because evenings at home with a book had started to pale. Besides, I was only slightly attracted to this guy. No danger. Or so I thought.

However, I did remind Albrecht in my next letter that I didn't expect him to live like a monk just because we loved each other. Bob continued to hang around. By November when he invited me to go camping with him for a long weekend and I agreed, I realized I was lying to myself when I told myself this was casual and didn't count. Bob's quiet competence was growing on me. I promised myself I'd clear this all up as soon as I had time to think. Then I'd get a letter from Albrecht – a letter filled with such complete trust in us as a fact – that I simply couldn't come clean. Besides, I didn't really have to make a decision instantly. I could take some time to see where this thing with Bob was going? I'm still mortified when I remember the games I played with myself. At the latest, I'd break it off when I left to go back to Germany.

All winter my agony grew. On my twentieth birthday, Bob took me out to Clemson's only steakhouse. Albrecht wrote me a poem and sent me twenty red roses. How unfair of me to compare two men who didn't even know I was trying to choose. Albrecht was everything continental I longed for. He wrote from his vacation in Spain and talked of going to Paris. In answer to a request from me he mailed a picture of himself striking a dramatic pose in a black turtleneck – black was his signature color. Bob wore Levi's and shirts his mother bought on sale and showed me how to change the oil in my car. In my fevered guilt, the choice between the two of them took on symbolic significance. On the one hand, Albrecht represented a dream. How well did I really know him? As the months passed, he was only real whenever an envelope addressed in turquoise ink showed up in my mailbox. Bob was a reality I could touch. Together we cooked dinner and did the dishes and increasingly spent nights in my bed. I did talk to him of leaving for Germany the following summer, but that didn't change the fact that I knew I was being a jerk.

I had returned from Krefeld with my own copy of the German university information manual, and knew that the logical place for a textile chemistry student to apply was the Technical University at Aachen. I had an address for admissions, as well as a list of required documents, but the instructions assumed I would be applying after completion of a German *Abitur*. The paragraph-long sentences, written in the most formal German officialese, didn't make allowances for my case. Furthermore, they intimidated me. The fluency of my spoken German didn't equal an ability to compose business letters. I would need help. Of course, I turned to my father.

Despite his misgivings, my father discussed the matter with the owner of his company the next time he traveled to Germany. Jan Kleinewefers had connections to the faculty at Aachen. He agreed to ask them how I might make the transfer. While my father was in Germany, he spent a weekend in Mühlacker and instructed his sister to invite Albrecht over for inspection. I didn't find out about this until afterwards, and my urge to seethe subsided when I realized that the meeting had gone well. I couldn't quite shake my annoyance at my father evaluating Albrecht like a nineteenth century suitor, especially in view of my own mixed feelings, but if it served the purpose of reducing my father's resistance, I could shut up about it. My hopes rose.

Mr. Kleinewefers had promised my father that he would hire me between semesters. A wonderful offer. Why did I suddenly get cold feet? Was it the way my mother sucked in air at the news, a sharp hiss, the same sound she made when she suspected certain death approaching on the highway?

I tried to imagine living that far from my family. My sister was four. When I stopped by the house on the way home from classes, she squealed and hugged me, then settled in on the couch draped over my shoulder. Whenever I wanted, my mother set an extra plate at the table. If I needed to talk, all I had to do was settle myself nearby, in the kitchen if she was cooking or next to her on the couch if she was sewing, even on the toilet lid if she was bathing. I knew I could manage a few months on my own - the summer in Germany had proved it - but years at a time?

Then the verdict returned. The professor at Aachen said that he would accept me, but I would have to start over, because he had never heard of this Clemson University and thus had no way of evaluating the quality of my education.   And I would have to demonstrate Latin proficiency at a level German educators call "*das kleine Latinum*" - the equivalent of four years of Latin. When my father delivered this news, he tried to look sympathetic, but I could see the relief in his eyes. He knew I was terrified of Latin and he knew I wouldn't want to throw away three years of college. The German professor's reaction underscored what he'd been trying to tell me all along. Arrogance and inflexibility suffused the German culture. I hated that it looked like he was right. My mother consoled me with the idea that I could look for a job in Germany when I graduated.

I was angry and disappointed, but also relieved. My decision was made for me. I knew how to succeed at Clemson. One of the professors there had begun suggesting graduate schools in New England, the Midwest, and California. On my way to Germany the summer before, I had arranged a layover in New York and taken a limo to New Haven where one of my high school friends attended Yale. There, I was thrilled to discover the intellectual atmosphere I missed at Clemson. Those two days at Yale now burned as a promise that I could find a place in the US that felt like home. I would search for an American place of my own. At least provisionally.

After I received the news from Aachen, I wrote Albrecht a more direct letter. I still didn't admit to Bob, I told myself this wasn't about him. I just told Albrecht I couldn't afford Europe that summer, and that another year was too long to wait to see if our love could blossom. His reply was so understanding, that I felt even more worthless. In August, Bob and I packed a tent and took three weeks to drive Route 1 up the Atlantic Coast all the way to Maine, then looped into Canada to Quebec

City and Montreal and explored the Appalachians on our way back to South Carolina.

I still can't separate Albrecht and Bob from the decision I made that summer, even though I believe that the real decision was not about them at all. Albrecht represented a promise to me that I could find my way back into Germany if I tried. My relationship with Bob lasted for another year and began to sputter the following summer after he graduated and moved home to Charleston to look for a job.

The fall of my senior year, I flew to the Northeast to visit the three graduate schools that were my top choices: McGill, MIT, and UMass. A snowstorm prevented me from making it to Montreal, and the professors at MIT seemed entirely too certain that MIT was the only possible choice. I don't mean to make it sound as if I chose UMass by default. Bright, lively students filled the Polymer Science Department there and the professors glowed with the self-satisfied air of successful fundraising. But it was Amherst that clinched the deal. I thought I was a city girl. Boston or Montreal would be perfect, right? Apparently not. Amherst fit me perfectly. It was politically liberal, littered with bookstores and vegetarian restaurants, had free bus service, but the rents were reasonable and the countryside near and lovely. And I could fly back to South Carolina a few times a year.

*****

Darkness had fallen. I pulled off at the Stamford, Connecticut, rest area. When I left Clemson that morning, I promised my mother I'd spend the night somewhere north of New York City, and that I'd call her when I'd made it that far. The phone booth shook as trucks passed on I-95.

"I'm not going to stop and spend the night. I've made good time. It'll only take three more hours to get to Amherst." I had to shout into the receiver.

"But you've been driving for thirteen hours. Aren't you exhausted?" my mother asked.

I could barely hear her anxiety above the road noise. My jaws ached. I must have clenched them all the way through Brooklyn. But I was wide-awake, as if I'd had a couple of Vivarins and a gallon of coffee. I assured her I was fine. After one more cup of coffee at the rest stop, I buzzed on up to I-91 and headed west into the rolling hills of Massachusetts, where my new life waited.

Just past midnight, I swung into the Colonial Village Apartments parking lot. I dragged my suitcase out of my Beetle's front luggage compartment and fumbled for my key. When I opened the door, the apartment looked just like it had when my parents and I left a week earlier. We had hauled my few pieces of furniture in a U-Haul behind my father's Plymouth, unpacked them and spread them across the linoleum tile. Here they sat, the contents of a bedroom, trying to puff themselves up to look like they could fill an apartment. Under the ceiling light huddled the only addition, the modular plastic dinette set - yellow chairs and brown parson's table - that my mother and I had bought direct from the factory in Greenville for only thirty dollars. At the other end of the room a pile of large pillows pretended to be a couch. My steps echoed.

I opened the refrigerator door. Just as I remembered. Right in the middle of the otherwise empty fridge sat a partial jug of white wine. I poured myself a glass and headed for the bedroom. Sitting on the bed, leaning against the wall, smoking and sipping wine, I waited for the buzzing in my head to stop and the tension to drain from my body.

The morning after my heroic drive, I woke up, filled with energy and eager to get settled. I made lists of tasks to accomplish: unpack clothes, open checking account, buy groceries, hang pictures, measure for curtain rods, buy curtain rods, attach Indian bedspreads to new rods. When I made my moving plans, I left myself three days between arriving in Amherst and new student registration. I wanted to make sure I had plenty of time. I hadn't taken into account how quickly I move when I'm alone and in overdrive. I burned through my list on the first day.

The next morning, I woke up feeling a bit sorry for myself. What was I going to do for two days? I refused to feel homesick for Clemson. No way. This not knowing anyone was temporary.

Walking. That was the answer. A long and solitary walk along the edge of the Amherst College campus. As I passed a scatter of male students crossing the shaded lawns I wondered what it would be like to attend a college where one year's tuition exceeded the total cost of my education at Clemson. Would they sneer at me if they knew? Did they feel pressure to justify their parents' investment? Did they learn things in their 100-year-old buildings that I couldn't even guess at? I straightened my spine, and gave myself a mental pep talk. But instead of exploring the Amherst College campus further, I turned toward town.

Amherst lies in a lush valley that's a hotbed of colleges. In addition to Amherst College and UMass (the poor intellectual relation), Hampshire, Mount Holyoke and Smith are nearby. The free bus service shuttles hordes of students from one academic site to another. When I moved there in 1975, I inhaled the liberal atmosphere with years of stored up desire. On the streets, I admired the women in their leotards and overalls. Their legs sprouted dense hair above the upper edges of their combat boots. The bookstore on North Pleasant Street was crammed with books I had been dying to read and many unfamiliar ones that promised intellectual growth. In a nearby alley, skinny guys with bushy hair tied up in bandanas stacked crates in front of the food co-op. Further down the main drag, a silversmith operated a craft store. Next door you could buy Earth Shoes in all styles and sizes. There was even a Scandinavian import store, a Chinese restaurant, and an Asian grocery. I wandered in and out of stores, bought a book by Collette and circled slowly back on Triangle Street.

In the afternoon, I studied my Massachusetts map. The towns that surrounded Amherst sounded medieval: Belchertown, Pelham, Sunderland, Northampton. I drove off in the direction of Vermont via Belchertown, just to see whether the town looked as odd as it sounded. It didn't, of course. Belchertown is just a small collection of white clapboard houses with a small village green. The countryside unrolled before me, villages merging into each other, white clapboard houses, tidy in fenced yards. I saw no refrigerators on porches, no peeling paint, no rusting cars. The vegetation too looked comfortable. No kudzu or Bermuda grass. When I stopped to walk in a meadow, I found Queen Anne's Lace and grasses like those that grew in Germany.

On day three, I decided I was too worn down by talking to myself to explore. Instead, I invented errands to the hardware store and chatted with the checkout girl. Already, the stores along the shopping strip on Route 9 and the Cumberland Farms convenience store where I bought my cigarettes were familiar. My ears, too, were gradually acclimating to the local sounds. I observed that pronouncing Amherst as if it contained an "h" branded the speaker as an outsider. It was 'Amerst' with the emphasis clearly placed on the 'Am', the second syllable swallowed as if the locals were in a hurry. I learned to similarly shorten syllables and drop h's while pronouncing Northampton and Pelham. Since I was determined not to sound like a Southerner, I listened intently and imitated the tighter rhythm.

Over the next few months I added more landmarks and grew attached to them. The towering UMass library could only be approached via wooden tunnels that led through a barricade of chicken wire because of a construction defect that caused it to hurl bricks from the thirtieth story. The Campus Center's interior was festooned with swaths of plastic to catch leaking rainwater, another construction flaw. Several of the Polymer Science grad students who were raised in Massachusetts educated me about local politics. The state, they confided, was beholden to the Mafia, and the Mafia owned construction firms. None of this bothered me. The Graduate Research Center, which housed the Polymer Science Department, functioned adequately, and the department was rich in grant money.

On weekends, I continued to explore Amherst and the surrounding area, but I no longer did it alone. I had fallen in love. Matt represented everything I longed for in a man while I languished in Clemson's heat and humidity. The first time I met him was on my interview trip. He was one of the stops on my arranged tour. My host dropped me off in his lab in the Chem E building so Matt could spend a half hour describing his thesis research. I sat beside Matt's vintage wooden desk, its top brimming with a layer of papers. Engineering formulas spiked with Greek letters covered the loose pages that piled in drifts. Matt's blonde hair fell in long waves and when he wanted to show me details, he deftly fished a piece of paper out of the piles, then pulled out a battered pair of wire rim glasses and hooked them behind his ears. As he talked, he periodically ran his hand through his hair to clear his vision. When he finished his prepared spiel and found we had some time left, he asked me questions about my research interests and listened intently as I lurched through my vague notions. Then he told me about his life in Amherst. He played rugby and tennis, went to lots of movies and shared an apartment close by with a roommate. He missed Chicago. The restaurants, the concerts, the foreign films he'd enjoyed as an undergraduate. I came away from that meeting intrigued by the possibility that there might be guys who, like me, were good at science, but had cultural interests too.

Living in Clemson, I felt like I missed everything that was exciting about the sixties and early seventies. Matt hadn't. On his dresser, he kept a ticket stub from Woodstock. And he arrived in Chicago to attend Northwestern University in 1968 just in time for the Democratic Convention. He went along to the protests, though, unlike several of his friends, he avoided arrest. I thought that showed sense. I didn't understand the implicit faith America's youth showed in the police respecting their rights. I remembered the outrage and shock after the Chicago convention. Allegations of brutality and unnecessary strip searches. My reaction was *what did they expect? They are the police and while they've got you you're in their power.* Matt hadn't thought about that, he was just pragmatic enough to want no arrest record.

In the flush of our romance, Matt and I spent weekends hiking in the Vermont woods, or taking long walks around the Quabbin Reservoir. After he moved in, we found a Scandinavian furniture store in Florence, just past Northampton, where we bought our first joint piece of furniture, a teak queen size bed. By March, we sat upstairs at the Rusty Scupper, on the mirrored cushions imported from India, discussing marriage. I was surprised to discover that science at the graduate level was an international endeavor. Our department had post-doctoral students and visiting instructors from all over the world. Marrying a fellow scientist didn't have to mean committing myself to America completely. I'd still be able to hedge. The bigger obstacle appeared to be that he would be graduating two years before I did. How would we handle that? I was not going to live my life like my mother had, following my husband wherever he was moved to go. That much I knew.

When I went back to Clemson for spring break, I sat at the kitchen table while my mother peeled potatoes. I told her that I thought maybe Matt was the one, but I didn't see how we could get married for some time. He wanted to be a university professor, so he would be leaving either to take a post-doc or start a job as soon as he finished.

"Can't he find something at UMass until you're done?" my mother asked. She liked Matt as a potential husband. Even though she hadn't met him, she could tell he was smart and ambitious, both of which she found lacking in my previous partners. She had also tired of my ever-changing array of boyfriends and thought I needed to just pick one and settle down.

"I can't ask him to do that."

"What about you? Could you transfer somewhere else to finish?"

"I'm not going to do that. UMass is one of the best polymer departments in the country. Who knows where he'll end up."

She walked past me to empty the potato peel bowl into the compost bucket outside the sliding glass door. Then she sat down around the corner from me. "Well, maybe you could just get married and live apart for a few years."

I hadn't thought of that. The idea appealed to me instantly. It was so modern, so feminist. We could have separate addresses as well as separate names.

When I returned, Matt and I went out for a nightcap at the Scupper to discuss it. He liked the idea. It gave significance to our careers, made them seem so high-powered they couldn't be interrupted for anything. We decided to get married that December.

I avoided thinking about the implications of marrying an American. Whenever the realization sneaked up on me that I was committing myself to more than a marriage, I ducked. Going home didn't feel quite as urgent now that I lived in New England. Who knew what the future would bring?

Over the summer, I noticed that Matt had less and less time for hikes, walks, and me, but I blamed that on mounting pressure as he drew closer to completing his thesis. I tried to lighten his load by typing his required research proposals, hunting and pecking because I had steadfastly refused to learn to type in high school and college, since it was such a stereotypical female skill. I did have an attack of doubt the night before the wedding, but with Matt's relatives and friends packed into the Holiday Inn, cases of champagne in the basement, tulips and daffodils imported from Holland waiting to be picked up at the florist, and my custom-designed dress hanging from the closet door, I could hardly change my mind.

*****

"We have finally persuaded the East Germans to let us have one of their guys," Professor Vogl told me, his Austrian accent rumbling under his well-honed English.

He clearly relished being able to share this news with me. I was the only graduate student in the department who could possibly guess what obstacles he must have surmounted. Professor Vogl had made it his pet project to build bridges to Eastern Europe via science. That year, Professor Zhubov, on sabbatical from Moscow University, had been our lecturer for the unit on catalytic polymerization. Other Eastern European scientists worked on rotating post-doctoral fellowships in Professor Vogl's labs. Only the East Germans were too suspicious to allow their scientists out of the country. But Professor Vogl's persistence had paid off. The following semester, we would have a post-doc from the University of Jena. I smiled and congratulated him. I even felt vaguely pleased that an East German would achieve his impossible dream: travel to the United States. At the same time, I calculated that the fellow must be a true communist believer with impeccable party credentials in order to be selected for such a plum.

Except for a few trivial digressions, my relatives struggled to survive in East Germany without engaging in collaboration. My father's entire family had hooted at my grandfather Willy during his flirtation with communism right after the war. Willy's admiration for the Russian victors hadn't lasted more than a few years, and was the subject of family jokes by the time I was conscious of politics. When I was about six, one of my uncles entered a phase in which he defended the socialist position in lengthy speeches at the Poser dinner table. Helmut had a way of turning didactic and refusing to notice when his conversational partner showed signs of fatigue. Since no one else took him seriously, I didn't either. A few years later, Helmut converted his growing disillusion with communism into a fervent Christianity. No one took that seriously either, at least not until it stood the test of time. Willy and Helmut's excursions into Party support were memorable because they were aberrations from the family ethic. My aunts and uncles stubbornly avoided Party membership. And the Party took note. Officials dangled promotions that dematerialized upon refusal to join. My cousin's wife lost her chance at a career that involved travel to the West, simply because she'd married into our family. Because I admired my relatives' sacrifices, I not only intended not to like Professor Vogl's post-doc, I felt that friendliness would amount to betrayal.

With only twenty graduate students and half again as many postdocs, the Polymer Science and Engineering Department at UMass was too small to avoid anyone completely. Manfred was slight and sported the only crew cut I had ever seen on anyone who wasn't American. His English was technically perfect, though accented. I didn't want to recognize East German rhythms underneath, but they intruded on me anyway. He watched and smiled and quickly merged into Professor Vogl's group.

I would have had little to do with that group if it hadn't been for my husband. Matt began a joint project with Manfred. Matt thought European political suspicions had no place in the trans-global world of science. He assured me Manfred was a 'nice guy.' When Matt and I went to lunch at the Campus Center, Manfred occasionally joined us at Matt's invitation. I tried to balance on the edge of civility without tipping toward either 'rude' or 'friendly.'

Once, returning in the elevator after lunch, the three of us absentmindedly followed a stranger out the door a few floors too early. Manfred giggled and looked at me for help. "How do you say *'Herdentrieb'*?" But before I could translate he made a walking motion with his fingers and said: "One sheep goes and the other sheep follow." What better way to describe 'herd instinct'? I had to laugh.

After a few months, Matt said, "Let's invite Manfred over for dinner. He says he's getting homesick for German food."

"Oh, I don't know. I imagine he'd be uncomfortable."

"That's silly. He's really nice, and he's lonely. He never talks politics at all."

"He probably couldn't come. Associating with the enemy, you know."

"Well, I'm going to ask him."

I didn't keep arguing. I could tell I was starting to look like the bad guy. Instead I dug out my German cookbook and paged through it, looking for the dish that most acutely called up childhood visits to East Germany.

One of my fondest memories was the smell of roasting *Kaninchen* - rabbit - from my grandmother's kitchen. She'd pull out her speckled roaster at intervals to baste the meat and keep it from drying. When it was done the meat stretched brown and juicy between delicate leg bones. At the farm in Eilenburg, Onkel Otto still raised rabbits to supply inexpensive meat for the family. I had noticed a house with a sign offering rabbit meat at Amherst's fringe.

When I rang the doorbell at the rabbit house, I imagined a wrapped package dug out of a freezer. A man in overalls emerged and asked what I wanted. Then he took me back to the garage to a row of rabbit hutches. Some of the rabbits were white with red eyes, some brown. They turned their heads to get a good look at me and sat up sniffing the air.

"Which one do you want?"

I swallowed. Did he really want me to point at one of those creatures with the twitching noses and choose its death? They looked like commercials for the Easter bunny. The rabbit grower stood back, his face immobile, waiting. I wanted to run back to my car. Come on, I thought, meat comes from killing. Is it any better when you buy it at the grocery store? You've eaten rabbit lots of times, and each time Onkel Otto walked back to the rabbit stable, and picked a rabbit he'd been feeding every day for months. The image of Onkel Otto holding a rabbit up by its scruff so I could pet it flashed before my eyes. He never killed one in front of me. The only animal I had ever seen slaughtered and subsequently consumed was a chicken Omi Paula chased in circles in the courtyard. I watched from an upstairs window, thrilled and repelled, unable to turn away as the chicken's squawks and flaps increased in desperation until Omi Paula caught it and wrung its neck.

I grew intensely conscious of the rabbit man waiting at my side. Did I want a rabbit or didn't I? He'd think I was a real weirdo if I left now. I narrowed my eyes and pointed at the brown one in the top hutch. The guy's callused hand unhooked the cage, swooped down, and lifted the rabbit out in one swift motion.

"I'll be back in a minute," he shouted as he disappeared in the direction of the house.

I stood there, wrapping myself in my arms, staring at the live rabbits as they munched greens. They cared nothing about the killing I initiated. I wasn't consoled. Beyond the rabbit hutches, tobacco fields stretched away toward the woods. I stared into the middle distance and tried to stop thinking. It was too late anyway.

After five or ten minutes, the front door opened. The rabbit man held out a Styrofoam tray piled with skinned and quartered rabbit under a professional layer of plastic wrap. I groped in my purse for my wallet. As I reached to take the meat, I noted the sterile grocery store packaging with some relief. Maybe I'd be able to forget the way this rabbit had fixed me with his little red eyes when I pointed him out.

I was wrong. When I touched the top half of the package, heat shocked the inside of my hand. The recently slaughtered body poured blood warmth through my fingers directly into my heart. I tightened my lips, mumbled perfunctory thanks and fled to my car. When I got back to the apartment, I shoved the tray into the fridge and slammed the door. The distance between childhood and adult reality had never seemed greater. But I was a product of my post-war upbringing. I would cook this rabbit, because it was now food and food was never to be wasted.

The next day, when the doorbell rang promptly at seven o'clock, I was seasoning the gravy, hoping that a dash of vinegar and grind of pepper would erase the scorched undertone. I had underestimated how critical my grandmother's experience with proper basting had been. *Matt was the one who insisted on inviting him. Let him open the door.* A rush of sound bounced into the kitchen. Matt's welcoming laugh carried an edge of anxiety - Matt always tried a tad too hard to be the perfect host - and Manfred's East German accent protruded more intensely than normal.

"Can I get you a beer?" Matt shouted over his shoulder, on his way to the fridge.

"Yes, thank you very much." Manfred followed him into the kitchen. He pronounced his English carefully and almost perfectly. When he saw me he held out his hand for a shake. *"Guten Abend."* He inclined his head in a slight bow as we shook.

"We're having *Kaninchen* and I'm afraid I burned the gravy. I hope it's not too bad." Why did I have to blurt that out first thing?

Manfred smiled. "I am sure it is very good."

I turned the stove off and began ladling the sauce - it still tasted acrid - into the waiting gravy boat. Manfred settled at the table, while Matt carried in the potatoes and salad and I arranged the rabbit parts on a platter.

As I filled my beer glass, Manfred raised his and said: *"Prost!"* Matt laughed again, then clinked glasses with Manfred.

"Oh," Manfred exclaimed as he reached for the salad bowl. "When I was a child, my mother makes this salad."

I had counted on it. Steamed wax beans, cucumber slices, and diced onions in vinaigrette. Both of my grandmothers served this salad on summer Sundays. Manfred filled his salad bowl, his eyes gleaming in anticipation.

"Where exactly did you grow up?" Matt asked.

"I grew up in the *Erzgebirge*." He glanced at me. "What is that called in English?"

"I don't know." I turned toward Matt. "It's a mining region in East Germany. It's where they carve those wood angels I use for Christmas decorations."

"Yes," nodded Manfred. "It is very poor there. My father was a miner. If not for the State, I would be a miner too. It is because of the government I could go to university and study Chemistry."

Odd that it had never occurred to me before that someone might have benefited from communism. I had never met anyone who felt that way. The idea threw me off balance.

"Did you study at Jena?" I asked.

"Yes, that is where I became acquainted with my wife too."

"What does she do?" Matt asked, though we both knew the answer.

"She works for the Party. She had to stay in Jena because she has a very important job." Manfred said. Did he really believe that? Surely Manfred knew she was the hostage that secured his return? I looked down and watched my knife carve a chunk off the rabbit shank. He broke the silence, "And where do your relatives live?"

That sounded like a neutral question; one I could answer easily. When I opened my mouth, I barely caught myself. Usually when someone asked about my East German relatives I wove their litany of injustice into the factual detail. The farm expropriated by the State, my grandfather's battles to protect his factory from being nationalized, my relatives' frustrations with tightly controlled lives. How would that sound to Manfred? To speak of politics would risk crashing through the thin ice of politeness that made this dinner possible. And what would it prove? The underlying emotions were too deep and complex. He couldn't afford to look at the bargains he made to fashion a workable life anymore than I wanted to expose the anger and resentment I inherited from my family. There was another, more prosaic reason to keep the conversation impersonal: even if Manfred was trusted enough to be allowed out of the country, he might have to report a visit to my house and possibly the details of the conversation. I answered his questions factually, without my usual editorial comments. We drank a few more beers and maintained a strained conversation that relaxed when we reached the relative safety of scientific shoptalk leavened by a little departmental gossip. In this way, we managed to stretch the evening to a decent length.

Manfred stayed in Amherst for six months. By the end of that time, I forgot my resolve to be distant. When Professor Vogl's group arranged a goodbye coffee party in his honor, I stopped by, shook his hand and wished him luck. The next year, when Matt and I started planning a trip to East Germany to visit my relatives, Matt said: "Let's go see Manfred while we're there." I thought he was crazy. Manfred might get in trouble if we visited him. But Matt ignored my worries. Jena was only a short train trip from my grandmother's, and it would be interesting to see an East German university. He wrote to Manfred and made his own arrangements. When we arrived, Manfred met us at the station, all smiles. He promised we would meet his wife at lunch. I had never met a Party functionary, so I was curious how she would behave. My cousin's wife's father was a Party boss, but he was never allowed to participate in any family events where Western visitors would be present. Manfred showed us around the labs and offices at the university. It was in his office that a secretary delivered the message that his wife was "just too busy to get away" today. A shadow of disgust crossed Manfred's face. Then he put his smile back in place, and squired us around Jena for a tour. Somehow, probably using every connection at his disposal, Manfred had arranged for an outdoor table for lunch at a restaurant. Afterwards, we visited the medieval city hall, where couples in wedding clothes waited their turn to be married. Then we climbed a hill to gain a spectacular view. When we left Manfred behind at the Jena station at the end of the day, he had the same forlorn look my relatives always wore when we departed. I always ascribed that look to a sense that the outside world was leaving them once again, and they had no way to follow.

I realized Manfred had given me a gift. I had known only two kinds of East Germans: my relatives whom I saw as trapped victims and the police officials who patrolled the borders and kept them there. But Manfred forced me to expand my view. Until I met him it had never occurred to me that there might be another angle, a different way to experience East Germany's social experiment. Manfred forced me to see beyond the black and white child's view and admit adult shades of gray.

*****

On that first trip Matt and I took to Europe, I had been excited about finally sharing Germany with someone from my American life, but I hadn't thought about the strain of constantly translating. Instead of being able to fuse with my past and merge completely with my German self, I found myself constantly switching back and forth between English and German, between past and present. I hated the way my need to flip back and forth prevented me from indulging in the fantasy that I belonged.

We stayed at Tante Isolde's house in Bad Düben. Opa's factory and apartment building had been taken over by the state a year or two after he died, and Omi had moved to a one-bedroom apartment in Eilenburg-Ost at the opposite end of town. The house in Bad Düben didn't look as grandiose to me now that I was used to American proportions, but it was a house you could spread out in. Onkel Horst's newest project was a homemade swimming pool. He excavated a rectangular area and lined it with heavy plastic secured at the edge by bricks. It was large enough for an adult to swim four or five strokes. The patch of water gleamed under the trees.

Onkel Horst greeted me with a hug and a cynical: "Nice that you've come to visit us in our socialist paradise!" He swept his hands around the house and pointed out the flaws he couldn't obtain materials to fix. Matthias who was just a year shy of his *Abitur* and had a few years of English worked hard to communicate with Matt. The conversation was similar to what I remembered. Every other sentence contained a reference to shortages or items that just weren't available. What sounded hard and disgusted coming from Horst was tempered by curiosity with Matthias. He wanted to know what life was like in America - to him it must have seemed as unreachable as Pluto.

If I had been visiting by myself, we would have stayed in Bad Düben except for an occasional visit to Eilenburg to Tante Anni's farm or my grandmother's apartment, and the usual shopping trip to Leipzig to find some way to use up the East German money we were forced to buy at the border. In Matt's honor, we planned a trip to Berlin. Matthias and his girlfriend would accompany us on the train and show us around. Tante Isolde drove us to the Eilenburg station early one morning. We lined up at the ticket office. When the ticket agent told us the cost of a round-trip ticket, I turned to Matt who was carrying most of our cash.

"How much was it?" he asked me.

I repeated the price in English.

"Let's pay for their tickets too," he said. I glanced at Matthias who already had the proper bills in his hands. I wasn't comfortable with this, but I couldn't think fast enough to argue.

"We've got all this money we need to get rid of anyway, and it's a lot for them." Matt whispered.

Then before I could say anything else, he shoved 300 marks through the ticket window. To Matthias he said, "I will pay."

Matthias tried to argue. "I have it," he said and held up the bills in his hand.

"No, no. You be our guests," Matt said and laughed.

Matthias shrugged and stuffed the bills back in his wallet. Heat rose to the top of my head and rendered me mute. I couldn't have told you at that moment what agreement had been broken, but I knew there was a crack. It was only later, when I had time to think about it that I realized what it was. Matt didn't understand that my relatives did not suffer a shortage of money. They had plenty of that by East German standards. It was the wrong kind of money. Money that couldn't buy the Western products they saw advertised on West German TV every night. Money that had no value at the *Intershops* that displayed everything from oranges to Swiss chocolates, West German washing machines to canned tuna to blue jeans. You needed dollars or West German marks in those stores. The family agreement was that my mother sent coveted items or slipped dollar bills into letters. The only way they could return the favor was to shower us with what they called their 'play money.' If we didn't even let them spend their own money, we upset a barely functioning balance. Too late now.

When we arrived in Berlin, Matthias guided us first to Unter den Linden, the famous boulevard that ends in the Brandenburg gate. The four of us walked slowly as we approached the brick and concrete barricades backed by geranium planters. Between the barricade and the gate stretched several hundred meters of barren, empty asphalt. A dense row of streetlights marched away from us across the bare space. I grew up with the Brandenburg gate in countless pictures and felt a moment of frustration that I couldn't get closer. Soldiers with guns over their shoulders patrolled back and forth through the orderly stands of trees and expanses of red flower beds on either side of the lights. The space on the East Berlin side of the barricade was crowded with school classes on field trips and East German tourists. They rested their elbows on the waist high wall and leaned their heads across to get as close as possible. Between the gate's arches hazy trees stretched away into West Berlin. We were too far away to see the tourists that surely stared back at us from the other side.

Judging from the dialects I heard around me, I was certain that Matt and I were the only Westerners in this crowd. I tried to imagine what it must feel like to stand here, knowing the huge vertical supports that bore the gilded quadriga represented the bars of your cage. That you were looking at the perimeter of your jail. I gasped as a wave of instant claustrophobia threatened to pull me under. As a child my biggest fear on every trip had been that our papers would get lost and we would have to stay.

"Checkpoint Charlie is just around the corner down Friedrichstrasse. If you want you can cross over into West Berlin and look around," Matthias said this with the matter-of-factness of a good tour guide. My West German passport suddenly burned bright in my pocket.

"Would they let me back in?" was the first thing I said.

"Sure they would. If you have a visa you can take a day trip into West Berlin." I don't know whether I just assumed he would be feeling envious, or whether I detected a wistful note in his voice. I pictured him and his girlfriend standing behind the Wall as Matt and I walked away, passed through the impenetrable barrier thanks to the privilege conferred by the magic of our passports. No way. I already felt guilty every time I left. There was always that moment, when I realized I had passed the border. Suddenly my chest opened and air began to flow freely. A spark of joy entered me with each breath. It surprised me every time. Why me? Why did I get to leave?

A few days later, Matt and I were packing our suitcases to leave for Gera. "Let's give Matthias and the girls each a twenty dollar bill as a goodbye present," Matt suggested. "It isn't that much for us."

Twenty dollars? Matt's ways with money never ceased to surprise me. It would never have occurred to me to give away twenty-dollar bills to my cousins. We weren't that rich. But Matt liked my cousins and wished he could make their lives better with his money. What harm was there in following his suggestion? I took three envelopes and tucked a twenty into each one. Just after breakfast I handed them out privately, trying to catch each cousin alone. I was embarrassed but they accepted the money graciously.

It was on this trip that I noticed a paradox of attitudes for the first time. Yes, my Gera relatives groused about the government and the difficulty of finding plumbing parts and the ingenuity and connections required to procure a batch of *Rostbratwürstchen*, but they also found things to enjoy. When Tante Gina invited us to dinner, she showed us her pictures from a vacation in Prague. Her eyes glowed as she remembered the city's beauty. She did not say, "I'm sure you've seen better, but this is the best we can get," as Tante Isolde had after her visit there. Onkel Klaus showed off the cottage - he called it his *dacha*, the Russian word for country house - he had erected on my grandfather's leased garden plot, a ten-minute walk from their house. He swapped and bartered until he had a snug little one-room cabin, and he was proud of his accomplishment. Tante Bärbel showed off her brand new living room furniture with not a hint of self-consciousness. Why did they seem less frustrated even though they had it harder than my mother's family? The question flashed through my mind, but I didn't pursue it. That's the way it was.

We emerged from the gloom of East Germany into the technicolor world of Stuttgart University. We wanted to visit colleagues at several universities to nurture connections. Maybe we could move to Germany together? If not permanently, then for a year? I had met several German scientists who camped at American universities for years at a time. Why couldn't it work the other way around? At Stuttgart, we met with a professor who was an East German refugee like my parents. Over lunch he turned to me, an eyebrow raised beneath his grey shock of hair, and asked, "You say you were born in Krefeld, but your accent is pure Saxony. Why is that?"

I choked on my potato. Just a few years before, Professor Vogl called me in Clemson to interview me before admitting me to UMass. In the middle of the interview, he veered from questions of my qualifications to say, "Miss Poser, I must say I'm surprised. I expected you to have a German accent, not a Southern one." If only my personality could be as malleable as my accent. I could be at home anywhere in a matter of weeks.

*****

I played games with myself when I used the word 'home' now. Inside my head HOME referred to Germany, and 'home' meant my apartment, first in Amherst, then briefly in Maryland, and - once Matt and I graduated and settled into our new jobs - our condominium in St. Paul, Minnesota. I never discussed those distinctions; only I could hear them. My life felt provisional. I lived in the US, but refused to think of myself as American. I tried not to think at all.

Once, when Matt and I were returning from Germany, an immigration officer pierced the fog of my denial. We dragged ourselves off the plane, and stumbled into arrivals. Fluorescent airport lights bounced off white cinderblock walls and gray linoleum. The bumblebee buzz of one or two malfunctioning bulbs irritated my ears. Ahead of us, lines of drooping people in rumpled clothes inched their bags toward immigration officers who looked rested and alert. Here in New York it was four in the afternoon and my brain told my body to get used to it. Yet my body remembered breakfast at Tante Nanne's house, the train ride to Frankfurt, and the long hours wedged in tourist class that had followed.

Matt said, "See you in a bit," and headed toward the side marked 'U.S. Citizens.' I peeled off to follow the arrows for residents and visitors. I added myself to a line that moved surprisingly quickly. In my purse, I carried a *Brieftasche* - document carrier - of black leather that fit my West German passport exactly. I had to dig in my wallet for my Green Card - I kept it there, because by law I was required to carry it with me at all times. Not that anyone ever asked for it except in these vast halls that existed suspended in jet lag time. As my turn approached, I sized up the INS official. A young black man, light-skinned, with a thin mustache. I tried to stay away from women, because my mother always warned they were especially thorough, to prove themselves as good as the men. Did her rule apply to minorities?

I slid my Green Card inside my passport and handed it to the officer. He flipped the card into position and hesitated.

"I know it's an old picture," I offered.

"Yeah, I can see that. How old were you?" His forehead wrinkled as he looked back and forth between the card and me.

"Thirteen."

He checked the date on the card. "You been living here how long? Almost fifteen years?"

I nodded. My hands tightened on my purse strap. His challenge triggered my latent border crossing anxiety. He could claim he can't be sure it's me. My nails dug into my palm. Before I had time to hyperventilate, he shook his head and laughed.

"When are you gonna get your citizenship?" he asked.

My hand relaxed. I managed to chuckle. It did seem funny suddenly. Like being engaged for fifteen years and never having the guts to consummate the relationship.

He smiled as he handed back my documents and added, "I mean, what are you waiting for?"

I slipped the card back inside my passport. He had charmed me and I felt I owed him an answer, but I had none to give. What exactly was I doing? Living in one place and locking my heart away in another?

I carried the question close to the surface for months. Admitted to myself that my attachment to that German passport had slid into the sentimental. I cherished it as a memento of who I had been, but also as proof that I could still change my mind. If I gave up my citizenship, who would I be?

When the questions circled in on themselves and made my heart and head hurt, I followed Scarlett O'Hara's example. I'd think about it tomorrow. Life was about to provide me with plenty of distraction.

*****

The trouble started with my Christmas ritual. Every year, six weeks before the holidays, I'd roam the grocery store and buy three of everything that was difficult to get in East Germany and came in cans: pineapple, peaches, tuna, mandarin oranges. Then I loaded up on Lindt chocolate bars, aware of the irony that these had been shipped across the Atlantic and were about to make the trip back. I tucked in three packs of disposable wipes, and maybe some imported German cookies. At home, I dug up three sturdy boxes, filled them with my purchases and padded the empty spaces with plastic bags I saved for just that purpose. In East Germany, the stores still wrapped your purchases in recycled paper and tied them with string. Plastic shopping bags were in high demand. Finally, I taped my packages shut and addressed them to Omi Hedwig, Omi Paula and Tante Anni in black permanent marker. I lugged them down to the post office, collected the triplicate customs forms East Germany required and transferred my shopping list to the forms. The value of the contents – around fifteen dollars – was similar to the postage I paid, even though I sent them by the slowest possible boat. I had been lugging heavy boxes and filling out triplicate forms with grocery lists ever since I first moved to Amherst and continued the tradition in St. Paul. I dreaded doing it again.

On one of the rare occasions I managed to pry Matt out of his office, we went to Rosedale Mall for a bit of shopping. I remember riding down the escalator at Penney's and turning to him to sigh. "I suppose it's about time for the annual East German Christmas packages."

Matt nodded. "Why don't you try to think of something they can't get there? Something easier to ship?"

We stepped off the escalator and found ourselves in the small electronics department. Matt grinned. "How about a calculator? Those things are really valuable over there."

I wasn't so sure. "What would my grandmothers do with calculators?"

"Well, if they don't want them, they can pass them along to one of your cousins. I'm sure Matthias or Ulrich would be thrilled to get one."

I considered this. Matthias was in dental school and Ulrich was majoring in engineering. A calculator would be a big thrill for them.

What I liked best though was the thought of slipping a flat little package into a mailing envelope. I'd be able to carry these to the post office with ease. Not for Tante Anni, though. She didn't have any young relatives of her own. Besides, she had just a small pension and no access to Western currency. She relied on my mother and me for the occasional mandarin orange. I bought two basic calculators, and stuck with a food package for Tante Anni. That year, I bounced into the post office, whipped through the forms, mailed my presents and gave the matter no further thought.

Months passed. Every day, I returned home from work, grabbed the mail on my way in, flung off my jacket and kicked off my shoes. If there was no interesting mail, I changed into my running clothes and took off. I had at least an hour to kill before Matt came home from work, and he usually left as soon as dinner was over to work until bedtime. One day in late January, I found a package in the mail from Tante Isolde. Strange. Tante Isolde did not usually send presents. She managed to produce a brief card for birthdays and Christmas, but that was it. I dropped my briefcase on a barstool in the kitchen, and slit the package wrapper with a paring knife. Wrapped in one of my plastic bags, I found the calculator and a letter.

The letter was a direct assault. She didn't mess with any salutations. Not even a hello. It started right in:

Herewith the return of the calculator, Claudia!

Omi is very angry with you, because she clearly perceived that this was a mean-spirited insinuation!! Please apologize immediately to your old grandmother and set this matter right immediately. I would have thought it more appropriate as a granddaughter to inquire after your Omi's health than to insult her with your derision and to accelerate her mental decline. Consider your behavior and follow my advice! Only then can we look forward to your next visit.

Tante Isolde

What the hell was this all about? I read the letter at least three times, and I still didn't know what she meant. How was I insulting my grandmother? I lurched to the phone and dialed my mother. After I read her the letter, a sob escaped me.

My mother said, "It sounds like she thinks you sent Omi Paula a calculator because you didn't think she could add any more."

"Doesn't she know me well enough to know I'd never do anything like that?"

My mother fumed. "She's like that. She doesn't think before she lashes out."

I had never seen that side of Tante Isolde, but I was in no mood to question my mother. I was blubbering like a kid who had been unjustly sent to her room.

"Let me handle this," My mother said. "I'll write her. You just stay out of it." Her voice snapped like an over-tightened guitar string.

I still couldn't let it go. "What would even make them think of such a thing?"

My mother considered this. "I haven't seen old ladies in Germany carrying calculators in their purses like they do here." After a pause she added, "Omi Hedwig said in her last letter that she thought it was an odd present. Said she gave it to one of the boys for school."

"See," I shouted, "she didn't think I was trying to insult her."

"I have trouble believing that Omi Paula did either. That sounds more like Isolde and Horst."

When I hung up the phone, I needed to do something. Anger coursed through me so intensely that I couldn't hold still. I flung my work clothes off and almost ripped my running shorts tugging them on. Slamming the door, I burst onto the back deck of our St. Paul condo, resenting the need to slow down long enough to fit the key into the hole. I crashed down the back steps and took off through the parking lot. I pounded the pavement with my feet, imagining I was delivering blows to my aunt with every move. For months my run had not varied. Arundel from Marshall to Summit, then down Summit to Lexington and back. Four miles. When I reached the Lexington stoplight, it was green, and I decided to keep going. There's a wide park-like median that starts at Lexington. Down the middle of it, legions of runners have worn a dirt track that runs through a patch of bushes and emerges into grass flanked by tall trees. I crossed over, checking for cars, without breaking my stride. It wasn't until I reached Snelling that I had calmed enough to turn around. This run would come in at six miles, my longest ever. Yes, it was unjust to accuse me like this. But surely, once my mother wrote to set things straight my aunt would see she had made a mistake and apologize.

I was wrong about that. I did not see a copy of my mother's letter, but I do remember that instead of apologizing my aunt escalated the attack. I was now a selfish spoiled brat, we were all self-centered and insensitive, and my mother was just making excuses for my rude behavior. My grandmother's quiet letter to my mother admitting that she had been a little confused by this present, but hadn't thought much of it until she mentioned it at Isolde's, just confirmed my mother's hunch. My miscalculation had set a match to the tinder of Isolde's frustrations. All the injustices her family had incurred by choosing to remain on the wrong side of the Iron Curtain were suddenly our fault. I hadn't realized until then that they had chosen. Apparently my father had located a job in West Germany for Horst in the early sixties. Back then it was still easy to get out as long as you were willing to abandon your possessions, but Horst hadn't wanted to "start all over." My mother and Isolde exchanged several volleys by letter across the Atlantic. They only served to further fan the flames.

"I'm done. I'm not having anything further to do with her," my mother finally announced on the phone one day. My father was as stunned as I was.

A year passed and neither sister showed signs of budging. My father couldn't stand it when people were unreasonable. He believed in the power of the intellect, the ideal that every conflict would yield to talk. During the winter of '82, he took up the mantle of peacemaker. During a business trip to Germany, he planned a few days in Gera at the end, and decided one day to point his rental car to Bad Düben. I suspect he called ahead to ensure that he wouldn't meet a closed door. Over coffee and torte, he convinced Isolde that we could treat this all as a misunderstanding, one that certainly wasn't worth breaking blood bonds over.

While I was glad to hear the news, the effects on me were not reversible. Eventually, I would visit Isolde and we would both act as though the letter had never been written. But this rift - and even though I believed that it was primarily between the sisters, I couldn't help but take it personally - had exploded the bedrock of my universe. The spring it happened I upped my running to six miles every other day. I still pictured Isolde on the ground under my pumping feet. What was the point of anything if you couldn't count on your family to love you? All my life I had trusted that we would stick together, despite the obstacles created by the communists. And all my life I could count on unconditional love from my family. Well, not unconditional. I knew I had to be a good girl in exchange, but I did my part. Isolde's attack on my character destroyed that certainty. I had plenty of time to think on these runs. I realized that I had never really given up my belief in justice. I often joked about it, "I grew up as an only child, so I have this illusion that life is fair. Nobody ever punishes you for something you didn't do." Well, here I was, being accused of something I didn't do. I was 28, and reality hit me with the force of an earthquake.

It took months of thinking and running, but by June I decided to quit smoking. It was my life, and I was going to take responsibility for it. I smoked a pack a day since about high school graduation and had tried to quit at least three times before. I was no stranger to picking through the trash for a butt with another puff or two on it when I finally gave in to the craving during the small hours of the night. This time there was no looking back. I smoked my last cigarette the day before Isolde's birthday. I was a little worried that I might start again when Matt left for his six-month sabbatical in Paris, since I couldn't take a leave from my corporate job to join him. To my surprise I was not lonely. Matt was so absorbed with trying to get tenure he wasn't home much anyway. When he was home, we fought over our different perceptions of how much time together, and more importantly how much attention paid, made a successful relationship. He'd make promises to change and I discovered the frustrating role of enforcer. I was surprised how much his absence eased my breathing, almost as much as leaving East Germany always did.

I wondered what was keeping me in this marriage. My fears of what my family would think? I knew my parents would be outraged if I considered divorce. But if Tante Isolde could judge me so unfairly for something I hadn't even thought of doing, then why was I worrying about pleasing other people? Apparently you couldn't count on them to hold up their end of the bargain. No, Isolde had taught me a lesson. The only person I could count on was myself.

I had never risked my mother's love. The move to South Carolina had left me so shaken during my teenage years, I couldn't. But Tante Isolde's undeserved attack pulled my sense of security out from under me, and I had survived. I didn't need to trade my life for safety.

*****

A few weeks before I left Matt, I sat on a battered chair in Mr. Wolkowicz's basement office. Mr. Wolkowicz ruled his rental empire from behind an ancient metal desk. I guessed he was in his sixties and his words carried an Eastern European echo. He probably fled Poland to escape the Germans, but now his continental manner gave me comfort. I twisted my hands, stalling, even though I had come here to pay a two-hundred dollar security deposit for a one bedroom in one of his buildings.

"Why is this so hard?" he said, with a grandfatherly smile, "It's not like getting married. It's just an apartment."

I coughed up a strangled laugh.

"Yes, but if I take the apartment, I'm leaving my husband." I couldn't believe I was telling him this, even if he had kind eyes. I hadn't said it out loud, even to myself, as I sneaked off to look at apartments all over St. Paul on my lunch hour.

Mr. Wolkowicz's expression sobered. "How long have you been married?"

"Five years," I answered.

"That's longer than a lot of them last these days."

I don't know why that made me feel better. I reached for my checkbook and filled in the blanks. When I gave him the check, he shook my hand and wished me luck.

On the way back to my office, I took a detour past my new apartment building. It dated from the twenties, when F. Scott Fitzgerald roamed St. Paul. A stonemason had hewn its name - Cecile Court - into a sandstone lintel above the door. It presided over the corner of Chatsworth and Goodrich just a few blocks from Summit and the Governor's mansion. I loved walking through the grid of tree-lined streets in the neighborhood. (My knees had informed me clearly that I had to give up running a few months before.) The apartment itself was a tiny one bedroom with sloping wood floors. The kitchen had a foot of counter space, and the bathroom, though it looked stately with its pedestal sink and spacious bathtub, suffered from an unreliable hot water supply. I learned never to take a shower during peak times in the morning or late evening. But generous windows flooded the eating space and the corner living room with light filtered through tree branches. Later, when I tried to grow flowers in window boxes, squirrels dug up my violas as fast as I planted them. I would spend hours reading in my living room, looking up to watch birds and waving branches, and listening to the chuk-chuk-chuk of quarreling squirrels.

It wasn't easy to bear up under the pressure of my mother's opinion even though it was all delivered long distance. She acted like getting divorced was an American fad and as soon as I remembered my German roots, I'd buckle down and make the best of my marriage. The way it felt to me at the time, I was struggling for survival and I didn't care if my methods were German or American, as long as I got out. When she threatened to withdraw her love if I divorced, I had gone too far to turn back. I clung to the new insight I gained from the calculator incident. This was my life. My mother was bluffing, but I couldn't know that until she capitulated.

Now that I wasn't always waiting for Matt to come home, I systematically filled my time by inviting friends for dinner, and arranging dates with other women to go shopping, visit museums, and attend plays and concerts. Even though I sensed my stay here was temporary, I sewed curtains for all the windows, and searched for pieces of art that matched my furniture. After years of wishing I could learn to draw, I signed up for an evening class at the College of Art and Design in Minneapolis. My self-generated whirlwind of activities proved exhilarating.

After a few months of fruitless telephone fights, capped by my refusal to come home for Thanksgiving, my mother accepted the inevitability of my divorce. We tiptoed around each other in conversation, trying to stick to mundane details for a few weeks. Then she shocked me with an unexpected angle. She wanted me to move home.

"Home?" I said. "Do you mean move back to South Carolina?" You have got to be kidding!

"You must be lonely there. If you looked for a job somewhere closer like Atlanta, you'd be near your family at least." Her voice sounded forlorn.

I stood in my kitchen, phone in hand, silent, staring through the window into the frothy crabapple preening for spring. A surge of affection wound through that tree and spread out through my St. Paul neighborhood. I felt airborne, yet space was fractured too, as all my favorite places conjoined into a jumble of Summit Avenue, Mississippi River, Downtown Minneapolis, Maplewood Nature Center, Lake of the Isles, the Walker and the Art Institute, the Guthrie, and twenty or so of my favorite restaurants. This sense of attachment - where had it come from? I hadn't noticed its growth.

"No," I said, suddenly at a loss how to explain. "I'm staying."

The truth that I liked the Twin Cities better than any place I had lived since Krefeld sneaked up on me gradually. I first visited Minnesota in early '77, just after Matt had received a job offer from the university. Before we got on the plane, I needed to find a map. Minnesota. A state somewhere in the unmarked middle, jumbled together with Missouri, Kansas, Nebraska, the Dakotas - states I imagined as endless open plains, populated by buffalo herds and frontier towns. I knew cities existed there, but I couldn't picture them. From the map I learned that Minnesota was practically in Canada, further north than I would have guessed. My mother sent an article she found in a newsmagazine that rated Minneapolis one of the ten most livable American cities. Under a picture of the IDS Center - oh, yes, Mary Tyler Moore, I remembered - a gushing article described the Guthrie Theater and Walker Art Center, downtown skyways, and city lakes and parks. It went on to tout the low crime rate and well-maintained neighborhoods.

The article attributed the flavor of the city and the state's healthy social service system to its Scandinavian heritage. I later discovered that the bulk of immigrants to Minnesota were of German descent. They had learned to keep quiet about it during the First World War. In passing it mentioned the one disadvantage, a lengthy winter which routinely exposed the inhabitants to subzero temperatures. That all sounded good, except for the cold, of course, but what bothered me was the way the state sat right in the middle of the continent, days of driving away from either ocean. I couldn't imagine being landlocked. All my life, I lived within a few hours of driving from salt water, even if I only took advantage of that fact a few times a year. The idea of being surrounded by thousands of miles of land in all directions gave me vertigo.

I put on my warmest coat and boots before Matt and I drove to the airport and climbed into the plane. As the pilot touched down he announced, "Don't forget to set your watches back an hour. It's a little chilly here in Minneapolis. The temperature is 14 below zero and falling. Bundle up and have a good stay."

Matt smiled at me, then squeezed my hand. "They tell me you get used to the cold. It's dry cold, so it doesn't feel so bad. And you can dress for it." He really wanted this job.

The cold didn't scare me. At least not until I emerged from the terminal to feel the air reach out and punch me in the lungs. I flipped up the fake fur on my collar and hid my nose and mouth inside it. The Chemical Engineering Department head waited for us with a warm car right outside baggage claim. He whisked us toward downtown Minneapolis, where they had booked a room for us at the Marquette, then the fanciest hotel in town, and right in the IDS center. They really wanted me to like it here.

The icy air concentrated billows of steam around the cluster of skyscrapers that rise in the center of the city. Gleaming glass reflected street lamps like a thousand icicles against an inky winter night. The next day, I explored the skyways that connected our hotel to a network of indoor shopping. We dipped in and out of the frigid air, relentlessly sunny by day, to tour the university campus and the cities' neighborhoods. Blankets of snow and layers of ice obscured the public parks, but the sun glinted through lacy tree branches and cross-country skiers and skaters littered the landscape. The place had possibilities.

Over the next two years, while I lived in Maryland to complete my thesis research, I flew to Minnesota for the weekend every other month. There must have been visits that took place in the summer, but I remember standing in line for movie tickets on a succession of 20 below zero nights outside the Cooper Theater on Wayzata Boulevard. While Matt worked, I explored downtown. In 1978, most visitors from the East Coast complained that Minneapolis didn't have any ethnic variety. Two overpriced Chinese restaurants comprised foreign cuisine. Pale skin, blonde hair, and blue eyes predominated on the streets. Matt's colleagues warned me to avoid the 'seedy' part of town, Hennepin Avenue. I spotted a couple of strip joints and a gay bar, but saw no sign of urban decay. No graffiti, very little litter, and just a few winos. Just like the cities of my childhood.

People acted very polite, even though I sometimes couldn't understand a word they said. I always thought a Midwestern accent meant no accent, sort of like TV Anchors, but I learned differently in Minnesota. One day, I waited for Matt in his office when the phone rang. I recognized his secretary's voice, and offered to take a message. She burst into a rapid-fire sequence of sentences, her voice squeezed tight and pitched high as if she was gritting her teeth and holding her nose at the same time. I had to ask her to repeat her message three times. Since then I've learned that 'beg' means 'bag' and that a 'binder' is a rubber band, and that Minnesotans routinely say 'come with' when they mean 'come along.'

But how did I get attached? After I moved and landed a job at 3M, I complained about the introverted social ways of Minnesotans. In South Carolina, if you invited people to a party, this implied a social contract. Your job as a party participant is to find ways to interact with other partygoers. That rule did not appear to apply. Parties that involved Minnesota natives could get very quiet, because if I approached a Minnesotan with any of the standard icebreakers I learned in the South, they mistook this for a serious question instead of an invitation to start a conversation. If I asked how long they had known the hostess, they'd say something factual, like "not long" and return to examining the contents of their drink as though the interplay of ice cubes was an intriguing display they did not want interrupted. For a few months, after attending several work-related 3M functions, I wondered whether I had lost my social skills. To be fair, most 3M'ers are not only Minnesotans, but also engineers and scientists, a double whammy on the introversion scale. I also found native Minnesotans fairly resistant to forming friendships. Most of them had standing dinner dates with their parents, grandparents and siblings, and high school friends. It only took a few exceptions, though, and between these and fellow imports to Minnesota, I soon gathered a small collection of friends.

The sense of attachment I glimpsed in my conversation with my mother was based not just on those tendrils of friendship. It wasn't just that I knew my way around after three years of living in St. Paul, though it was a factor. The thought of packing up and starting all over in a new place was daunting. When I had done it in Amherst, I thought of it as an adventure. When I moved to Maryland to finish my graduate work, adventure took on an edge of necessity, and by the time I settled in Minnesota I did with a sense that at least this time the knowledge I gleaned from driving around with a map in my car would serve me for some time. And, there was much I liked. I love art museums, and here I had access to several. I love well-groomed city parks - they echo our Sunday afternoon promenades in the Krefeld's *Stadtwald* - a park with gravel lanes, ponds and swans. The Twin Cities is studded with green spaces. I love to eat. By the time I sat in my apartment, watching the squirrels and birds in the crabapple, Minnesota had transformed from a monoculture. A rapid influx of Southeast Asian refugees in the early eighties broke up the uniformity on the streets, and added spice to the restaurant selection. I believed that citizens should provide social programs with their taxes so that the streets were not filled with the destitute. While Minnesota had gotten less civic minded as the movement to cut taxes was taking hold, I still felt less guilty here than I would in most other states. A friend of a friend quipped that this was the "Socialist Republic of Minnesota." In 1982 that wasn't true anymore. But I approved of the motivation that led to the joke.

Looking back, I ask myself why I didn't even consider going back to Germany. I know it never occurred to me. Proof, I suppose, that I had made the transition. I still didn't think of myself as an American; I thought of myself as a German that lived in Minnesota. Who spoke better English than German. Who knew how to be a child in Germany, and an adult in the US. I can make up excuses in retrospect. During my separation and right after my divorce, I felt like a hermit crab exposing its tender flesh to predators as I searched for a new shell. The first few weeks in my apartment, I woke in the dead hours of the night, every night, shaking from a recurring nightmare. A masked intruder with a gleaming blade crouched in the window, ready to plunge toward me as I lay defenseless on my futon. I was in no shape to take risks, or even to imagine them. My instinct insisted I swaddle my crablike soul in comforters made up of the familiar. I needed to shop at the Maplewood Byerly's on the way home from work, to load up my basket with imported German cold cuts, and then drive west on I-94, just one exit further than before. I needed to bike down Summit Avenue to the Mississippi, and across the Ford Parkway bridge all the way to Lake

Nokomis, just as I had done on other summer Sundays. Most of all, I needed to stay at the same job, where I knew just what degree of independence was allowed, and what level of dissent was acceptable.

I stayed in the apartment for three years. When it was time to move, I dismantled the curtains joyfully. I had fallen in love again, this time for real. I knew, because I felt not a twinge of doubt despite the fact that the object of my passion was totally unsuitable.

*****

Although I've often felt rebellious, I've usually tempered my impulses with enough caution to pass for a good girl. Before I got divorced, I never did anything major that embarrassed my parents. They had barely reconciled themselves to that shock when I dealt them another.

I visited Clemson for a week at Christmas. My parents had taken up their customary spots, side-by-side on the couch, facing the TV. I sat on the Scandinavian metal and canvas sling chair, my feet propped on the matching footstool. My father leaned forward, lined up three wineglasses on the coffee table and uncorked the bottle. He poured exactly equal amounts into each glass, then distributed them.

I took a sip and leaned back into my chair. What was the best way to sidle up to my awkward news of love? The best way to arrange the details so they wouldn't shock? How could I highlight my certainty that this time, it was right, and keep unattractive facts in the background?

I cleared my throat. "I've started seeing someone."

My father's eyes opened a fraction of a millimeter wider. My mother's spine straightened, her face tilting so she wouldn't miss any details.

"It's someone I met at work. In fact, you've met him," I added glancing toward my father. Just a few months before, he had stopped by my lab during a business trip to 3M. I remembered introducing him to Ron.

My father puzzled over this for a second. "You mean the tall guy with the mustache?" I nodded.

My mother wrinkled her forehead. "How old is he?"

I sighed. Now what made her ask that, first thing? "Well, he's a bit older than me."

"How much?"

I should have known evasive action wouldn't work. "Fifteen years."

My mother gasped. Before I could explain that he didn't look or act that old, and that I was so deliriously happy that I didn't care, she did some quick thinking of her own.

"Is he divorced? Does he have kids?"

I admitted to both.

"How many?"

I hesitated. I had lost control of this conversation, and I didn't know how to get it back. My intentions to swaddle the hard data in the rosy light of my adoration evaporated under the harsh light of my mother's interrogation.

"Well, there are five of them." Shocked silence. I charged into the breach with explanations. Told them that the three older ones were his biological children and the two younger ones were mixed-race children he had adopted. That the youngest was eleven and the oldest twenty-two. That he'd had primary custody of them since the youngest was six months. I was consumed with admiration for this man who took it upon himself to raise five children. How could they help but be impressed? They were not.

"Claudia," my mother said, just barely stopping herself from raising her right forefinger and wagging it at me, "you can't. You just can't." Her voice shook. My father nodded agreement.

I stopped trying for diplomacy instantly.

"Why not? I know it won't be easy, but we get along so well, we can deal with anything." I couldn't explain how I felt when I was with Ron. Anchored. Rooted. Supported in who I was. Not to mention the passion that rose up between us at the touch of a fingertip. No, I couldn't describe any of it to my parents - they wouldn't want to hear it now.

What finally won my mother over was Ron himself. When my father had to go to Germany in May, I used frequent flier miles to bring my mother to Minnesota for Mother's Day. On Saturday night, I made a reservation for three for dinner at the Nicollet Island Inn. As my mother and I arrived, Ron met us in the entryway. He was dressed to impress in an Italian suit and silk tie I had helped pick out for work. The cut of the suit emphasized his tall, slender build. I know my mother saw how his face lit up when he spotted me - a slow, deep smile that spread to the corners of his blue eyes. His hair and mustache showed barely a sprinkle of gray. After we ordered our food, I excused myself to go to the restroom. By the time I returned, my mother's posture had softened and she was giggling. Later that night, as we got ready for bed in my apartment, she said, "He is very nice, but I do wish the situation weren't so complicated. You'll have a hard time with those kids, especially the girls. It's difficult for girls to share their Daddy with a new woman. And they've been through so much already."

I agreed, relieved at her switched focus.

As soon as I let myself fall in love with Ron, I knew I had made a commitment. His vital statistics were so contrary, that I couldn't just mess around. In fact, I spent weeks trying to talk myself out of it. My intellect failed to convince my heart, and I plunged in not caring what price I would have to pay. About a year and a half after the conversation in my parents' family room I moved into Ron's house and six months after that we celebrated our wedding in the backyard. While my mother was right that some of the children would struggle with my presence, I was also right that together Ron and I would survive. I hadn't foreseen that I would eventually count most of my stepchildren among my closest friends.

Ron had grown up in Minnesota, left briefly to go to graduate school in Iowa and returned home to a job at 3M. Married to him, Minnesota would likely be my permanent address. Not that he was unwilling to consider moving somewhere else someday. Whenever we discussed it, say after a long weekend in Seattle or a trip to Vancouver, I ended the conversation by declaring that one rootless person in the family was enough. I couldn't imagine Ron anywhere else. His mother's parents had emigrated from Ireland and farmed a section near Hutchinson, about forty miles west of Minneapolis. Family lore handed down a story about Chief Little Crow rushing the O'Fallons to safety during the Indian Wars. Although Ron's mother had moved from 'Hutch' to marry his Norwegian immigrant father and settle in Excelsior on Lake Minnetonka, the family center of gravity remained the farm and the cemetery nearby where Ron's grandparents and aunts and uncles, lay buried under aged trees on a wind-swept hillside.

No, the only way I could consider returning to Germany was temporarily. Maybe once the kids were grown, we could work for 3M Europe? Or, once Ron retired, we could spend summers there? Those were the games I played in my mind; a habit I couldn't quite lay to rest.

Within a few weeks of our marriage, Ron's family absorbed me into huge Catholic funerals and weddings. I thought I might feel strange in the bosom of devout Catholicism, but the family interpretation is inclusive. Ron's mother approached me with the attitude that she loved anyone who made her son happy. The rest of the family followed suit. Over the years, I've accepted that I will never be able to tell all the Ebert "boys" apart unless they're standing next to each other and that there are many relatives of varying degrees named Mary and I may mess up on knowing which one is Mary Claire and which one Mary Eileen. Always, I can be sure of one thing. I can count on a friendly word no matter which way I turn, just because I'm a relative. I may bathe in this warmth at the local VFW or, for fancier weddings, at the Holiday Inn, but if the settings are strange, the atmosphere is identical to Poser family weddings and birthdays. The similarity brought me another few steps closer to feeling settled, but I still needed to bring the new part of my life to meet the old.

*****

During the 1980s, East Germany became a darling of many women's studies and political science professors. On paper, it looked like the best place on earth for women. My step-daughter Cori showed me how the state measured up in her copy of *Sisterhood is Global*, a book that catalogued the status of women using the following criteria: availability of day care, birth control availability, abortion law, pregnancy leave policies, women's literacy rate, women's employment rates, percentage of women professionals, percentage of women living in poverty, access to health care. All the socialist countries shone, but East Germany looked practically perfect on paper. Day care was universally available and paid for by the state. Abortion was legal on demand during the first trimester at no cost. Free universal health care provided access to birth control. According to government statistics, 100% of East German women were literate, almost all adult women worked, more than half of all doctors were women, there was no poverty, and women who had babies received a year off with full pay. Paradise.

How could I explain the price paid? I didn't know where to start. How do you stack a polluted landscape against universal health care? They probably cancelled each other out, I thought. And do generous pregnancy leaves make up for the shortage of fruits and vegetables? Is the right to leave your country, to travel and see the world, really as important as universal day care? How much does it matter to the psyche to know that the state has spies everywhere and anything suspect you've ever said in public is filed in a *Stasi* office somewhere? How do you weigh a police state against low and stable rents and guaranteed full employment? After all, I had always looked at those questions from the point of view of a winner in the land of capitalism - I had educated parents who could provide the necessities and support my pursuit of an education. How would an illiterate homeless woman feel about this? Wouldn't she be better off in East Germany?

I was willing to consider it possible. I ended up feeling like I had to change the subject to explain the heart of the problem. I struggled to find words for the depressing atmosphere in East Germany, the way no one had the freedom to think without looking over their shoulder, and the way they carried the absence of hope. People were unhappy. You could see it in their faces - what the Polish-born New York journalist Eva Hoffmann called their 'mugs.' She was talking about Poles, but her description applied to East Germans as well. If someone had set you down on an East German street anytime before 1989, and asked you to describe what you noticed about the people, this is what you would have said: They scowl. Their shoulders sag. They don't look at each other. When they bump into each other they do not apologize, though the one who got jostled might yell something like 'watch where you're going!' They move as though they're both in a hurry and worn out. Every one of them carries their own personal rain cloud above their heads.

I told Cori a few stories about shortages and the reality that most East German women spent their lunch hours in line at the stores trying to buy a few grams of meat for dinner. That the government controlled wages so as to force women into the workforce, whether they wanted to be there or not. I could tell I didn't sound convincing. She would have to come with us and see for herself.

Ron and I had intended to travel to Europe that summer taking the youngest, fourteen-year-old Tony. Cori had been dreaming of foreign travel and suggested she come along to be his roommate. East Germany promised to be a more exotic destination than Austria, Switzerland and Italy.

Cori's eye for unusual detail reframed my vision of familiar places. She arrived equipped with a camera and copious rolls of film and approached picture taking with the passion of a documentary maker. She snapped pictures of the strangest details. West German haystacks piled up by pitchfork instead of rolled by machine. The intricate window displays at bakeries and butcher shops. The pedestrian zone in Stuttgart and the tram stop where we waited to ride to the *Funkturm* - the landmark TV transmitter - to get a view of the valley. When Tony's braces required emergency repair and Tante Nanne's orthodontist friend invited us to his office, Cori photographed his dentist chair. She appeared determined to record all the minutiae that made up Germany; the mundane pieces I recognized with relief each time, but would never have thought to record.

After we crossed into East Germany, I saw her pull out her camera while I was stowing our visa.

"Don't take pictures now!" I yelled.

Cori froze. I'd shocked myself with that visceral yell. In all the years I traveled back and forth, it had never occurred to me to record the mine strip and guard towers. I looked around. We were pulling away from the border post in our rental car. Could anyone see her aiming a camera at the border fortifications? No. Then why was I so intimidated? Suddenly I wanted a picture. I told Cori to just be careful and not let anyone see her. She snapped a few banners with political slogans on the Autobahn bridges as well as the guard towers that hovered above major interchanges. I didn't know then that the mine strip and towers she recorded would be gone in five years. They were permanent to me.

In Gera, she took a picture of the buckling, cobbled pavement, the decaying exterior at Calvinstrasse, the indoor toilets off the staircase. She snapped my grandmother standing in the narrow strip of her kitchen, the casement window wide open behind her. When we went to the cemetery to put flowers on Opa Willy's grave, the crematorium caught her eye. Sooty black stones and art nouveau grillwork.

Cori did not bring her camera when we all went to register at the police station on a hot August morning. The police station in Gera was compact, brown stucco with stout iron bars on the windows. The building stood apart on a sandlot invaded by scruffy weeds. Flies buzzed in and out through the door propped open by the line of people waiting.

The station not only registered visitors, but also processed travel permits for East Germans hoping to visit the West. The government had been loosening up those restrictions lately and everyone was having a go at a trip abroad.

I peered into the waiting room gloom. Thirty people at least.

"How do we know this is the right line?" Ron asked.

"There's no one to ask," I said. "We'll just have to wait and see." A familiar leaden attitude flowed into my body: waiting without question.

"How long do you think this will take, Claud?" Cori asked.

"There's no way to know. We'll just have to wait and see." I knew I was repeating myself.

Every once in a long while, a voice came over a speaker, metallic, female, announcing a room number. I whispered to the woman in front of us as we shuffled forward a few steps. She pointed to a small hand-lettered sign by the door. The directions, illegible from more than a foot away. The room was packed with irritable, anxious people, fanning themselves with passports and forms, patting the sweat off their faces with crumpled paper tissues that left little threads of cellulose stuck to their skin. We wouldn't get close to those instructions for at least an hour.

A man emerged from the door, holding his passport out like a trophy to one of the women in the crowd. "I got it!" She squeezed his hand as they pushed out, past me to the end of the line. A rushing murmur, lively though suppressed, splashed through the room. I could make out only "maybe they're in a good mood today." We inched forward as the line extended at our backs. Tony found a wall to lean against.

The lucky passport recipient had left the white door that appeared to be our goal open behind him in his excitement. One woman, about eighty and bent from softening bones, pushed toward the door without being called. The crowd held its breath. She advanced into the corridor. We could see four doors back there, all white, all closed. She knocked at one. A male policeman cracked the door, and she asked why no one was calling room four, that was the one she needed. He frowned and shouted at her, "You are not to come into this hall until you're called. What kind of disorder are you trying to cause? Now go wait with everyone else. The colleague who handles room four is on her break." Even though my American family didn't understand him, they flinched at his voice. She shuffled back out closing the door behind her, muttering. Someone said, "See. It's no good trying to talk to them. Now she'll just have an extra cup of coffee before she goes back to work."

Nothing happened for at least half an hour. Finally, the door opened. A plump, red-faced woman, who had looked defiant on her way in, burst out, tears tracking down her cheeks. Three women, who might have been her sisters, broke from the crowd and surrounded her. "They won't let me go," she sobbed, as they stroked her long limp hair. I translated in whispers, as we watched, as helpless and stunned as the rest of the crowd.

At least with that group gone, we got close. I could finally read the sign and determined that we needed room two. I glanced at my watch. We'd been waiting a little less than two hours. The smell of linoleum and other people's anxiety had settled in my nostrils. The intercom barked out its crackly summons more rapidly. Soon we faced the entrance. "Room two" hissed out from above. We entered. Number 2 was at the end of the hall. I depressed the black plastic handle and pushed into the room. Bright light slapped my eyes. A picture of Erich Honecker - the East German leader who replaced Walter Ulbricht - smiled benevolently between two tall windows. Below him sat a young woman with stylish dark hair under her uniform cap.

"Please sit down," she almost smiled. There were only two chairs. Ron and I perched at the edge of them, clutching passports and quadruplicate forms. "May I please see your passports?" There was an edge to her polite voice. She studied our photos, then us, then the photos. I put on the same clenched smile that is standard for passports. She handed Tony and Cori's passports back and sent them out. Only their raised eyebrows hinted at their concern. What did she want with Ron and me?

After the door shut, the policewoman spread the forms out in an orderly line and asked me a few brisk questions.

"You are both chemists?"

"Yes," I answered.

"Where do you work?"

"For a company called 3M." I said. What was this all about?

After getting a few more details about our jobs, she seemed satisfied. She selected the proper stamp from a spidery round stamp caddy, flipped the top off her stamp pad and positioned it below the line of forms. Her wrist flicked back and forth between paper and stamp pad as she pounded the stamp down on our forms. Within seconds she had accurately landed the State Seal in the appropriate circle on every form without a single wasted motion. She looked proud. "I hope you have a pleasant stay in the DDR," she dismissed us. We sailed through the door, through the gloomy hallway, slid through the crowd and emerged into the sandlot. Tony and Cori greeted us with relief.

"We were trying to figure out if we could find our way back, if they kept you." I had been so puzzled by the policewoman, I hadn't registered Cori and Tony's anxiety. Just like my mother, I thought. She never realized the East German police scared me either.

A few days later, we gathered at Onkel Klaus's *dacha*. This time the long table set for coffee with three kinds of torte impressed Cori. She also took several pictures of my cousin Uwe's wife Viola. Viola is blond and blue-eyed like Cori and only a few years older. In school, she'd majored in Import/Export business and had acquired a working knowledge of English. Viola and Cori spent the afternoon in a corner, comparing lives. In the evening, Cori recorded Onkel Klaus's famous techniques for grilling *Rostbratwürste*. He'd shake up a beer bottle with his thumb over the opening, then squirt the sausages, and turn them by hand; the beer flavored the meat and kept his fingers from burning. After the meal, we sat inside around a small table, drinking cognac. Onkel Klaus leaned toward me and chuckled.

"Would you believe it? One of them, you know one of the *spitzel* - stool pigeons - at work, approached me. He asked me about you and your job. Then he said, if she's ever interested we'd like to talk to her." He guffawed at this.

"Talk to me?"

"Oh, you know. They're always looking for people to spy for them."

"You've got to be kidding." We laughed together. Creepy, I thought. That the East German State would track me like this. I had never felt so exposed. For an instant, I had a glimpse of what it must be like to live in such a state, constantly aware that your every move is recorded.

Cori knew better than to use her camera a few days later, when the police stopped us on the Autobahn on our way to Bad Düben. Before we left, Onkel Klaus had cautioned us, "Be careful on the Berlin Autobahn. The police are always trying to catch those rich West Germans speeding." I knew. Tante Nanne had complained about the East German police and their speed traps. We were determined to avoid them.

We followed a rattly truck toward the Autobahn entrance ramp. "My mother says the pavement on these ramps is still the original, from the time Hitler built this Autobahn," I said. Ron didn't answer. He was stretching to look for traffic, because those same original ramps were too short to allow for easy merger with traffic moving at the speed limit of 100km/hr.

At first, we were too tense to chat, but after a Mercedes going 150 km/hr had passed us, we relaxed a bit. By comparison we should be safe, since we were being so scrupulous. The sun was even trying to break through the clouds.

We crested a hill. Way down at the bottom, we saw several police cars on the right shoulder, and a police officer with binoculars stood in the median, waving only the West German cars off the Autobahn. I scanned the road for a reason. At first I saw nothing. Except, there was something, yes; there was a speed limit sign - an official sign on a portable easel, just inches above the grass in the central divider. 30 km/hr. Why would they need traffic to creep along at 15 mph in the middle of nowhere? Those jerks. I'd been expecting rigid enforcement of reasonable laws, but I hadn't expected this. Ron slowed down at my shout, but it was too late. The policeman with the spyglasses waved us off to the shoulder.

Ron blanched. He gripped the steering wheel and slowed to a stop.

"What do we do?" Ron and Cori asked simultaneously. Out of the corner of my eye, I noticed Tony shrinking deeper into his corner.

"Pretend you don't speak a single word of German. I won't say anything either." Maybe if they thought we didn't have a clue they'd give up.

Another policeman climbed out of the van parked behind us. He walked slowly along the shoulder, gravel crunching under his black boots. Ron lowered his window. *"Ihren Führerschein."* Ron looked baffled.

"Ich spreche nicht Deutsch," Ron answered with a convincing accent.

"Your Driver's License," answered the officer, equally convincing in his way. Ron pulled out his international license. After leafing through it, the officer demanded his passport. Reluctantly, Ron handed it over. The officer took both documents and walked away, back to his police van. He disappeared inside.

Ron's knuckles whitened on the steering wheel. "What's he going to do now?"

I tried to be reassuring, though I wasn't sure exactly what was happening either. "Probably he's writing you a ticket," I said.

"They can't keep his passport, can they?" Cori asked.

"Oh, I don't think they'll do that. They do this for the money." I was pretty sure.

We sat, looking in the rearview mirror, waiting. The officer climbed out and slammed the door behind him. He carried a book in his hand. Back at Ron's window, he bent down and held the open book into the car. It was a book of international traffic signs with descriptions in several languages. He pointed at a speed limit sign.

"You go too fast. Here: 30 km/hr." His finger tapped the picture. Then he pulled out a traffic ticket. He had filled it out with Ron's name and the car's license number. An involuntary scowl passed across Ron's face, replaced immediately by tense neutrality. "How much?" he asked. "Fifty marks." Ron shifted his hips to pull his wallet out of his pocket. He handed the officer fifty East German marks.

"No, no. D-mark. Fifty D-mark." I pulled the West German cash from my purse. The officer took the money, handed Ron the ticket, his passport and license.

We waited for an extra large gap in traffic before pulling away. My heart was beating hard; both from the adrenaline jitters that shook my body when I was in the power of East German officials, and from the anger I couldn't help but feel at being tricked so shamelessly.

"Whooee, that was scary!" Cori called from the back.

We all started talking at once, hashing over the incident's details, until Ron suddenly asked: "And what would they do if you said you didn't have any D-mark with you?"

I laughed. Tante Nanne had answered that question a few years ago. She said she was staying in Gera and had used the Autobahn to visit an old friend in a nearby town just for the afternoon. On the way home, a policeman had stopped her on some pretext and given her a ticket. She had only East German money with her. The police officer followed her all the way back to Gera to Calvinstrasse so she could pay her fine. Anything to get Western Currency.

After we arrived in Bad Düben, Cori's camera got busy again. She aimed it at the fountain under the willow tree, the homemade pool in the backyard, and the exotic Eastern European cars: the old Wartburg and my uncle's Moskwitch, both of which were rare East German status symbols. They stood out in the crowds of *Trabbis* - the two-cylinder tin cans that were the only cars available without special status. Onkel Horst had access to these 'luxury' cars not because he was a party boss, but because he was a veterinarian, a professional the government desperately needed. Cori is fascinated by anything medical. She had Onkel Horst open his trunk so she could photograph the giant syringes he used on cows and the well-organized contents of his medical tool kit.

On my cousin Matthias' wall hung a saber my great-grandfather discovered while plowing the fields. It dated from the Battle of Leipzig, when the Prussians fought Napoleon. Snap. She captured Heidi, the wirehaired dachshund in her hiding place under the dresser in the entrance hall, and recorded the bullet holes on the outside of my grandfather's factory. I grinned unconvincingly (you're supposed to smile when you get your picture taken, whether you feel like it or not) as I stood in front of the locked gate, next to a sign that identified Opa's building as the "People-owned Jewelry Manufacturing Facility - Eilenburg." Two square, spackled indentations were all that remained of the sign that had read "Gustav Sieg und Söhne". When we visited my grandparents' grave in Bad Düben, Cori posed Tony, Ron, me and Matthias in front of the *Pesttor* - the gate erected in 1577 to mark the end of a particularly vicious wave of the bubonic plague.

The next to the last East German image from that trip is carried in my mind, not on film. Our car idled in line at the East German border, waiting to cross back into the West. Concrete pavement, aluminum-sided buildings, guard towers on all sides. The soldiers behind banks of windows holding machine guns at a stern angle. Nothing shadowy here. Everything lay revealed. I shifted and sighed. Ron looked pale, not certain that his American passport provided protection in this space of systematic intimidation. Cori and Tony craned their necks in the back, trying to make out what lay ahead. At the front of the line we saw a VW Rabbit, all four of its doors open, people and luggage spilled onto the pavement. One guard, stiff in his gray-green uniform and polished black boots, directed several others in removing the seats and wedging the door panels, shining flashlights into the remotest crannies. With an angled mirror on a pole, he inspected the wheel wells and the undersurface of the vehicle.

Off to the right, in the commercial lane, the border police were inspecting a line of grain trucks. A guard climbed onto the back of the truck, boosting himself up with a long metal pike. Then he climbed in, stood on the grain, and jabbed the pike through the grain as hard as he could. He shifted his position by two feet and jabbed again. Ron asked me what he was doing.

"Checking for people trying to escape." I answered and pictured the pike striking flesh.

"Holy shit!" Cori gasped.

Tony mumbled under his breath, "Oh my God."

Their disgust made me feel tough, as if taking such inhumanity for granted made me worldly.

The guards reassembled the VW, slowly, methodically. It lurched away. We inched forward. I wondered whether we'd have to get out of the car and unpack our suitcases. My mind took inventory of the presents we had bought with our East German money. We were not carrying any contraband. I had long ago learned that for me it was not worth the fear.

The guards had used up their desire to harass for the moment. Maybe they'd met a quota. The cars moved through at a steady pace. The guards asked questions, bent over to peer into backseats, then waved permission to continue. Our turn. Silently, Ron handed our passports through the open window. The guard's face flashed from bored to alert as he spotted the blue and gold U.S. passports on top. He leaned into the car and took in Cori's fair skin and golden hair next to Tony's café-au-lait complexion and black curls, then scanned Ron and me, as if trying to connect the puzzle. Another look at the passport. He shrugged. He even managed to sound polite as he asked how long we stayed in the DDR. I called out the answer from the passenger side. We escaped with a cursory examination of our trunk. As he handed the passports back to us, he startled us by using heavily accented English to say, "Good-bye. Have a good journey."

As soon as we crossed beyond the guard post, Cori's camera clicked, framing the metal bridge railing and the strip of mined no-man's land below.

The rest of Cori's pictures showed a typical European vacation: Andean street musicians in Munich, the fountains at Linderhof, Juliet's balcony in Verona. Cori's eye for unique detail did not desert her even here. In my photo album are pictures of an abandoned radioactive spa in Merano, wallpaper sprigged with rococo roses in a tiny Austrian hotel room, and, my personal favorite, a portrait of Tony attempting to consume the largest ice cream confection on the menu at an Italian sidewalk café.

When Cori returned, her friends were unhappy with the impressions she had gathered. Vehemently, she argued that East Germany might look good on paper, but she'd never want to trade lives with the women who had to live there.

*****

"You speak German. Why don't you just give her a call?" As Joe - my boss at 3M - said it, he grinned, obviously pleased that he could offer our German research partners a bilingual contact.

Easy for him to say. Yes, I could speak to Frau Dr. Körner in German, but what was the proper etiquette for a business call? When I was still living in Germany, I had been a child and so intimidated when my father's boss called him at home, that I involuntarily curtsied as I asked him to hold. One curse of still sounding native after twenty years was that if I mishandled the call, Dr. Körner would think I was rude instead of merely ignorant. And then there were the technical terms. I only knew those in English.

I didn't want to admit those doubts to Joe. Especially since I wanted to find a way to exploit the connection between German and science. And here it was: a German materials conglomerate wanted us to evaluate their new polymer for use in our medical products. As the only trained polymer scientist in the department, I was the perfect person for the job. I would just have to overcome my fear of sounding foolish. So I nodded as I took the letter that was crafted in Dr. Körner's careful English, and promised to get right on it.

For several mornings, I sat at my desk, rereading her letters, studying all the technical articles on the new material in the original German to accustom my brain to the vocabulary, but hesitating to dial the long string of numbers that would force me to confront her voice. I called up overheard phone conversations between my father and his German colleagues. You answer the phone not with a greeting, but by announcing your last name. The caller does not use the German equivalent of "This is" to identify themselves but starts out with *"Hier spricht"* - here speaks. When you are finished you don't say *Auf Wiedersehen,* since you are not seeing the person at that moment, you say *Auf Wiederhören,* which translates roughly as "until we hear each other again." These phrases were so creaky in the deep storage chambers of my brain that they sounded bizarre once I dragged them into consciousness. If I thought about them too much, I began to wonder if I hadn't imagined them after all. Obviously I had to stop dithering and get it over with. I took a deep breath and punched the buttons on my phone. I listened to the characteristic German dial tone - a froggy staccato. Nothing. They didn't have answering machines? Apparently not. By the time Dr. Körner picked up the phone three days later, I had stopped fretting. We stumbled through a conversation that felt endless to me. Afterwards, I felt my body soften, releasing tension I hadn't been aware it held.

I never once asked myself why it was so important to me to appear in complete command of German business vernacular. Why couldn't I cut myself some slack? I had left when I was thirteen. Surely, Dr. Körner wouldn't be aghast if I used awkward sentence structure or had to appeal to her superb knowledge of technical English to describe the details of my experimental results? Despite my superhuman attempts, I did fumble a phrase here and there, and I had to throw in an English technical term once or twice. Every time it happened I flinched, haunted by the specter of my mother. Her accent in English would have suited Hollywood's idea of a Freudian psychiatrist's, but after twenty years, she struggled with German as well. On visits to Germany, she searched openly for German phrases and sometimes substituted English ones while talking to her sister, who had no English and thought my mother must be showing off. I saw her stuck in language no-man's land: stumbling between rusty German and unwieldy English, not at home in any language on earth. What I hoped to accomplish was the opposite - a seamless flow in which I could express myself elegantly in Germany or America. But there was more to it than that. I pretty much accepted Minnesota as home, but I was terrified of seeming "Americanized." Whenever a slip of the tongue or the wardrobe caused a cousin or aunt to say - always good-naturedly "you have become American!" - I cringed.

In my soul, I carried two stereotypes of "American" remembered from the time before I got to know Americans as individuals rather than seeing them as a group from a distance. The earliest image, derived from my mother's stories about the war, was the good one. Americans as embodied by the Marshall Plan and the decent behavior of American GIs that contrasted so sharply with the rape and pillage perpetrated by the invading Russian soldiers. In this view, America was a kind and generous nation that believed in fairness and justice. This America was modern, the source of new inventions. Its people exhibited a childlike humor, were almost naïve in their belief in the goodness of humanity, yet they were clever, self-confident, and egalitarian.

The other stereotype of Americans - the ugly one - grew from caricatures of tourists and from American foreign policy in Vietnam and beyond. These Americans were simplistic politically, hyper-patriotic and pious, materialistic, arrogant, and sloppy in dress and table manners. They were insensitive to other cultures. They assumed it was everyone else's job to learn English. In short, they were rubes. I was forever afraid to be identified with this "ugly American."

By the summer of 1988, my boss suggested I travel to Germany to meet with Dr. Körner and her colleagues. Secrecy agreements had been signed; careful levels of disclosure negotiated. I was to fly to Frankfurt, arrive on a Sunday afternoon, and spend Monday in meetings. I knew I'd be hard-pressed to stay awake, let alone hold an entire day's worth of technical discussion in German. As I pulled my suitcase through the Frankfurt arrival hall, scanning for the driver who would be holding a cardboard sign with my name on it, I felt as if I had morphed into my father. The driver's resemblance to the company chauffeur who had taken us to the airport years ago when my father returned from his trips heightened the sensation, and it intensified even more when the car he drove turned out to be a gray Mercedes. Too bad I couldn't just press my nose to the window in the back and sing songs. Instead, I got to use the driver to unfurl my German language brain cells. He informed me he was taking me to a hotel that sounded like an Islamic religious observance. It dawned on me that he meant the "Ramada", but the word becomes barely recognizable when pronounced with the accent on the first syllable and the other two dragged along in a rush. RA- ma-da. *Oh great,* I thought, *they've put me up in an American chain hotel!*

By the time Dr. Körner picked me up, I had managed to revive myself by means of a shower. Even though I knew she was a brand-new Ph.D., I was surprised that she showed up in career woman drag: navy blue suit with conservative blouse, very tailored, 2 inch heels. When she spotted me, I detected a flicker of disappointment on her face. I tried to see myself through her eyes, and had to agree. I hadn't dressed to impress. I was slipping, becoming casual. I was wearing a dress and an off-white raw silk jacket with beige flats. Probably what a German housewife would wear shopping. I sensed the familiar panic going for my throat. I was certain I could hear her thinking *Those Americans. They have no style.*

For an instant, I wished I had brought my most formal suit, but then I glimpsed the outline of a revolutionary thought. Why was I so convinced the German way was superior? What was wrong with choosing comfort? Why couldn't I be proud of my own style? I thought of all the male German visitors who showed up at our lab in the last few years, every one of them wearing white socks and loafers with their business suits, because that was the height of fashion in Germany. How silly that looked, yet I hadn't heard anyone judge them for it.

Dr. Körner recovered quickly and ushered me into her car. She drove me to the best restaurant in Heidelberg for an expense account meal, and we managed to chat with only the usual amount of discomfort that results from two introverts trying to make conversation without dwelling exclusively on the work that brought them together. She asked me a lot of questions about women in technical careers in America. The only part of the meal I remember clearly is the dessert, and that only because it was a gourmet version of *rote Grütze* - a berry gelatin concoction my grandmother occasionally fed me. German nouvelle cuisine. Now that was interesting.

The next day triggered memories of visiting my father at work. Rows of offices with closed doors, people knocking to gain admission, coffee brought in at ten in the morning and served in china cups and saucers, instead of gulped all day from mugs. I held my own somehow, and by the end of the day, I knew the proper German words for every variation of data collection relevant to this project. If nothing else, I convinced myself that I could learn to adapt and quickly. The rest of the trip I switched back and forth between German and English constantly as I visited several of 3M's German sites.

Just before I left for a quick trip to the East, I found myself with a talkative cabbie, a German woman in her early twenties. When she heard that I was German, but lived in America, she was intrigued. As she started and stopped her Mercedes at what felt like every stoplight during Frankfurt's rush hour, she said, "I've always wondered why Americans are so arrogant. Why don't any of them ever bother to learn any foreign languages? Almost everybody else tries to speak at least a few words of German when they're here."

Arrogant? To my surprise, I felt a wash of defensiveness. "They're afraid."

"Afraid?" She cast a quick glance into the backseat before shifting gears.

"Yes, they think learning a foreign language is really difficult, and they worry about sounding stupid." I could tell she didn't quite believe me. I needed her to understand. "When you live in the US, the country is so big that you never really go anywhere where English isn't spoken, so there's no pressure to learn other languages. When you live here, you bungle other languages on every vacation, and you learn that it doesn't matter if you get it perfect, as long as you communicate."

She shook her head. "And I thought they were just being narrow-minded."

I sat in the back of her cab, astounded at myself. It wasn't so much that my identity was shifting. I felt a splitting in my sympathies. I couldn't have been more shocked if I had glanced in a mirror and discovered multiple heads.

I had no hint that the forces of politics were about to demolish more of my lifelong certainties.

TECTONIC SHIFT

I dragged my suitcase down the sweep of marble stairs to the Leipzig train station lobby. Tante Isolde carried my handbag. At the bottom of the steps, she leaned close to me and whispered: "Those two, they're bolting. They're taking off for Hungary."

I turned in the direction her eyes signaled. Two young people - a boy and a girl, neither more than eighteen - stood in a dark alcove in front of a ticket counter. Matching orange frame packs rose high above their heads. The sign over the counter read *Sozialistisches Ausland* - socialist foreign countries. I searched their faces. They looked like hikers, off to the mountains. He stowed his wallet, while she checked her watch. Weren't they afraid? It was true the Hungarians had gotten lax about enforcing their borders, but in 1988 escape still required sneaking through dark forests, evading border patrols. If my aunt saw their plan, so would the border guards. Would they even get to Hungary? I telegraphed thoughts of luck.

Isolde grinned, her eyes excited behind thick lenses. Did she wish herself young and able to take such a risk? Would she want her son and daughters to make a run for it? We couldn't talk about it here, in the middle of the Leipzig train station.

Isolde and I crossed the vaulted hall. Layers of grime dulled its nineteenth century splendor. Leipzig had once been an elegant European city; its present-day dowdiness was due to decades of communist neglect. My aunt and I checked each other out with sidelong glances. In recent years, I had spent little time alone with Isolde. I had been busy translating, first for Matt, later for Ron. Isolde looked good for a woman in her late fifties, plump enough to smooth out the wrinkles. She had let her hair return to its natural color - dark brown with a shake of gray. Her red short-sleeved sweater and gathered flower-print skirt were a little girlish for my taste, but Onkel Horst had always liked that in his wife.

When I stayed with them as a child, I asked her once why she wore baby doll nightgowns to bed. She giggled, "It's what he wants me to wear." Although she and my mother were sisters, I couldn't imagine my mother doing or saying such a thing. Her nightgowns were high-necked because she hated getting cold shoulders during the night.

What did Isolde see, when she glanced at me? My business clothes were stuffed into my suitcase; I was done with that part of the trip. I was thirty-six years old, in jeans and a t-shirt, my body trim from regular trips to the gym. If I hadn't known that no amount of careful blow-drying would hide the streak of gray hair in front, I might have tried to pass for a young kid myself. When I saw myself through her eyes, I looked more American than I realized.

Isolde and I chatted a little too brightly, dealing in travel practicalities. I had forgotten what a major undertaking a drive to Leipzig was for her. Bad Düben was almost an hour-long drive away. From my American perspective, a one-hour drive was, if not exactly trivial, certainly reasonable. But in East Germany even the farthest distance took less than a day to drive.

We stepped through heavy doors into bright, June sun and a barrage of diesel fumes and crackling motors. Mopeds buzzed past lines of idling buses. Tinny Trabbis and an occasional Lada or Moskwitch sputtered by. Crowds of surly pedestrians crested on islands between traffic lanes and rushed across with the signal lights. Bland five and six-story concrete buildings surrounded the square; they were erected in a hurry after World War II, because American bombs intended for the station had wiped out the surrounding neighborhood. The big *Konsum* - a state-owned department store built in the seventies - provided the only visual thrill. It flashed a sculpted aluminum exterior. The people of Leipzig called it the 'tin can' and avoided it in the summer. The architects had neglected to take into account the interior temperatures a windowless aluminum-covered building would generate in the absence of air-conditioning. My relatives ridiculed it as a prime example of socialist planning.

My aunt's red Wartburg clanged as she opened the trunk. The sharp tang of gas stung my nostrils. We squeezed my luggage in next to the spare gas cans that every East German carried. Gas stations had limited hours and long lines. Isolde peered anxiously behind her before backing out of her spot. We clattered away from the station on an old boulevard, whose surface was a jumble of cobblestones, asphalt patches, sandy potholes, and slick tram tracks.

Since my cousins had grown up, Isolde worked part-time running the office for the veterinary collective. Both she and Horst were on salary now; gone were the days when he was still able to have a private veterinary practice and collect a portion of his pay in meat, vegetables, sometimes even mushrooms. Once the government had sealed the borders in the sixties, it no longer needed to cater to scarce professionals to keep them from escaping. Vets and doctors were collectivized.

We entered the house through the sun porch with its jungle of hanging plants and worn Vietnamese grass rug. Horst sat waiting at the kitchen table, his chair tipped back against the wall. He was still tall, handsome and deeply tanned as every summer, but the many glasses of vodka consumed in front of the TV every night had thickened his middle. He stubbed out a cigarette as he shouted out a jovial welcome, then rose to give me a hug that was slightly too tight. His cigarette smell mingled with a whiff of cow manure.

Isolde tied on an apron and told me what she planned to fix for lunch: cucumber salad, boiled potatoes and scrambled eggs. A workaday meal my mother used to fix once a week in the summer. I peeled cucumbers at the table while Horst lit a new cigarette and tipped his chair back again. He wanted to hear all about my trip, but within minutes the conversation veered to the fools who ran the East German government.

"Those idiots, those Reds, all they know is how to harass people and make life difficult." He told me that the West Germans were only propping them up. "If all the relatives would stop sending hard currency and goods, the whole economy would collapse on itself." I had never heard this theory before, so he elaborated. The only way to get a carpenter or hire anybody else anymore was to pay them in West mark.

"And the Russians, those poor dogs, do you see how they lock up their soldiers in their barracks? Whenever they let them out, you can see how hungry those poor suckers are, and what rundown trucks and old tanks they rely on. The Americans could blow them over if they had the guts. Your President Reagan's got the right idea."

I couldn't let that one go. "Reagan? He doesn't have a clue about foreign policy."

Horst laughed. "Of course, I can tell he's dumb. But he's right about standing up to the Russians." His voice rose and he reddened slightly. He got up and paced back and forth. "*Ist doch alles Quatsch -* it's all nonsense," he spat out. Then he growled, "Call me when we're ready to eat, I'm going out to the vegetable garden."

I slid the cucumbers up and down on the slicer, creating thin, perfect cucumber rounds. I added oil and vinegar, dill, mustard and sour cream, just the way my mother did.

After lunch, I hauled my suitcase upstairs, and pushed it into the room Omi Paula had used on weekends. Omi had died in this house from a stroke a few years before. Some of her old furniture - dark wood living room pieces, too big for a bedroom - greeted me. I peeked into the bedroom next door. Matthias's old bedroom. Matthias was living in his old room again, since his divorce. He'd be back later, Isolde had said. I never met Matthias' wife. His entire marriage took place during the time Isolde and I weren't speaking. Matthias' furniture came from Tante Anni's living room. She'd given it to him when she moved into a rest home. For just a second, I envied my cousin for being able to inherit the tangibles of our childhood.

Matthias arrived just in time for *Kaffeeklatsch*. He fumed about the heat. He baked in full sun on the highway for three hours on his way back from meeting his thesis advisor in Dresden. Within a few months he would be a doctor of dentistry. He looked flushed, his black hair sweated into strands. His round face and big brown eyes marked him as my mother's relative. In fact, he looked more like her than I do.

He gave me a big sweaty hug, apologizing for being so sticky, and settled in for coffee at the kitchen table. I was anxious to hear whether Matthias might consider sneaking out of the country. When he was in kindergarten he collected model airplanes and dreamed of traveling the world.

"Not now," he said. He took another sip of coffee. Then he straightened his spine and leaned forward. "It's tempting, but if I'm going to leave I want to wait until I finish my degree." He paused again. "One of my friends applied for an exit visa. Of course, if you do that, you can't find work and you have to sit there with your suitcases packed waiting for who knows how long. Somebody I know in Leipzig had to wait three years. And then they tell you to leave and you have twenty-four hours." He shook his head. "The problem with escaping through Hungary is that you can never come back."

Isolde nodded. "You could never see your family again." She looked at Matthias, her lips tight. "At least they're loosening travel a little. It's getting easier to visit relatives in the West. I hope Horst and I will get a visa to come to your mother's sixtieth birthday this winter."

Matthias left to take a shower, and I offered to wash the dishes. Isolde stayed to dry.

The next morning, by the time I got up, Matthias and Onkel Horst were gone to work. Tante Isolde had taken the day off, so after breakfast we decided to go to Eilenburg for some shopping. On the way, Tante Isolde lamented that you could never find what you wanted in the stores. It was such a familiar litany that I heard echoes of my grandmother's voice, my great-aunt's voice, and the voices of the workers in my grandfather's factory. Scarcity was the background of every shopping expedition in East Germany. "There's nothing in the stores, and what there is isn't what you want."

Tante Isolde said that little black cotton sweaters were all the rage, and she was hoping to find some for her daughters in a new boutique in Eilenburg. The word boutique caught my attention. I had never heard it in connection with an East German store before. I was stunned when we climbed the stairs to the second floor above one of the stores along Eilenburg's main street. When we stepped into the salesroom, it looked like a real clothing store. There were round racks crammed with dresses and skirts, shirts and sweaters in all sizes. The clothes were imported from India, the kind of clothes I might buy at home in St. Paul. Tante Isolde swept through the racks wrinkling her nose. "Nothing. They've got nothing. Not a single thing in black."

Outside, I struggled to explain how amazed I was. Tante Isolde dismissed my surprise. "Oh, it's all from India. That's one of the few countries poor enough to sell us stuff for our funny money." Then she shrugged and admitted that the government was trying to have more goods in the stores, but they just couldn't get it right.

We crossed the street and walked around the corner to a small square shop I had never noticed before. Tante Isolde explained that it was a *Privatbäckerei* - a private bakery. She wanted to pick up pastries for that afternoon's *Kaffeeklatsch*. Limited free enterprise appeared to be another government experiment. The bakery appeared plain on the outside - not like the West German bakeries that displayed pastries on mirrors and on crystal stands festooned with lace, but the selection inside was surprisingly large. The store was empty of customers. A few years earlier, there had been a line at every store that had anything worth buying. As we carried our apple and strawberry tarts back to Tante Isolde's car, past the people with their closed, tight faces, I wondered if it was a problem of too little too late, or if people had gotten so used to complaining that they didn't know how to stop. Or maybe grousing about shortages was a way to grieve deeper needs, frustrated longings that were harder to quantify.

When Matthias returned from work late in the afternoon, the two of us set out for the nursing home where Tante Anni had moved after she sold the farmhouse. In her letters, she complained that Tante Isolde and Onkel Horst and the girls never came to see her, just Matthias, whom she loved dearly. He said Tante Anni was still as sharp as ever, but her world was shrinking to the nursing home news now, since it was getting harder for her to make the walk into town. She obsessed about the caretakers, the other residents, who lived and who died. In her shared room she had a picture above her bed that once hung over the sofa in the old farmhouse. In it, summer was endless. A girl in a straw hat sat on an old log at the edge of a stream and dangled her feet in the cool green water.

Tante Anni sat at the edge of her bed, dressed and waiting. She was shrinking, but her eyes were sharp. Some of her hair was still brown. She watched us with a smile in her eyes, as her roommate hailed us in a loud voice. Frau Ferber was an amputee, and as Tante Anni put it "a little vulgar," but I guessed they liked each other. They lived in the same room for many years. Tante Anni pulled herself up with her worn wooden cane to receive my hug. I'm only five-two, but I had to bend down a little. She turned and rummaged on her windowsill, then offered me some chocolates I had sent for her birthday.

She whispered: "Thanks for sending two packages. That way I can give a little something special to the nurses. You know they won't treat you well if you don't give them something from the West once in a while."

Matthias and I escorted her down the long linoleum hallway, past men propped up in chairs next to dusty green plants. We settled her in the car's back seat as one of the male residents called out to her: "You get to go for a visit today, eh?" Tante Anni wrinkled her face and said, "Some of the people here are not too well bred."

I sat next to Tante Anni while the family gathered around the big dining room table for pastries and coffee. I noticed that her voice trembled even more than it always had, and that her hearing was getting dimmer. Onkel Horst shouted jovial questions at her. "How's old Ferber getting along?" and "Are they still trying to kick you out of your room?" Tante Anni answered his questions at length and with great emotion in her voice, but Horst was focused on his cake and coffee. She ended up looking at Matthias and me. After Horst left to work outside, Tante Isolde tried to make conversation with Anni. She asked about Thea, Tante Anni's old friend and neighbor, but Tante Anni's complaints that Thea had been too busy to come visit lately clearly irritated her. "You can't take it so personally. She's been sick," Tante Isolde said. We passed around more chocolates, and loaded Tante Anni back into the car.

The next morning dawned bright and sunny again. It was time for me to leave. After breakfast, I hauled my luggage back into Tante Isolde's car. As we drove to the train station, she asked about my mother. She told me she didn't like what she saw on her last visit. "She looked so tense, not happy at all."

"When she comes to Germany, she always has mixed feelings. She's glad to be here, but upset that she can't stay," I said.

Tante Isolde nodded and sighed. "It must be hard for her. She clearly isn't happy living in South Carolina. At least I never had to move away from home, and I have my children close by."

I sat up to listen more closely. All my life, I had heard only how awful it was to live here, how lucky we were to have gotten out. This was the first hint I ever had that Tante Isolde knew there had been a price to pay.

She went on to talk about the accommodations that my mother had had to make for my father. Not just moving, but how she had to spend weeks and months alone while he traveled on business. Then she surprised me by going further. "Your father's pretty miserly, too. She didn't grow up like that. I remember in the fifties when I could go to West Germany for a visit once. We went shopping one day. Your grandfather had given me some West mark. I found a blouse I really liked, so I bought it. Your mother really liked it too, but she wouldn't buy one for herself. She said they couldn't afford it right now and her husband would get really mad."

I had to puzzle over this story for a moment before I understood. For Tante Isolde's family in East Germany, there had never been a shortage of cash. A shortage of goods to spend it on, yes. But the money had always been there. When I was small, my parents had the opposite problem - trying to wrap my father's earnings around our needs. Was it possible that Tante Isolde didn't realize my parents were poor at first?

We pulled into the small parking lot. Concrete containers in front of the station bloomed with red and blue pansies. The bathroom was as old as I remembered, but it smelled clean and there was toilet paper. As we paced on the quay waiting for my train in the railroad station wind, I told her how nice it was to see flowers and a clean bathroom. "Honecker and his government know they have to do something to try to satisfy people. But it's only window-dressing. They still make people jump through hoops like they always did," she answered.

Then she told me how nice it was that I came for a visit. That she was glad I wasn't forgetting my relatives, stuck here in this old hole, and that she and Horst would probably meet me in South Carolina for my mother's birthday if they got government permission to travel. Their application had been handed in over a month ago. She thought they should hear soon. She was hopeful. I knew it gnawed at her that my parents would have to pay for the plane tickets - only Western currency was acceptable. Neither of us knew then that Isolde and Horst's visit to Clemson, to the house on the lake, would only stoke their sense that we were the clear-cut winners in the game of chance that was History. We hugged as the train pulled in.

I waved from the open window when the train began to move. As I watched Tante Isolde recede on the platform, I felt a surge of affection - a pull of blood and memory. Or perhaps it was nostalgia for the days when she had been a student nurse home on a visit, and I had admired her singing as she watered my grandmother's plants. I hoped that our falling out had been an aberration we could safely forget.

*****

"The German Democratic Republic, half of a divided German nation, is...the most stable socialist state in Eastern Europe." I found this quote in a book published in 1988, written by Mike Dennis, a British Researcher who specialized in East Germany. I felt better when I read it. I wasn't alone in imagining the East German state to be eternal.

During 1989, as more and more East Germans braved the implicit threat of a crackdown and gathered on the streets I held my breath. How bloody would the outcome be? The Chinese crushed the hope that was Tiananmen Square on June 4, 1989. Would tanks leave stiff bodies lying in pools of blood in Leipzig and Berlin? Would it be like June 17, 1953 in Berlin or like Hungary in 1956? I was too young to remember either of those uprisings, but I'd been reared on stories of tanks rumbling across cobbled squares to aim their guns at people armed only with paving stones.

I was old enough to remember the Prague Spring in 1968. That thaw in the socialist ice age had lasted just long enough to permit me to nurse sprigs of hope. If the Czechs could melt the edges of Soviet control, slowly, carefully, then maybe the East Germans could widen the patch of soft ground and plant a few flowers of their own. So, although I was only fifteen when the Russians sent in their tanks that time, or maybe because I was fifteen - it is after all an age where we feel injustice keenly, and are often choked with a sense of powerlessness - I felt intense shock and defeat when Dubcek toppled and Prague returned instantly to the deep freeze.

Of course, the East German government, whether alone or with help from the Russians - who could have believed that Gorbachev would keep his army immobile in their barracks? - would eventually put a stop to the demonstrations. Each week, as the numbers grew and the demonstrators' voices strengthened, as more and more East Germans voted with their feet by making their escape through the dismantled Austro-Hungarian border, my feelings grew more conflicted. I teetered between abandoning myself to hope and reigning myself in with caution. I was like a reluctant lover trying to protect myself from pain. Surely, I couldn't trust this building joy. Any minute now, they would bring on the tanks.

When I look back now, I calculate that events moved so swiftly that I couldn't have suffered these emotions for more than a few months. The last trip we took to East Germany before the Wall fell was in late September of 1989. Ron and I had arranged to join my parents in Bad Düben, at Tante Isolde's. On a Monday, Isolde, Ron, my mother and I decided to drive to Leipzig to sightsee and shop. Ron drove our West German rental car. Isolde got in the back with my mother, and we set off on Route 2, dodging potholes.

We emerged from the narrow streets of town to a sudden back up at the Mulde River Bridge. Several police officers had propped a wooden board on sawhorses to create a makeshift barricade. We waited in line, speculating. Although our windows were closed and we were still two cars back, Isolde leaned her head forward and hissed her guess into our ears, "They're checking who's going to Leipzig because of the *Montagsdemonstrationen.*" The Monday demonstrations. All summer, growing numbers of people had been gathering to demonstrate on Monday evenings at one of the Leipzig churches. The East German police probably had pictures and names of every participant. They were no doubt controlling all the roads leading to Leipzig to get license plate numbers and to intimidate. What surprised me was that they set up checkpoints this far away from the city. From here the distance was thirty-four km, a good fifteen miles.

"Are you scared?" I asked Isolde. I noticed that my body was going into habitual East German police response mode - if someone had tried to bend me, I would have snapped. And I didn't even live here. What, really, could they do to me? But if Isolde wanted to turn around, I would understand.

"What can they do?" Isolde said. "Get the number of your rental car?" Her voice had a jaunty air, like a kid laying down a dare.

We reached the front of the line. We'd never know what the police were telling their own citizens, since we drove a Western Opel with Düsseldorf plates. The police officer politely asked us our plans for the day. He bent down to smile at me as I shouted answers from the passenger side. He may have even wished us a nice day, before waving us through. Isolde sighed and leaned back into her seat.

We hadn't lied. We were going to Leipzig to shop - we had to spend our East German money. We hunted through the usual craft stores in the first-floor arcades, bought a few antique print reproductions at a bookstore, and a classical record or two. At lunchtime, we jockeyed for position in line at a state-run restaurant and waited most of an hour for a table. When our turn finally came the hostess yelled at us for trying to cut in front of someone she considered more deserving - we hadn't - and we had to wait another ten minutes.

After lunch, we decided to visit the church that sparked the demonstrations. We first noticed the secret police at the crosswalks. Men in windbreakers, holding briefcases, stood as if waiting, but when the lights changed, they stayed in place. More of them dotted the square in front of the Nikolai church. Sprinkled through the milling crowds they stood, some wearing gray jackets, some wearing blue, some with nylon shopping bags, some with brief cases, trying hard to look casual. Isolde made sure we were out of earshot before explaining, "They're *Stasi*." Would they be that obvious? Isolde said they probably wanted people to know they were watching. I hesitated. Isolde said, "Come on. I want to go in. They can't stop us from sightseeing."

The interior of the church was painted pure white. I had never seen an East German church so crowded with visitors. Whispers echoed in the tall space. The air hummed with tension and excitement. I barely registered the lovely palm frond columns that stretch up to the leafy Gothic vaults. In the narthex, wooden boards displayed invitations to the weekly 'peace gathering.' A manifesto issued by a dissident political group, complete with supporters' signatures, hung from another wall. The huge church dwarfed these brave posters, and I felt very small reading them. Where did people find the courage to resist against such overwhelming odds? I felt constrained just by the windbreakered agents that wound through the crowd inside the church. They kept their eyes wide open to let you know they saw. If I had grown up being watched like that, would I shuffle out of sight? Or would I ever reach a point of saying, enough?

We read every word on the posters before we even made a show of studying the paintings at the altar. The crowd outside thickened as we left, just two hours before the service. As we walked back to the parking lot near the train station, trucks crammed with soldiers rumbled past. What would the police and army do? That night, watching the West German news on the TV in Isolde's living room, we saw 5000 people crammed into the square, every one of them more daring than I could imagine. The government forces stood by and watched.

A few days later, after we left East Germany, Ron and I lay on a narrow bed in a small West German hotel room. We watched the *Tagesschau* - the daily evening news - complete with footage of an even larger demonstration and the latest totals for the number of East Germans seeking political asylum at the West German embassy in Prague. They were gathering in Czechoslovakia, because after the loss of ten thousand through Hungary, the DDR stopped issuing visas for that country. After the program finished, I amused myself by flipping channels. Suddenly, I saw the logo for the East German news, *Aktuelle Kamera* - Topical Camera. We were close to the border, but it had never occurred to me that you could watch East German TV in the West. "I bet none of the people around here buy high-powered antennas to get this channel," Ron said. In East Germany, every apartment building bristled with antennas designed to catch West German TV channels.

On screen, Erich Honecker, the East German head of state, stood at a boxy podium at the front of an auditorium. Behind him hung a bright red velvet curtain decorated with a gilded DDR seal. The podium also bore the State Seal. On the floor, in front of the podium, bloomed a huge bouquet of flowers. Party officials in identical gray suits filled a row of red chairs on the stage. Almost all the men wore glasses, and their frames were identical. Identical to the ones worn by their leader. I had seen those frames on East German border guards. The voice-over described preparations for the fortieth anniversary celebration of the DDR. An envoy from North Korea climbed the stage, shook Honecker's hand and read a statement in laborious German. He congratulated the East German people on their stable, peaceful and prosperous state. A rush of applause followed. Honecker shook the Korean's hand and thanked him with another short speech. End of scene. The announcer continued with his routine of nightly news, none of it even glancing on the real news East Germans were making.

"They're just going to pretend nothing's happening," I told Ron. "The news is the same as ever. Glorifying the DDR, complaining about capitalist, imperialist countries, touting the latest factory production quotas. Not a word about the growing refugee problem or the demonstrations. Do you suppose they think that if they just close their eyes, it will all go away?" I didn't really believe that, though. I was afraid that this silence was meant to hide preparations to bash the protestors' heads before sealing the borders more tightly once again.

We watched the news - the West German news - nightly in our hotel rooms as we made our way to cousin Ulrike's house in Düsseldorf. Every day, more East German families sneaked through the woods in back of the Prague embassy, then climbed across the walls to get in.

Rains turned the grounds into a morass. Prague citizens passed food to the East Germans through the iron fence. The numbers grew. By the time we sat in Ulrike's living room watching once again, the number had grown to 4000. The TV cameras showed a sodden group, shivering, packed close. Then the cameras shifted to the balcony to show the West German foreign minister as he stepped forward. Hans-Dietrich Genscher, himself an East German refugee - you could hear the echoes of Saxony in every word - only made it through the first sentence of his speech. *"Liebe Landesleute, ich bin gekommen um Ihnen mitzuteilen daß heute Ihre Ausreise...*- Dear countrymen, I have come to inform you that your emigration has been negotiated...a cheer drowned out the rest. The cheer leapt from the TV into our throats. Ulrike and I shouted - I tossed a quick explanation to Ron, then laughed and cried, and laughed and cried some more. I didn't stop to analyze why I was so elated. Knowing that the crowd, all 4000 of them, could leave was all that mattered. They were free, and the East German government wasn't going to stop them. Every single one who could get out was a victory.

I hated to leave Germany the next day. I was excited and hopeful, although I still feared the worst. Nothing like this had ever happened before. I had no way to imagine where it was going. I didn't want to miss a thing.

Back in Minnesota, we decided to take a dramatic step. For years, we kept the TV in the basement - a compromise we preferred over getting rid of it entirely. This way, we had to go to some trouble to watch it, which we only did for major events like the Olympics. But now, we wanted to watch the news every night. I felt breathless every evening, as I watched report after report on the growing streams of refugees, thousands each week. Germany set up special *Auffanglanger* - reception camps, to temporarily house the swelling tide. Every Monday the crowds in Leipzig grew larger, though the threat of violence did too. Now there were almost 100,000 shouting, *"Wir sind das Volk"* - we are the people - but soldiers and the Party faithful encircled them. There were arrests. But mostly, the soldiers stood and watched. And the crowds kept growing. The demonstrations spread to all the major East German cities. My parents and I called each other daily instead of once a week on Sunday morning. We repeated the news back to each other, and speculated what would happen next. Every remark Gorbachev made we turned inside out for significance. On October eighteenth, the Party tried to stem the tide of protest by forcing Honecker to resign. Our heads spun with the speed of events. And yet, I still held back, knowing that at any moment the tanks could roll. Until November ninth, when the Wall cracked open. Even I knew then that the change was irreversible.

Years before, trying to fall asleep in my bed in Krefeld, I had dreamed of the East Germans crashing through the Wall, but had put away that dream as a childish fantasy. I sat in front of my TV, sobbing, not even trying to control my tears. I installed a box of Kleenex next to my chair, because it didn't matter how often the news replayed those scenes of celebration, it didn't matter how many different East Germans they interviewed, each time I started crying all over again.

My body felt weightless. Being in East Germany felt like struggling against increased gravity - like walking on Jupiter. The very air had weight. What I hadn't realized was that I carried some of that weight with me, just knowing it existed for my relatives after I left. Suddenly my body could expand. I would never have to fight that extra weight again.

The next day, still shaky from joyful tears, Ron and I boarded a plane for Washington, D.C. It's hard to remember that in 1989, I had concerns that had nothing to do with Germany. The Religious Right looked to be growing ever stronger. To me, their attack on women's rights felt viscerally threatening. I had dreams of being cornered by crowds of tight-lipped men carrying guns, men who wanted to kill me for being an affront to their vision of womanhood. Ron and I had decided to participate in a rally for abortion rights on the Capitol Mall. I had never protested before. During the Vietnam War, South Carolina hadn't exactly been a hotbed of activism, but when opportunities presented themselves I avoided them because I was afraid I might get deported. Back then, I still thought of myself as a guest in America, a temporary resident.

My parents, my sister, and Cori decided to join us. So we converged - the day after the Wall fell - on a corporate suite near Dupont Circle that Ron had managed to procure at a discount through his job.

The carpeting was thick and beige. Nica and I spread poster board on the floor and settled down with purple markers. *Every Child A Wanted Child, America is Based on Choice,* and *Keep Your Laws Off My Body.* The posters took shape as we sipped white wine. Our mother sat on the couch watching. Cori worked at the glass dining table.

Finished posters leaned against dining chairs. Ron dug out the lath and staple gun he'd carried from Minnesota in his luggage. Time for the eleven o'clock news. Images of East Germans dancing on the Wall, drenching each other with champagne, and leaning laughing into water cannons splashed across the screen. I thought this time I might not cry. It was the accents that did it. Underneath the translation, I strained for voices thick with accents I never expected to hear on TV. East German accents that belonged to the private sphere of family visits, not the public sphere of TV news.

I sneaked a blurry peek at my mother and saw glistening tracks down her cheeks. My sister sniffled and even my father's eyes were about to brim over. We passed the tissues and smiled until our cheeks ached. Ron and Cori couldn't help but grin.

The protest on the Mall was a giant picnic. A few hundred thousand of us crammed around the reflecting pool, too far away from the stage at the Lincoln Memorial to hear the speakers as more than a wavering wisp in the balmy air. Nica and I decided to make our way closer to the stage. We worshipped Alice Walker, who was the featured speaker. We got close enough to identify her round, beaming face and expansive braids, but her voice rode the wind and dispersed before we could catch it. People smiled, shared soda pop, and waited in orderly lines at port-a-potties. Toddlers waddled around women and men supporting themselves with canes. Many wore t-shirts from previous marches. We sat on the grass, our posters stacked. There was no one to convince.

After a few hours, the thin sound from the far away speakers stopped, and the crowd dribbled back toward the city streets. We ambled past federal office buildings, past the park rangers who were directing traffic. Later, we heard estimates that the crowd had been between 280,000 and a half million strong. Did it matter?

At the last protest in Leipzig, the count had been a little over 200,000. Every one of those people had risked their lives to be there and they had changed the world. We risked nothing more than a sneer from the few counter protesters we encountered on the way back to the hotel. If we were lucky, our rally would merit a picture and an article in the Washington Post. I wasn't complaining. I was glad I had come to Washington. I did feel better having done something instead of sitting at home fretting and stewing. But mostly I was glad that I had come so I could share the Berlin Wall's collapse with my family.

If the Berlin Wall could fall, anything could happen. Precisely because it had seemed so permanent before its collapse, its sudden cracking and dissolution filled the world with possibilities. The East Germans could develop a new kind of government, a third way between capitalism and socialism. Women there would retain the protections that had made East Germany look so good on paper: universal subsidized childcare, a fully paid maternity year for each baby. My parents could move home, we could resurrect my grandfather's factory. I could live in both places at once. I could become a potter and a writer and have a baby and... Logic had nothing to do with any of it. I felt like the doors of my heart were thrown wide open and I could merge with the world.

In the months that followed, our international long distance charges took a huge leap. My mother called Tante Isolde, my father called his brother Klaus, the only one in his family with a phone, even I started calling my relatives, just to hear directly from them how it felt to be let out of jail. It didn't matter what we talked about. We beamed good will toward each other and everyone else. When the Velvet Revolution in Czechoslovakia followed we didn't even mind too much that suddenly the Czechs were considered the experts in bloodless revolution, even though the East Germans had modeled it first. Peaceful revolution clearly didn't fit with the international image of Germans. We were busy trying to figure out who we were now that the border was porous and rapidly dissolving.

*****

Omi Hedwig turned 90 in June of 1990. Attendance at the celebration was close to mandatory, but I wouldn't have wanted to miss it anyway. Omi Hedwig loved to party. Whenever I visited as a child, she found an occasion to push all the tables together and invite everyone in the family and a few old friends. Twenty or more people ranging from two to sixty squeezed into the living room. Somehow the commotion and crowding didn't bother me as much when there was an official occasion. There would be platters of cold cuts, hard-boiled eggs, pickles, and cases of soft drinks, beer and bottles of liqueur. Later in the evening, Omi Hedwig disappeared into her bedroom for a visit to her locked wardrobe. She'd return carrying a box of West German pralines and some Lindt bars for the children. If someone threatened to leave, she'd call out "Oh, why don't you stay. Let's stay up all night!"

I loved that idea, but I knew my mother would never go for it. I bunched up with the other cousins at one end of the table. We'd get Onkel Dieter - he was Tante Gina's husband - to tell jokes. He could reel off one after another with a straight face. At first they started out gentle like this one: Once the Russians were our friends, now they are our brothers. Why is that? Answer: Because you can't pick your siblings. As he worked on his beer and enjoyed our laughter, he got more reckless. Why is the toilet paper in the DDR so rough? So every last ass turns red. We egged him on until he ran out. By midnight, Tante Gina yawned. "No, no, we need to go home and go to bed," she said, as she kissed Omi Hedwig goodnight and pried Onkel Dieter away. "Go find your son, he's bouncing off the walls, he's so tired." Those who could still stand washed the last glasses and put them away in the living room cabinet. I crawled off to bed, but I lay awake listening to the bongs from the grandfather clock, too excited to go to sleep. For me, Omi Hedwig and a proper family party were synonymous and I suspected her ninetieth birthday might be my last chance to see her in action. So Ron and I booked flights to Düsseldorf and lined up a rental car.

Although the Wall, the most potent symbol of the East German border had fallen, the border itself still existed and we were going to cross it one more time. As we got close, I felt myself tighten up out of habit, but I expected the crossing itself to be a breeze. After all, the East Germans had voted for reunification and it was scheduled for the fall of that year. Instead, we experienced the East German border police in their last hurrah. We swooped around a curve to encounter a huge line of cars. When we finally approached the border post, the inspection officer closed down his post and left us to linger in the June heat while he took his coffee break. We lost almost two hours.

The sense that nothing had changed evaporated as soon as we drew near the first rest area. A hand lettered sign advertised *Rostbratwürste*. Ron slowed the car a bit, so we could gawk at a battered trailer, next to a portable grill. A plume of seasoned smoke broadened out to the sky. A customer stood next to a car, munching a sausage. Free enterprise sending out shoots right on the Autobahn.

As we drove into Gera, we looked intently for other signs of change. Bright cigarette ads and Western-style election posters stood out against the drab cityscape. East Germany's first and last free elections had been held that spring, and they had voted overwhelmingly for reunification. On one wall, painted freehand in red letters, a slogan read: *Wer SED wählt, wählt ein leeres Land* - a vote for the Socialist Unity Party is a vote for an empty country. I chuckled as I pointed it out to the others. Except for a few Marlboro signs and pyramids of red and yellow peppers in the vegetable store windows, Calvinstrasse looked unchanged. It wasn't until the next day, strolling in the shopping district that I felt the change in atmosphere. Gone were the dour faces and furrowed brows. People weren't exactly smiling at strangers, but they did not look like they'd explode into pedestrian rage if you accidentally bumped into them. They walked taller, their shoulders straight, a bit of bounce in their step. I smelled hope.

Omi Hedwig's ninetieth birthday would have been a big party anyway, but now it fairly bubbled. Every single child and grandchild was in attendance. My aunts and uncle had arranged to rent a restaurant in walking distance where we could party from *Kaffeeklatsch* until the last bottle of wine had been consumed in the evening. The restaurant had paneled walls and lace curtained windows. The tables that lined the walls were covered in white cloths and decorated with bouquets in an assortment of vases provided by the family. My cousins' young children played recorders and recited poetry. My father, as the oldest son, gave a short speech and toasted his mother for keeping the family close in hard times. Hedwig, who was still physically fit enough to wear me out on a walk, but whose mind had suffered the incremental losses associated with small strokes, basked in the occasion. In her younger days, say her sixties, she would have insisted we party until breakfast, but now she settled for a late evening. The only attendees who didn't exude complete happiness were a few distant second cousins who had been among the Party faithful.

When the restaurant owner began to serve dinner, he sought out the *Wessis* - Westerners - in the crowd, and placed platters of steamed, sauced cauliflower in front of us with a flourish, "Now that we can get vegetables over here too, I just want you to know that we too know how to prepare them." I had never doubted that East Germans knew how to cook. Did he think we held *Ossis* - Easterners - responsible for shortages caused by socialist "planning"? Maybe there were West Germans ignorant enough to blame the victim. It never occurred to anyone I knew.

As I shifted tables and caught up with cousins I had only briefly glimpsed since childhood, I noticed that all our talk was of the future. Much of it was optimistic - they talked of trips they wanted to take - but uncertainty caused worries to creep in. When Germany unified its currency, would they have enough money? That worry was offset by the prospect of having real money and access to Western goods. How many factories would have to close, because they couldn't compete? When all was said and done, who would have jobs? One West German newspaper editorial had suggested that the way to avoid high unemployment in the East was to close all the day care centers and send all the women back home. While that wasn't official policy, day care centers were closing down for lack of money, and women were getting laid off in higher numbers than men. And what about property rights? How would the state settle what belonged to whom in a country where most of the real estate had been expropriated by the state thirty or forty years ago? What about social policy? When unification happened in October, would East German women lose their *Babyjahr* - the year of paid maternity leave - they had come to take for granted? Anxieties swirled just under the surface. No one wanted to spoil the mood by complaining. After all, even with worries, this was better than before the *Wende* - the turning point.

After the party, my father's siblings got down to business. The state had not requisitioned the Calvinstrasse house - my grandparents had remained the outright owners. One of my cousins wanted to buy it from Omi Hedwig so he could take out a mortgage and renovate the building. Uwe had trained as an electrician and intended to use the ground floor to start his own business. In principle, everyone agreed with his plan. The problem was how to put a value on the building. I heard rumors of intense arguments between my aunts and uncles. These spilled over to the rest of us. Pretty soon we were all weighing in on whether we would feel cheated if property values skyrocketed and Uwe alone profited. The majority of us agreed with my father that East German reconstruction looked likely to be a long slow process. Besides, no one else wanted to live in the house, take out a loan, and supervise construction. The faction that felt Uwe owed us future profits was defeated after a few days of sometimes acrimonious debate. The house would go to Uwe for a sum approved by the bank.

My father rejoiced that he had been instrumental in preserving family unity against the threat of greed.

*****

While we were in Bad Düben, the government announced that property expropriated by the East German state would be returned to the original owners. What would that mean? We sat around Tante Isolde's dining room table, faces rosy in the copper lamp's shine, speculating. Our first thought was of the factory. The sisters put their heads together to reconstruct events.

"He arranged to sell out to the state in the event of his death," Isolde was certain. "He didn't want to risk the state simply taking over without paying his widow."

My mother nodded. "She told me she got sixteen thousand marks. But what about the apartment house?"

By the time Opa Gustav had died in 1971, the house was in terrible disrepair, because of the shortage of building materials that plagued the DDR throughout its existence. He had transferred ownership of that to the state too, so Omi Paula wouldn't have to bear the cost of renovation. "The only way to challenge the state's ownership is to argue that they didn't pay Omi Paula for the full value of the property. That could work."

My father nodded. He rubbed his hands and sat up straighter. "I bet it would. Especially since they need help figuring out how to run businesses. But what exactly did the factory produce? And what kind of equipment did it have?"

I closed my eyes. That way I could take better inventory. I counted the women upstairs and the men downstairs, then felt my way along the machines that lined the assembly room and pictured the big equipment in the carpentry shop. To my surprise, I now had names for the machinery, though only in English. What was a router in German? Or a drill press? Isolde and my mother confirmed what they could, though they hadn't been allowed into the factory as often as I had.

My father drooped a bit when we figured out that most of the equipment dated from 1933 or before. Isolde added that she saw Frau Mauser, who still handled shipping, while shopping in Eilenburg. "She says they're losing money."

"It's still worth a try," my mother said. "At least we could get the house back even if the company goes bankrupt."

We stayed up late into the evenings, drinking wine, eating snacks, talking and talking some more. Tante Isolde's daughter Annett, an agricultural engineer, came one night and poured out her worries about the future. Her collective farm seethed with confusion. One day they talked about finding ways to turn themselves into a profitable agricultural company, the next they worried about whether they would get sued by the former property owners for letting the property run down.

"The former owners all fled because they didn't want to work for the collective. They abandoned their property. Now they want it back, they can ruin us by suing us for not maintaining it. That's not fair either," Annett said. She thought she would surely lose her job, and there wouldn't be any other jobs for her with her training. She'd probably need to go back to school.

Onkel Horst returned from work ecstatic one evening. The West German government had announced that it intended to fund the veterinary collectives for several years to ease the transition. He had a job, at least for the foreseeable future. His voice boomed, as we toasted his news. We spent hours that night discussing the pros and cons of the choices Horst and my father had made, trying to weigh the costs of rootlessness against government intimidation and stunted lives. My mother went so far as to wonder out loud whether we would have been better off staying in Eilenburg and waiting it out. I thought she must be insane. Just trying to imagine having been born and raised in East Germany made me feel like my body was trapped in a vise. She couldn't mean it. I waited until we were alone to challenge her. She looked surprised by my ferocity, but she did start to back-pedal. But she would only go so far as to admit that the situation looked different in hindsight. Could she really mean she would have preferred forty years of East Germany to the life she'd had? She wouldn't answer.

The next afternoon, we picked up Tante Anni at the nursing home and drove her to Isolde's. After strawberry torte and whipped cream, we rested in the living room, on the couch and easy chairs grouped around the coffee table. Tante Anni sat next to me, her hands grasping the top of her cane, her eyes bright, as she recalled her girlhood on the farm.

Isolde leaned forward and shouted, "Did you hear about the government planning to give us our property back?"

"Yes. Anything they took after 1956. They didn't steal our fields from us until 1959."

Isolde asked, "Where did your parents own land, exactly? I know there was a field along the road to Leipzig, but I don't remember the rest."

Tante Anni's voice grew intent. She catalogued the fields for us. There were several hectares by the railroad tracks and that piece next to the nursery was theirs too. The nursery owners had been great-grandfather's cousins, so he gave them a break on the rent. There was another field by the cemetery, and the one Isolde remembered. "We should be able to get all of it back," Anni's voice crackled with excitement; her right index finger stabbed at the air. "Don't let them steal it. Get it back."

When Ron and I drove Tante Anni back to the nursing home, she directed us along a different route, so she could show us. Her voice wobbled and her eyes filled as she pointed out the fields. All were in walking distance of the farmhouse, plots of land I had sped by many times in my grandfather's car. Ron slowed down so we could get a better look. Tall grasses swayed over one field; another shimmered with potato shoots. For a moment, I felt dizzy as I surveyed this land. Land that connected me to the past.

*****

Just a year later, I steered a tiny Opel rental along the right lane of the Autobahn. My plan was to reach Gera just after lunch. I had gotten a small car because I knew I'd be traveling alone. Ron was roaming around Europe trying to interest companies in a new technology he was managing. I grabbed the chance to satisfy my curiosity about how East Germany was changing. I hadn't considered how much the car would vibrate at 140 km/hr nor how it would shake when a Mercedes buzzed past at 200 km/hr. The road noise was so bad I could barely hear the radio. Soon, I would reach Herleshausen. According to my cousin Ulrike, the border was vanishing rapidly. Would I recognize it?

I didn't expect the landscape to be familiar until right at the last moment, because I was coming from a different direction. Surely, there'd be some signs? I knew the guard towers were gone and the landmines had been removed, but it should take time for the earth to heal. The fields on both sides of the road looked green and healthy. My hands tightened on the steering wheel as I searched the hills for a telltale scar. Was that it, over there? The ground looked whole, but at the top of a rise I could make out a gap in the trees. I wasn't sure.

Why was I holding my breath? I looked ahead, disappointed. Could the border really have vanished in just a year? The car's tires rumbled as I drove onto a bridge. The bridge, yes, I remembered the bridge. Just a year ago, our car had rolled across at a snail's pace, one car in a long line. The railing flashed past on this trip. Empty flagpoles lined the road and the pavement broadened out into a plaza. The metal buildings and the awnings that had marked passport control and customs had been torn down. The old state-owned Mitropa restaurant just beyond the border still stood, but someone had turned it into a snack bar. A large sign proclaimed its new name, "Checkpoint Willi." I grinned at the joke, my feelings all in a muddle. I had slowed down without noticing. I stepped on the gas and left the old border post behind. A huge sigh escaped me, and got my attention. I inhaled once again, deliberately, exploring the state of my body. I dropped my shoulders and wriggled my fingers. Even my toes were tight. I forced myself to laugh. The border was nothing now - I had passed by it in a minute - but my body remembered differently. With a shudder, I realized I would carry every East German border crossing to my grave.

Gera, too, was changing. A mix of good and bad. A MacDonald's greeted me at the freeway exit. The road was newly paved. In the city itself, the main department store had been converted to a Horton's, a big West German department store chain. The historic *Rathaus* - city hall - had been restored and freshly white-washed, and the market square bustled just like any square in the West. The changes hadn't much affected Calvinstrasse. The biggest potholes had been patched, but the street still buckled under old paving stones. A few houses had received a coat of paint, but major renovations were still stalled because clarifying property ownership often proved complicated. Number 41 was the exception, bristling with scaffolding. I spent a few days visiting aunts and uncles and then drove on to visit Ulrike's younger sister Saskia in Berlin, a trip I avoided before because crossing and re-crossing the border would have been too complicated.

Another cousin who lived in the former East Berlin invited us to a party. The trams had been quickly reconnected to crisscross Berlin, so we could use public transportation to get there. As we rode, Saskia tried to show me where the Wall had been, but it was hard, because construction from both sides was filling the gap. Yet I knew immediately when we crossed into the eastern sector of the city. The houses looked ancient and worn, the roads were bumpy, and the occasional splotch of advertising color couldn't hide that it still looked like a third world country. I hadn't appreciated the magnitude of the job. The numbers I had been seeing in German news magazines, billions and trillions of marks required to rebuild East German infrastructure suddenly made sense.

The apartment teemed with people ten years younger than me. They were comparing trips they'd taken in the last year. One young black woman struck me particularly. She was a native German, the product of a love affair between an Angolan student and a German woman. She described an experience she'd had on the Turkish coast, where some German tourists were behaving like - well, stereotypical tourists. Speaking loudly in German, complaining about something, prices, or food, or some such boorish tourist behavior.

"It makes you embarrassed to be German, doesn't it?" she said. I saw myself as if from above, sitting in an East Berlin living room, in a newly united Germany that had changed so much from the Germany I knew in the fifties and sixties, that surely it was a whole different country? How alien this country had become.

The next day, I was back on the road, back in what the German press now called *'die neuen Bundesländer'* - 'the new states.' I still thought of it as the East. The worst stretches of the Berlin-Leipzig Autobahn bore fresh coats of asphalt and the speed limit had been increased from the 100 km/hr deemed adequate in the days of socialism. Once I passed Leipzig, I needed to watch for the turn-off to Bad Düben. Since I was driving alone, I had spread my map out on the passenger seat, so I could check my progress. Despite paying extra attention, I realized I had been driving much too long. I decided to pull off at a rest area and study my map. A bratwurst grill wafted spicy smoke from inside a mobile food stand that was parked in dirt at the edge of the pavement. My stomach perked up. I checked my watch. Almost two o'clock. Maybe I should eat. I checked the map first. I had gone a good fifty km past my exit. I was annoyed with myself. How could I have missed it? And worse, why did it take me so long to notice?

I grabbed my purse and got out of the car. There were no other customers. I greeted the vendor, and was gratified that he sounded like a local, not an opportunistic *Wessi* taking advantage of the local lack of experience with free enterprise. I asked the price of a sausage with bun. A double-semi roared by on the road.

"Excuse me?" I said.

"A mark fifty. Or isn't that expensive enough for you?" His voice delivered it as a tough jab, the sarcasm aimed at my Frankfurt license plate. I had no idea how much they charged for a roadside sausage in the West.

I felt around in my wallet for the right change, absorbed by my struggle to count out change that had grown foreign to me over the years. I could no longer distinguish between a one mark piece and a two mark piece by touch, the way I could feel the difference between nickels, quarters and dimes. When I looked up, the challenge in the vendor's eyes confused me.

"I just didn't hear you," I said.

He didn't look satisfied, but he took my money, opened a bun and fished for a sausage. It wasn't until I got back to my car that I noticed he gave me one that was dried out on one side from being kept warm for too many hours. I felt like the victim of a case of mistaken identity.

Back on the road, I mused about my place in the world. How hard it was becoming to pass for a German, to remember the correct polite phrase, to deal out change quickly enough, to remember always to arrive for a visit with a bouquet of flowers or some chocolate. Yet I looked and sounded like I belonged, so nobody would cut me the slack they might allow a foreigner. And now there was a whole new set of tensions developing between the parts of my homeland. Like any set of prejudices, they stung.

On my way to Bad Düben, I stopped at my great-uncle's house for a visit. I was surprised to find not just my great-uncle and his wife but also their son Peter. I had only one shadowy memory of having seen Peter when I was very young. He was a student then and I think he either twirled me around on the front lawn or let me ride on his back. After that he disappeared. He was in jail. Omi Paula and Tante Anni and my mother had talked about it in taut voices while sitting at the kitchen table. When I asked my mother about it, she looked uncertain. She sounded like she was about to tell me a story, like a fairy tale, but this story didn't have much of a plot or a happy ending. She said the police had arrested him, but it was because he was in the wrong place at the wrong time, not because he had done anything bad. I had seen enough of the East German police not to question her much further. Because she used the word *eingelocht* – a German slang term for jailed that literally means put in a hole – I pictured Peter sitting at the bottom of a pit while someone lowered a chunk of bread and water.

Peter was quiet and friendly with an undercurrent of tension constraining his movements that I might have missed if I hadn't been looking for it. During the afternoon, we drifted out into the yard and sat in the sun together. Like most conversations at the time, our talk soon veered toward the *Wende* - the collapse of socialism - and Peter's feelings about it. When I asked him if he minded telling me what happened when he was arrested, I was a bit tentative, because I didn't want to reopen his wounds. I needn't have worried. He poured out his story with the energy of someone who can think of little else, but has run out of people who want to hear about it.

In August 1961, when Peter was in his early twenties, he had been vacationing with other students at the Baltic Sea. The Friday night after the Wall was built, he joined some students at the *Haus der Deutsch-Sowjetischen Freundschaft* - House of German-Soviet Friendship. He described it as a social center with a bar where students hung out. Eventually, whether it was planned or just the result of a few beers, the students vented their frustration and anger about being trapped. There was shouting and a scuffle, but Peter left without incident. On Monday night, when he returned for a drink, he noticed a few men standing at the bar watching the room. They snatched him when he returned from the toilet and arrested him. He was charged with 'defaming the state,' and placed in detention to await trial.

"I got horrible claustrophobia sitting in a cell by myself day after day." Peter's eyes locked onto mine, willing me to understand. I nodded. I get claustrophobic sleeping too close to the edge of a tent, or having to stay home for a few days with a bad cold. I couldn't imagine being locked up in a little room, not knowing how long I'd have to stay. I could feel my heart rise into my throat as I tried to picture it. Eventually, he was sentenced to several years for 'Agitation' and 'Propaganda' and put to work in a jute factory. Peter visibly relaxed as he described how he gained the protection of a fellow prisoner nicknamed Pasha. He survived his sentence reasonably well, and intended to resume his studies at Jena when he was released. But his troubles were far from over. I always assumed that his difficulties after his release were due to the emotional toll his jail experience had taken on him. Now I learned differently.

As soon as he had re-enrolled in Medical School, the *Stasi* began to pressure him to inform on his fellow students. Peter refused. The agent made it clear that he couldn't expect to pass his exams if he didn't cooperate. Peter continued to resist. He studied hard and stifled the panic that insinuated itself into his days. He never knew when they'd be waiting for him. He failed his anatomy exam. He couldn't believe it. He had worked hard on his anatomy. He worked harder during the next semester. And still the Stasi agent materialized on his way back to his rented room, pressuring him for information. He would learn his anatomy so well, that they couldn't fail him. He failed again. I admired his persistence, even if in retrospect it seemed naïve. How could anyone resist when the Stasi held all the cards? Peter's story echoed my father's with one major exception. The borders were sealed, so he couldn't take my father's way out. He moved home for a while, depressed and unsure what to do.

I considered asking him if he was ever tempted to just give in. Before I could, Peter, who was hanging his head, looked back up and said, "One simply cannot participate in that kind of thing." Of course, not, I thought. But how hard it would be to remember that when your future is at stake.

Peter knew that being a doctor was considered a high privilege. Maybe he could try for a less prestigious job. He had finished most of the course requirements for chemistry, and he managed to get a job in the lab at Leuna, one of East Germany's large chemical factories. The trouble never really stopped. Every time someone sought to promote him or increase his job responsibilities, a *Stasi* agent materialized at their door. He experienced sleep disturbances and panic attacks. He was now down to part-time quality control work. For a moment, Peter looked deflated, his shoulders hunched, and his head heavy. Then he tightened his muscles, sat up and smiled. "At least I don't have to worry about the Stasi anymore. Gorbi is like Jesus for me. I never thought I would be free."

As I took in the rubble of Peter's life, I wondered if Gorbi had arrived soon enough to make a difference. I often thought in recent months that nobody could ever make up for the time my relatives had lost in the prison of East Germany, but at least most of them had been able to build islands of private happiness. Islands they could build on now. I guess it was a matter of degrees. Peter's story unleashed a vast sadness in me. A sense that the damage done to the people in the East would take generations to repair.

I drove the short distance to Bad Düben, feeling relieved that I'd be going someplace I felt at home. Isolde greeted me cheerfully, the guestroom was sunny and welcoming, the pool promised a cool haven in the July heat. My cousins and I took turns cooling off in the water and warming up on the patch of grass scattered with *Gänseblümchen* - tiny white daisies - precious to me from trying to weave them into chains as a child. I rested and restored myself.

I was ready to leave. It wasn't just Ron I missed, though he supplied a Nordic calm in my life that was sorely lacking. Without him, I felt unbalanced, off-center. But I also missed the elements of our life together. The food we bought at the local co-op and the farmer's market and cooked together whenever possible. My favorite restaurants - I couldn't wait to go to Café Brenda for vegetarian and seafood, or to the White Lily for mock duck salad. I had grown satiated with meat and gravy, smoked ham and sourdough rye. I wanted to dive into the pool at my health club and bask in the sauna, even if I had to listen to the weightlifters bitch about the Minnesota Vikings' record. I couldn't wait to walk our Golden Retriever around Lake Phalen, past the willows and oaks and the conflagration of Canada Geese.

*****

A few months later, my mother and I stood in the lobby of Lucio's Ristorante in Basye, Virginia waiting for a table. We were vacationing together at my parents' time-share nearby. Ahead of us, Ron listened intently as my father described a business opportunity that interested him. A small business for sale in West Virginia - my father wanted Ron to help him evaluate it as a project for his retirement. Ron bent toward my father to catch his voice in the Saturday night din of the restaurant.

"What happened to your plan to buy an apartment in Germany when Papi retires?" I asked, turning toward my mother.

"He doesn't want to." My mother pointed at my father with her chin. "He says it's a waste of money."

How could buying real estate be a waste of money? My mother added that my father also argued there was no good way to choose a place. They no longer had connections to Krefeld. She considered Eilenburg, but she knew even fewer people there. She added, looking sideways at him, "I tried to tell him I just want to be in a city, someplace we can use as a base when we travel in Europe. Munich maybe. But he won't have it."

Before I could work myself into righteous anger on her behalf, she straightened up and smiled. "So we made a deal. I gave up the apartment in Germany for a new kitchen. All new appliances, cabinets and a new floor." She was beaming. She loved to cook and had grumbled about the kitchen since the house was first completed.

I frowned. "A new kitchen?" This hardly seemed a fair exchange. "But then you're stuck in Clemson. You've always hated it there."

She looked at me, her eyebrows crinkled. "Hate Clemson? I don't hate Clemson. We've got a lot of friends there."

My budding outrage leaked away. She didn't hate Clemson? I tried to listen as she chattered on about their social life, and her shopping trips to Atlanta, their outings to the symphony in Greenville. How long since I had left Clemson? My eyes wandered to the illuminated fresco style painting on the restaurant's far wall. They followed grapevines winding around faux Corinthian columns and came to a stop on Bacchus' dimpled cheeks. He looked frozen on the wall. I moved away sixteen years ago. For sixteen years, I held on to her anger on her behalf while she found a way to let it go. I felt betrayed.

That night, I tossed and turned. I remembered several conversations in the early '80s when my mother insisted she wanted to return to Germany when my father retired. He was fifty-eight then - she must have wanted to get her bid in early. A few months later, when my father was in St. Paul trying to sell equipment to 3M, he took me out to dinner one night. We sat upstairs in the white frame house on Grand Avenue that was the Little Apple Deli, eating overstuffed sandwiches with piles of salad. At the end of the meal, as we faced each other over our demolished plates and sipped the last of our beer, I asked about their plans.

"Your mother thinks she wants to move back to Germany, but I keep telling her there's nothing there for us. You're here and you're staying, and Nica will get a job somewhere in the US once she graduates." He waited for my reaction. I hadn't thought of that. How sad, that my sister and I could function as hostages. I knew that was a harsh way to see it, but that's how it struck me.

"Couldn't you at least spend part of the year in Germany? That's all she wants," I said. I held onto my glass and looked into his eyes. He shrugged.

"It doesn't make sense to buy a place just for that. We'd be better off using the money to travel to different places, not tie it up in an apartment."

I shivered with a swift rush of frustration. Didn't he see that this was symbolic? That he'd had it his way all along and it was time for him to let my mother have a turn? Who cared if it made sense?

I took another sip of beer. "If you don't let her have her way, she'll be angry all over again, the way she was when we first moved. It's only money, but you can use it to buy peace between you."

My father's eyes flickered and his mouth opened. He sat still for a moment, staring at me. Finally he said, "But it doesn't make sense."

I wasn't giving up that easily. I had learned a thing or two about ways to do permanent damage to a marriage, and I was determined to pass my new knowledge along. I kept talking. The words I imagined to be sharp and convincing bounced off and turned limp as the coleslaw left on our plates. When I wound down, exhausted, my father muttered, "She'll get over it eventually. She always does."

Now, as I lay in my strange bed in Virginia, wrapped in my nighttime obsessing, I was furious at both my parents. I couldn't exactly put my finger on why. It shouldn't have upset me that my father knew my mother better than I did. The hardest thing for me was to give up my solidarity with my mother. She had deserted.

The next morning, I woke up at six. The house was quiet. I fixed myself a cup of tea and slid onto the deck to soak up the already hot Southern sun. Inside the house, someone clattered. I expected it was my father - an early riser. I was wrong. My mother emerged and sat down on the thin plastic chair next to my lounge. We talked about my mid-life crisis, if a crisis at thirty-seven could be considered mid-life. I had just quit my job to try to figure out what I wanted to be when I grew up.

She leaned forward and said, "Your father never did that. He never looked at the place career had in his life. It was the only thing that mattered." She clamped down on her lips and the two vertical creases above her nose deepened. "The only thing. All this talk about family - family always came second."

I asked her why she thought he wanted to live in the United States so badly. I thought I was reconciled to it, but the changes in Germany stirred up all my pain. Along with the joy that came with thinking the future was wide open, I was overcome with grief for what I had lost. She insisted again, it was all about career. His boss wanted to send him, it was a promotion, and that was that. I was disappointed, hoping for something deeper.

She leaned closer still and whispered, "He's been coming clean about his tactics. He told me that his boss offered him a job back in

Germany as branch head about two years after we moved to Clemson. He turned it down without telling us about it."

I gasped. Two years! A whole parallel life opened before me. I saw myself back at the *Gymnasium* growing up to study at a German university. An alternate self, hurrying down a divergent tunnel, disappearing into another reality. I was so stunned I couldn't react. My mother just looked worn. Fine and not so fine wrinkles webbed her face. More of them were frown lines than laugh lines. I was so sorry for her I stopped feeling pity for myself.

*****

When my father talks about his time as a "guest of the American government" as he refers to his POW years, his stories drift to Virginia, and his eyes glow. Our stay in Basye led me to wonder if I could find the key here. I told him I wanted to see this place where he picked apples. He was surprised I wanted this. He behaved like a polite dinner guest who didn't want to take the last piece of pie without being urged.

The Holiday Inn in Waynesboro sat high on a mountainside above town. From the rooms, you could see the mist on the valley and row upon row of dark rounded mountains across the gap. We floated in the pool. Above us puffy clouds sailed past. After dinner, my father said he wasn't sure he'd recognize the place. The first time he came back, in the sixties, he stopped at a gas station and found an old man who could tell him where the barracks were. He asked my father whether he'd been a guard there. When my father told him he was a prisoner, the old man chuckled. "Well, I'll be danged."

Sometime in the early eighties he checked by again, but the barrack foundations had disappeared underneath some new apartment buildings. I told him I didn't care whether we found the exact spot. He drove down into the valley toward the village of Lyndhurst and pointed into the haze above the valley floor. "It was just slightly up the hill there." The view was stunning. Blue mountains rising above an open valley filled with orchards.

He guided the car into town. An old railroad station, white clapboard, with prominent porches, still stood. This was where he had arrived. "I couldn't believe the prosperity when I got here. There was a huge war going on, and in Europe signs of it were everywhere. But here, there was plenty of food and the people had new clothes. The war didn't seem to touch them at all."

As we coasted down the street, he pointed out houses he remembered. "People were so polite and kind. They didn't treat us as if we were enemies. They'd offer us Cokes when it was hot."

Dusk settled over the valley. My father drove back toward Waynesboro on a two-lane road lined with bushes and pines. An occasional white house hid behind rhododendrons. He told us more about his life here. The apple orchards hired them as pickers and paid the government the going rate for four bushels picked a day. The prisoners got wind of the deal and slowed down their picking to exactly four bushels. The farmer complained. They had been picking six or more. They worked out a deal. They would go back to picking faster, but would be paid for the extra apples. The camp commander vetoed cash payments to POW's. Instead he banked the money and gave them a Sears catalogue. They could order anything they wanted with their extra earnings. By the time the army clamped down on these arrangements eight months later, they had ping-pong tables, badminton sets and a homemade still. "Only in America," my father grinned. His wrinkles had softened. He was seeing ghosts in the haze. He loved it here. I got goose bumps when I thought of the short drive between Clemson and the Blue Ridge Mountains.

Southern birds screeched in dark pine tops. We sat on my parents' deck sipping wine, a citronella candle flickering between us. I asked my father questions about his childhood. He tried to explain how a family of five, his family before all his siblings were born, could live in a two-room apartment. He and his two sisters shared a bed - the parents slept in the living room/kitchen. Then he reminisced about his parents. His mother always sewing, sewing. When he talked about his father, his voice became less certain. He searched. "Your grandfather was good with children. He was a lot of fun, but he didn't want any responsibility. I couldn't let my wife support me, the way he did."

I asked him whether he remembered what he wanted to be when he grew up. He smiled, "I wanted to be an agent for a German company in South America." We looked at each other. This was it, I thought. That was all there was to it. The candle flickered and jerked shadows across his face. "The continent was slightly off, but that's pretty much what I've done."

This was my answer.

Fate had held me in its capricious hand and given me a father with youthful dreams of adventure. How could I blame him for following his dreams when I was in the middle of searching for my own? I was too old for the righteous anger of adolescence. Instead I struggled to glimpse the possibility that he had done the best he could for himself without intending me any harm. I might be able to release my anger at my father. But could I ever give up the habit of longing?

*****

In 1992, the US government issued new rules requiring aliens to update Green Cards. Despite the bureaucratic nuisance - filling out forms, locating a photographer who could produce a picture that conformed to INS regulations, and waiting to get fingerprinted - I welcomed the new requirement. First of all, it meant I wasn't alone. There were enough of us to require a regulation. I also liked the idea of an up-to-date picture. Every time I returned to the US from my biannual pilgrimage to Germany, my card with its ancient photo and its dog-eared innocence drew a reprimand. The New York immigration officer who drew my attention to my dithering was only the first. Each time, the looks I got grew more impatient. Why hadn't I grasped the chance to trade in my Green Card for an American passport as soon as the required five years were up?

As I waited at the INS processing center in a suburb of Minneapolis, number in hand, I scanned the recent immigrants perched on the edges of hard plastic chairs. Somali men in somber suits, Russian women wearing stylish shoes, and Hmong grandmothers decked out in colorful patterns. I wondered how they felt.

Was it my privilege that conferred the luxury to waver? Would I have made the switch more quickly if we'd been driven by war or hunger?

I guessed that the elderly Hmong woman also woke at night aching for the smells of her childhood home. I wanted to ask the Russian in her stylish mini whether a full belly and money in her purse got her past the hollow moments when her ears searched in vain for sounds she had taken for granted in her old city. I knew most Americans assumed that immigrants applied for American citizenship as soon as they were able and that they would gratefully swear to give up all other allegiances and previous loyalties. Were there others like me who couldn't bear to shed their past?

On the fourth of July, the newspapers showed people that looked like us being sworn in as new citizens. They held tiny paper Stars and Stripes; they smiled, and assured the reporters that they were thrilled to be American. I searched the photos; examined their eyes. Did I imagine the mixed feelings reflected there? Or did the deprivation and violence many had experienced at home overcome the ambiguities that plagued me? They said they were thrilled to be citizens. Were they saying the words they knew the reporter wanted to hear because they'd learned anything else sounded ungrateful?

My number came up. I strode to the proper window, surprised the agent with my flawless English, pressed my thumb into ink as instructed, and left. As usual, I had found no answers, only questions.

A few months later, I spotted a series of newspaper articles on the Hmong community in St. Paul. The writer commented on the generational divide between the original immigrants who arranged their lives with the intent to return home and their children who have no interest in returning to Laos. Later, I found interviews with Somalis who hoped for nothing more than stability for their country so they could move back. The only thing keeping them here was the chaos at home.

Ron's grandfather had gone back to Norway after a few years in the United States. He had been so homesick, he left his children behind. I wondered if there were others who found the new world too strange. Good data is hard to come by, but once I started looking I was amazed by what I found. He wasn't alone. I had always assumed that returning home was not even an option until recently, when travel became relatively cheap and safe. But even some of the earliest immigrants changed their minds. Three of the original passengers on the Mayflower went back to England. Some researchers estimate that as many as a third of immigrants eventually returned home. There's also evidence that some who went home changed their minds - they show up twice or even three times on immigration records. My mixed feelings had hundreds of years worth of company.

Could I pinpoint the year the balance had tipped? The moment I knew my fantasies of returning 'home' were just that: sweet daydreams I nurtured with no intention of turning them into reality? But was I American? Could I be both?

*****

When my daughter was born in 1993, I became the mother of an American. I couldn't deny the evidence on her birth certificate. She was born in Minneapolis, Hennepin County, Minnesota. A Minnesotan by birth. I was so drunk on lactation hormones that nothing but the baby mattered. She was a Minnesotan, I was a Minnesotan, anything was okay as long as she snuggled against me and didn't cry. Accepting the truth felt like relaxing into the pillowy drifts of our new existence. A life in which only primal matters counted. I'm alive, you're alive, I'm healthy and so are you. I didn't have the energy to question why I was speaking to my baby in English, but singing her German lullabies as I rocked her in the moonlight.

Oh, I had hedged a bit. As the baby explored the limits of space inside my body, Ron and I agreed we should stick to names that would work in both languages. We knew we were expecting a girl and settled on Anna Sophia, which honored a combination of my German ancestors and his Norwegian/Irish ones. The name proved too serious for her impish spirit, so we quickly took to calling her Sophie.

The first year, I didn't even feel guilty about not speaking to her in German. I was almost forty, and had a baby for whom sleep was a foreign concept. It was enough to be able to speak at all. At the same time, I was lost in the wonder of this new territory. It seemed I spent most of my days in one of several chairs with a baby fastened to my nipple, sensations of contentment radiating through me from her sucking mouth.

When my mother reported trouble brewing between her and Tante Isolde, I didn't want to know. Nothing could really be that bad as long as Sophie's growing weight pressed on my lap. I didn't want to see frown lines on my mother's face. I preferred to see the joy that transformed her whenever she entered a room that held Sophie. So I pretended to listen - probably did listen - but wanted harmony so badly, that I heard only the most hopeful interpretations I could imagine and then changed the subject.

My mother tried to respect my desire to dwell in the positive, but the pressure to share her turmoil grew. Now that they had a grandchild, my parents traveled to Minnesota more frequently. On one visit, Sophie was about a year old, I noticed my mother's features had sharpened and her eyes were ringed by dark shadows. She confessed that she woke frequently at night, so angry she could hardly breathe. She'd stay awake for hours, inventing arguments with her sister, imploring her not to disinherit her. "I feel like she's trying to cut me off from home."

Her pain pierced my baby-induced nirvana. I tried to reconstruct what had happened. I remembered that the two sisters had seen a lawyer in 1990, to discuss not just the factory, but also their grandparents' land. The attempt to regain the factory consumed a few thousand marks in lawyers' fees, but sometime in 1992, the *Treuhand* - the management corporation formed by the government to deal with East German property - ruled against the family. They deemed the family to have been fairly bought out. Onkel Horst blamed my father for the loss of lawyer's fees, since he was such a clever Western businessman. The land was a different story. Even in 1990, the lawyer had been clear that Tante Anni should have no trouble regaining the land. "We'll share in all of it," Tante Isolde had promised.

Tante Anni's health was failing in1990. She lit up when talking about the past, but began to drift in the present. We all knew that her will - drafted in communist times - named Tante Isolde as her sole beneficiary. East German law discouraged Western beneficiaries. At that time, Tante Anni had imagined her sole property to be a few pictures and pieces of jewelry and her savings account. She was thrilled the family would get the land back, and constantly talked to all of us about 'our fields.' When my mother suggested to Isolde that they discuss the need to change her will with Anni, Isolde brushed her off. "She's getting too confused. We'll settle it among ourselves after she's dead."

In 1991, when Tante Anni was ninety-two, she fell and broke her hip. Her brittle bones resisted healing. Anni decided she'd lived long enough and stopped eating. It took her six weeks to die. I remember sitting on the steps to my greenhouse reading the letter telling me of her death. The December sun warmed me and melted the drifts of new snow on the roof. As I sat there, trying to absorb that she was gone, I watched rivulets drip down the windowpanes. I extended my right hand and focused on the ring Tante Anni had given me when I was eleven. She had called me into her bedroom and opened her jewelry box. She pulled out a simple gold band with a tiny sapphire and held it out to me. "This was my engagement ring. I hope it brings you better luck than it did me."

She had never even alluded to her divorce in front of me before. I touched the ring gently, and slipped it on. It fit perfectly. Since then, I had switched the ring to my other hand to make room for a wedding band, but I still wore it most of the time. Drip, drip, drip. Water hit the deck outside. I touched the ring to my lips, and hoped she knew I had been sending her thoughts of love these past weeks.

The trouble started a year and a half later, when my mother inquired how they would go about transferring title to her share of the land. Isolde responded that Anni's will was legal and could not be changed; it named Isolde as the sole heir and furthermore that was consistent with conversations between her and Anni at the hospital while Anni lay dying. Since Anni had explicitly told her she wanted no change made in the will, Isolde intended to respect that and expected my mother to understand her position.

My mother felt cheated. I tried to temper her reaction by reminding her of the building resentment that could be stoking Isolde's reversal. I knew from the distance of Minnesota my understanding was probably sketchy, but I had gone to dusty college auditoriums to see movies made by former East Germans and I pored over German news magazines to keep in touch with the German mood. As the euphoria of

German reunification had worn off, suspicion and prejudice between East and West rose rapidly. More and more East Germans traveled and as they did, they truly understood how disadvantaged they had been. Yes, the West poured in billions of marks to rebuild the infrastructure, but the task was too enormous. Even billions couldn't wave a magic wand and transform East into West overnight. As companies collapsed and refugees returned to claim their property, former East Germans felt they were fighting a losing battle to catch up. They saw the ones who had left as deserters; they'd gone off to enjoy the good life and now they were coming back trying to grab what little was left away from those who stayed and suffered. In their view, the refugees didn't need compensation. They were rich already. Both Horst and Isolde knew they would have to retire early, and while the government promised them pensions, they were probably panicked about the future.

"It's not about the money," my mother had answered. "I just don't want to be disinherited. Before my father died, he told me that he made Isolde promise him that no matter what the legal arrangements had to be, she would find a way to share whatever was left with me. That land was our grandparents' land."

The conflict escalated rapidly. The Vesuvius of Isolde and Horst's frustration spewed warning plumes of a coming eruption. They lobbed insults. "You yourself severed your relationship with your supposedly beloved home when you left forever." Trying to acknowledge the difficulty of the past forty years was as effective as trying to douse a volcano with a bucket of water. Every attempt to negotiate only turned up the heat. Apparently the 'Calculator Incident' from years before had been a warning rumble. My father hoped to repeat his peacemaking success and made a pilgrimage to Bad Düben to settle the matter face-to-face. He had a hunch that Horst was the main source of pressure, so he tried to concentrate his efforts on Isolde, while Horst steamed on the sidelines. He was persuasive; he is after all a salesman by trade. Isolde agreed to split the land 3:2 with my mother. An equal share for each of the two sisters' children. They shook on the deal and shared coffee and cake. The sky cleared. Until the next phone call.

Horst exploded, flinging streams of invective across the Atlantic. After he relieved his need to scream, he finished by forbidding my mother to speak to her sister. "I forbid you to further intimidate my wife!"

I tried to understand all the details, but could only make out the emotional trajectory. The euphoric sunshine of family unity that had warmed us in1990 was gone. By the spring of 1994, my mother, who absolutely hated litigation, consulted a lawyer and weighed a lawsuit against her sister. She decided against the suit in the end, because she thought legal action would only deepen the pain. I hadn't been directly involved, but I felt wounded. I was ambivalent about the land itself. It would be nice to own a swatch of land my great-grandmother had worked hard to buy. When I first heard of the possibility, I briefly entertained a dream of building a house and living in a revitalized Eilenburg. In reality, owning property in Germany would be an administrative nuisance. No, the damage I felt most keenly was to my love for my aunt and her family.

As I prepared to take my daughter to Germany for the first time, I confronted the shift in terrain. I couldn't imagine ever going to Tante Isolde's house in Bad Düben again. For Sophie, my father's family would be the center of German gravity. I knew I would eventually take her to Eilenburg and show her my great-grandparents' farmhouse and Opa Gustav's house and factory. Once she was old enough to understand, I would take her to Omi Paula and Opa Gustav's grave in the Bad Düben cemetery. But Sophie's first visit to Germany set the pattern: we went to Gera and attended a huge family celebration with every Poser in attendance. Like her great-grandmother Hedwig, Sophie would love nothing better. She couldn't feel the absence of a visit to Eilenburg and Bad Düben, an absence that plagued me like the pain in an amputee's phantom limb.

*****

I assumed since my mother had inherited hair that refused to turn gray from Tante Anni, she would live as long as my great-aunt had. Clearly, I'd been wrong. My mother looked drawn and skinny from the week of liquid diet she had endured just before surgery, but she was "recovering." They'd stopped giving her the Demerol that my father said disoriented her so that she could no longer understand English and tried to talk to the nurses in German. While Sophie and I were at the hospital, she got out of bed. My father supported her while she slowly forced herself down the hall to the nurses' station and back. She was an odd sight in the glamorous silk robe I had given her for her sixty-seventh birthday. Dramatic deep green and crimson orchids, flowers she loved, lined in crimson terry cloth. When I chose this robe I was not picturing a hospital hallway. She was getting stronger. My mind had trouble uniting that idea with what my father had told me when he picked Sophie and me up at the airport. The tumor in her colon had been removed, but there were others that couldn't be. Cancerous growths studded both lobes of her liver.

"Is Omi going to die soon?" Sophie asked me on the way back to my parents' house from the hospital. Yes, I screamed inside my head. Yes. But what is soon to a three-year-old? Tomorrow, next week, next month at the latest. So I said, "No, not soon."

On every visit, I was surprised to find that my body remembered the exact angle of the driveway. I slid to an effortless stop in front of the garage. Sophie watched with interest as I got out to push up the garage door. In Minnesota, everyone she knew had a garage door opener. When I released her from her car seat, she shot toward the Japanese Maple in the front yard and climbed into its low fork. The miracle of this trip for her was that she could be outside without a snowsuit in February.

Sophie climbed higher into branches too skinny to support her weight. I reached for her and pulled her toward me. "Look at Omi's daffodils," I said, "they're getting buds already. And so are the azaleas." I pointed to the bushes my mother had planted under the tall pines that edged the lot. When she first arrived in South Carolina, my mother had despaired of the scorching summers and acid red clay. She struggled for a while, until she decided to stick with the plants other Southerners grew. She gave up on roses. In Germany, we had a hedge of pale pink polyanthas that bloomed through June and July and had to be trimmed back so they wouldn't crowd the garden path.

South Carolina wasn't as cold as Minnesota, but the February chill was just damp enough to drive us indoors. We entered into stillness. I felt strange trespassing in my mother's house in her absence. She was there in the entrance hall, in the antique map of Saxony that showed Eilenburg. She smuggled it out of East Germany rolled up and stashed between her underwear on one of our long ago trips. She was in the Blue Onion Plates she hung along the open stairs to the basement. There was the cherry wood cabinet in the living room – one of the few pieces we moved from Germany. It was the first good piece of furniture my parents bought when they transformed from penniless East German refugees to West German taxpayers. My mother had filled its glass vitrine with her grandmother's mocha cups and her mother's Meissen coffeepot. There were a few traces of my father. He had brought back the rug under the coffee table from his first trip to Pakistan, along with an oft-repeated tale of haggling. Some Chinese customers had given him the print that hung framed in bamboo above the dining room buffet. But she decided when it was time to move the rug to its spot under the coffee table to hide its wear, and she had placed the nail for the print. Back in the bedrooms, she had not only chosen the wallpaper, but installed it herself, by herself, when my father was away on his many business trips.

I couldn't remember when I had last stayed here alone. My father was sleeping at the hospital in a recliner, so Sophie and I kept house. I couldn't find anything in the new kitchen. Since my mother had remodeled two years before, she had moved the garlic press to the drawer next to the fridge, and the wooden spoons to another drawer below the oven. Each time I tried to cook something, I had to open every drawer and cupboard.

As I hunted through drawers for utensils, Sophie pulled up a chair to the counter to see. She was fascinated by cooking, and had to be right there in the middle, helping test ingredients and stir. My brain was buzzing, I thought I longed for quiet to absorb what was happening to my mother, but I could think of nothing that would bring me more comfort than cooking with my daughter. I liked that Sophie rubbed against me as she reached. I needed to feel her close. Celery half-moons slid evenly off my knife.

"Can I try?" Sophie asked.

"Celery is too hard to cut. I'll let you cut the canned tomatoes with the tomato knife," I told her. The tomato knife's rounded tip and gentle serration couldn't do much damage in the event of a mishap. I found it, right in the knife block.

While she worked on the tomatoes, I looked out the sliding glass door. Past the deck, the lake looked gray through the maze of tall pine trunks. Whenever my mother grew homesick, my father pointed out that they would never have been able to afford a house this big on such a large wooded lot on a lake. "You'd have to be a millionaire," he said. My mother couldn't argue. It was true.

When we sat down at the kitchen table to eat, I put Sophie in my little sister's spot, and sat down before I realized that meant I'd sit in my mother's chair. Every time my attention drifted, Sophie demanded I come back to her. All we had to do was get through the evening together.

Until bedtime, I thought I was coping pretty well. I didn't think Sophie could know that I felt like I was stumbling across an Arctic ice field snow-blind. But she clung to me talking, twisting, and singing, unable to sleep, hours after her usual bedtime. Sophie never was a sleeper, and whenever she was troubled, sleep was the first thing to go. The only remedy I ever found was to drive. So, at ten-thirty in the evening, I slipped back into my clothes, grabbed my mother's keys, and installed Sophie in her car seat. It was the first of several nighttime drives. I turned the radio on - my mother kept it tuned to the classical station - and navigated through Clemson by adolescent memory. One night, we drove out to the high school, turned around in its parking lot and looped back on a side street that I hadn't taken since I had a high school friend who lived there. I drove out toward Seneca and came back along the lakeside road that passed the Y, where I danced the night of graduation. I rediscovered neighborhoods I had no reason to visit in the last twenty years, and tried to remember which house used to belong to which friend. I took the twisting street through the university campus and pictured myself trudging across, carrying a few pounds of chemistry books, headed for the canteen to meet my boyfriend.

As Sophie subsided in the back - I kept turning to see if her head had rolled forward yet - memories crowded me in the dark. I conjured up the thick sense of possibility and sexual tension that I would always connect with the sticky heat and chirping crickets of Clemson summer nights. I grew up in Germany, but I had to admit that a chunk of me had been formed right here, in this place I could hardly wait to leave behind. My feelings about Krefeld were uncomplicated; it was the paradise of childhood. Clemson was harder to define. While I lived here, I had nothing but contempt for its culture and its size, even as I adapted to its ways and absorbed its limits. Whether I liked it or not, Clemson lived inside me, its particulars a part of many a vivid experience. The intense memories called up by our night drives distracted me a little from my mother's illness, though I felt guilty at letting them. Sophie reliably succumbed to the rhythm of the car. Once I transferred her to bed, I'd sit alone on the couch in the living room, hunched over a book, or just staring at the night-blind windows.

Once my mother returned from the hospital, my father and I installed her in my old room. Her abdomen was too sore for her to withstand my father's tossing and turning on their king size mattress. She slept a lot, but when she was awake, I sat with her for hours, barely noticing I was uncomfortable on a wooden folding chair, my feet braced on the serving cart we used for her supplies. She faced me, her head propped up on a wedge padded with two pillows. Our conversation veered from the mundane - where could she get a runner for the bathroom - to the deep topics that were dominating our thoughts - the future and death. We discussed how to distribute her needlework and quilts, who might want her quilting frame, and my mother's certainty that her husband would need a new wife. My feelings fluctuated wildly from one extreme - *she can't die, this is morbid* - to the other - *I'm glad she's not kidding herself.* I felt ordinary and lost one moment and outside myself the next. One of her hopes was that she'd live long enough to go to Germany as planned that September. I had been considering a trip in June, but I thought I should cancel. I mentioned to my mother that I had gotten a postcard from my great-uncle Ernst, asking when I was coming for my visit.

Her reaction took me by surprise. Her voice pulled itself up to full intensity. "Don't you write anybody in Eilenburg about my ordeal," she stopped to catch her breath and wagged her right index finger in warning. "I don't want them to know."

I swallowed. I had been thinking that Isolde might relent if she knew her sister was dying. It seemed a risk worth taking. When I persisted she added, "There's just a black hole inside me." She pointed to her gut. "Where all the warm fuzzy feelings about my family used to be."

I had to catch the breath her image had knocked out of me. Was that black hole the incubator that had let her cancer ripen? At that moment I was certain it was so.

I couldn't let go. "I wrote Ernst and Matthias at Christmas that I'd be coming this summer. I have to let them know why I'm not."

My mother sighed. "Promise me. Just Ernst and Matthias. Don't write Isolde."

As soon as Ernst got my letter, he was on the phone every few weeks, checking on my mother's health. I got a note from Matthias, but we heard nothing from Isolde.

When Sophie and I left to go back to Minnesota, my mother was able to go outside and walk the few hundred yards uphill to the mailbox. The oncologist said he couldn't promise anything except hope. Spring brought news that sent hope ebbing and flowing. Chemo weakened her, but seemed to be shrinking her tumors. I didn't know how optimistic I had allowed myself to become until the news that a spot of bone cancer had appeared on her pelvis sent me spinning back into despair. The treatments weakened and strengthened her in fits and starts. We decided to spend our June vacation in Clemson.

When we arrived, my mother was feeling better, slowly recovering strength after the radiation treatments for bone cancer. The highlight of her day was the mail. That's when she got a pile of get well cards, some from needle worker guild friends, some from church members, some from the Gourmet club she had helped start, and some from a women's club she joined after I moved. A big bowl filled with cards sat on the dining room sideboard. On the teacart next to her bedside, she kept a yellow legal pad with a list of notes she herself had to write. Doreen - flowers, Irene - sherry gelatin, the Crabbs - roses, Betty - meatloaf, Ilse - pound cake. Every afternoon, she propped herself up in bed, perched a lap desk on her knees and wrote careful thank you notes.

On days when there were only a few notes, her face fell with the mail. When she was napping, I sorted through the cards. I always thought of my mother as a loner and a woman who didn't make friends easily. When had she gotten so deeply rooted in Clemson's community? Hundreds of people cared enough to send cards, and scores inundated us with gifts of food. I couldn't help but wonder who might notice if I got sick.

Every morning, we ate breakfast on the deck. My mother appeared, her yellow skin and deep eye circles a stark contrast to the riotous flowers on the robe. She settled in the prime chair, facing the lake and the hummingbird feeder. The hummingbirds appeared to be putting on a show for her. Every morning, there they were, dancing around the feeder, fighting each other for the right to go first. I had never seen a hummingbird before. My father said that in past years, there had been one on occasion, but he had never seen anything like this.

One morning, an envelope arrived from Germany, bearing Isolde's handwriting and address. My father hesitated over it in the entryway. I followed him into my mother's room, but when I saw her eyes narrow, I decided to leave again so she could read her letter alone.

When I came back, she lay there, her arm limp, hanging over the side of the bed, the card in her hand. Even from the door, I could see only a few lines of writing. My mother pinched her lips together, her eyes hard.

"See for yourself." She waved the card in my direction.

I struggled to maintain hope. Maybe she was so disgusted that it was just a problem of too little too late? I scanned the scrawled lines. Even I could find no hint of warmth or sympathy. The words sounded as mechanical as a child's thank you note for a gift of pencils from a maiden aunt. *I am sorry to hear about your illness.* I looked into my mother's wounded eyes.

My mother's voice twisted. "*I know that can be difficult.*" Then she added, "Sounds like she's writing to a distant acquaintance. She only wrote it so she can tell Ernst she wrote me. I bet he's been pressuring her."

I looked at my father. He shook his head: "My God, that's heartless."

During the summer, my mother regained strength. The chemo seemed to be working, though her body remained tender and swollen. I sent her some loose dresses I wore when I was pregnant and she wore them on short shopping trips and to hold court at several Clemson social events. When she told me about these on the phone, I could tell she was amazed that so many people should be so pleased to see her. But her brief resurgence came to a precipitous halt in August. She developed blood clots from the drug that had been keeping her tumors in check all summer. My father canceled his tickets to Germany; I moved up my plans to go back to Clemson.

In the dark of night, my sister's hand touched my shoulder. I surfaced from a scattered sleep, knew it must be 3 am. My turn. I felt Sophie's legs on my stomach, so I slid out gently, and turned to cover her. Her head was on Ron's chest. I moved slowly, following Nica out the door, rubbing my eyes. We stopped in the doorway to my mother's room. She lay there, in a rented hospital bed, propped up slightly to ease her breathing, the bed angled toward the door. Nica whispered: "She's still making those sounds. I can't tell if she's in pain or just sighing." They were rhythmic animal sounds, with no change in pitch or volume. Other than that, my mother was "unresponsive," in the hospice nurse's words.

I sat down on the folding chair squeezed between the bed and the window. I propped myself up and watched my mother breathe. I thought of medieval death masks. Where had I seen those? Dante or Erasmus came to mind. I could no longer see lips and all the flesh on her face had melted away. Her skull shone through translucent skin. She seemed to concentrate on dying; her brow furrowed hard, two sharp lines cutting from the eyebrows upward. I hadn't known that the body fights death long after the soul has given up.

I talked to her, softly. Just a few words. That I loved her and would miss her. The things you try to fling into the void in hopes she might still hear you. I kept trying to read to make the time pass. The chair grew hard and fatigue crept over me. I grew impatient. With impatience came guilt. How could I want her to die just to get this over with? But what was the point? Surely she wasn't trying to hang on.

I looked up once from the page I had tried to read three times, and my glance fell on her forearm. She had a birthmark there, almost round, the size and shape as if someone had dipped a pencil eraser in ink and pressed it against her skin. It was blue-black. Suddenly I was three and she was my world. The gold bracelet she wore settled right there on her arm, right next to the birthmark. If I held very still, I could recapture her importance, my childish adoration. Her skin, her arms, the hands that had once done everything for me. If I could only ignore her sounds, those struggles with breath. Soon this birthmark would be gone. I'd never see it again. I blinked to clear my vision.

At five in the morning, my father appeared in the doorway in his pajamas, his hair rumpled, his eyes exhausted and alert. He walked into the circle of light made by the reading lamp. I got up and wrapped an arm around him.

Dawn barely registered as dark metamorphosed into gray skies that poured heavy rain. Late in the afternoon, my mother's labored breaths faded away. Just after her breathing stopped, the clouds broke to reveal a glowing sunset over the lake.

Two days later, we had a memorial service at the Presbyterian Church. My mother was represented by a picture taken around the time she met my father - waves of glossy dark hair and a smile that reached into her eyes - and the quilts she had poured her creative energy into in the last two decades of her life. She approached this American craft with German meticulousness - every stitch in her quilts was hand sewn in close, perfect lines. Nica and I read a poem by Goethe. I read it in German, Nica delivered the English translation. It wasn't until after the service that I wondered about the people that crowded the church. Here and there I spotted a familiar face: there was Mrs. Kelly whose drama lessons had nourished me for two high school years, and of course I knew the Olsons, Simons, and Duesenberries who'd been friends when I lived in Clemson. A few neighbors, too, were familiar. But most of the people hugging my father were complete strangers. As I stood in the receiving line, next to my sister, who knew everybody since she had grown up with them, I felt like a ghost. That feeling grew more eerie as one after another, upon being introduced to me, exclaimed some variation of: "Oh my god, you look exactly like your mother. For a minute, I thought that was Ingrid standing there."

I smiled, and admitted that, yes, we did have similar haircuts, and shook hands. When I escaped to the bathroom, I peered into the square of mirror and examined my face closely. Yes, I had my mother's eyes. Right now they were shadowed in dark circles and the fine lines that were undeniably webbing the corners looked more prominent than on a good day. The last few years, my mother and I had slid into similar hairstyles, short cuts that framed our faces, and neither of us took the time for more than a quick blow dry. And, though I had never thought about it before, the narrow lips I've tried hard not to live up to, those were like hers too. "Exactly like my mother?" No. All my life, I focused on our differences. My head was oval, not round, my nose was sharper than my mother's, and I was shorter, but down here, in the gloom of a badly lit church bathroom, it struck me that even though I could quibble about 'exactly,' my mother's friends had a point. I resembled my mother a great deal. For the first time in my life, I let that knowledge slide over me and settle without fighting it.

My mother had asked to be cremated and the Presbyterians were in the midst of planning to build a columbarium - a new word for me - so we would not inter her ashes until it was ready. Even after my father explained that a columbarium was a wall with niches that held urns, I felt compelled to look the word up in the dictionary and found that it derives from the Latin word for dovecote. The knowledge soothed me. I imagined dove-colored souls, dusty grays, milky blues, powdery browns gently cooing as they floated in and out of tiny cubbies. Like the pigeons Onkel Otto had kept when I was still very young. They lived just under the barn's roof peak and flew in and out in the dusk, dark shapes in the soft night air.

The columbarium was ready by the following summer, but we decided to wait until the anniversary of my mother's death to inter the ashes. The anniversary of her death fell on a Sunday, so we would hold a small ceremony right after the regular service.

And so it happened that one Sunday morning I found myself in charge of transferring my mother's ashes into the urn I had made from terra cotta slabs that summer. I stood on the deck in Clemson and inhaled the damp September air deep into my lungs, then exhaled deliberately. My hands shook. Sun glinted through the pines. The deck's wooden boards were stained dark from the previous night's rain. Ron touched my arm, and I leaned against him, resting for a moment. Then I pulled away and reached for the knife laid out on the bench. Ron slipped the lid off the urn and put it down next to the box that held my mother's ashes. I slid the knife under a plastic edge. The box held. I forgot my jittery heart when I realized I'd have to work to pry it open. When it finally popped, I was surprised to find the ashes sealed in a plastic bag. I picked up the bag and felt its weight in my hand. The contents were light and heavy, fluid and lumpy. I considered slitting the plastic and pouring the contents into the urn. Ron suggested we just leave the bag whole. I tried it. The box had been a flat rectangle; the urn I made to fit the columbarium niche was tall and slender. My mother's ashes resisted the drastic shape change. I cut a hole in the top of the bag to let air out. At first, I nudged gently but I ended up pushing hard. The bony lumps were light as pumice, but the ashes themselves proved dense. When I finished cramming them in, I took another breath. I was glad to be done, but sorry for being so rough. Then I reached for the stone Sophie had chosen, a piece of jasper for protection, and placed it on top. I ran a bead of glue along the urn's lip and seated the lid. Then I wrapped my arm around Ron's waist as he tightened his around my shoulders. I inhaled deeply and deliberately, and faced the lake. This had been my mother's view a little over a year ago, as she finished her breakfast and waited for the hummingbirds. My father had told me that one of those mornings in August, when she knew her time was running out, she sighed and said: "*Ach, es war ein gutes Leben.*" Ah, it was a good life.

Did she really feel that way? Or was this a case of my father's selective hearing? Over the years I had learned that he tended to forget the bad and remember only the good. I would never know. For my mother's sake, I hoped that she really had moved beyond the bitterness of the early years in Clemson. That the only reason those years figured so heavily in my memories of her was because that's a time we shared so intensely. For her sake, I wanted to believe my father. I hoped she felt she'd had a good life.

EQUILIBRIUM

In the photo, Sophie, age seven, wears an East German police hat. She is smiling her biggest smile as she perches on Cousin Rainer's shoulders. Rainer's eyes are closed and his arms extend out like a scarecrow's. He's braced his feet at shoulder-width. I notice for the first time how ugly this uniform truly is. Tall black boots, a brown belt with a brass buckle - why wouldn't they have matched the belt and boots? For that matter the buckle clashes with the silvery coat buttons and the badge at the front of the cap. The uniform color, a brownish green that most closely resembles baby poop after a large feed of peas doesn't match the gray-green cap.

Rainer procured the uniform as a gag for my father's 75th birthday celebration. My father had rented a restaurant at the green edge of Gera to accommodate the fifty relatives and friends. Poser tradition dictated some form of entertainment before the *Kaffeeklatsch*. Both Onkel Dieter and I read poems composed for the occasion. Just as we were about to start passing the cake platters - the tortes gleamed with glazed fruit in whipped cream, and we'd all been longing for them - an East German Police Officer walked in.

The grown-ups tensed instantly. I could feel the air crackle. Then a giggle broke the silence and grew into a roar of laughter. The children peered over the tables, wondering why the grown-ups were so amused. I whispered into Sophie's ear, "It's my cousin Rainer. He's dressed as an East German policeman. Those were the guys who used to scare me so at the border crossings."

I studied the uniform. In just ten years, I had forgotten the details. I couldn't have described it from memory, but when I saw it I recognized it instantly. Rainer had worked up a regular stand-up routine. He veered between admonishing us in a steely voice while wagging his finger and rendering anecdotes of my grandmother Hedwig's fearless interactions with the East German border police. I translated into Sophie's ear. There was the time Hedwig had attempted to smuggle a Beatles record into the DDR for one of her music hungry nephews. "What kind of record is this?" the customs policeman had asked. "Oh," my grandmother said, putting on her most addled face, and drawing a circle in the air with her hands, "one of those round ones." The officer had simply shaken his head and given up. We all laughed, even though the story had been passed around the family like a fable, and we could each recite it from memory. Sophie goggled at the story. "You mean they decided what kind of music you could listen to?" I nodded.

After cake, Sophie and my cousins' children formed a pack that roamed the restaurant's grounds, balancing on fences and swinging from weeping willow branches. They attached themselves to the adolescents in the family and for the first time ever she had the experience of being allowed to roam without my constant presence. I knew everyone was watching out for her.

My father's siblings had arranged to rent a streetcar, which was waiting at the nearest stop to take us on a nostalgic tour of the city. Sophie had already discovered her love of Gera's streetcars on our trips around town, but this was special. The antique car had wooden seats and polished wood trim, burnished brass poles and, just under the roof, a row of advertisements from the twenties. The conductor wore a spiffy uniform and hand canceled the children's tickets. Sophie was too excited to sit - instead she practiced balancing her weight against the swaying turns. We toured the parts of town that had mattered to my father's childhood, but for Sophie no set of buildings could compare to the thrill of the ride.

When we returned to the restaurant, it was almost time for the evening buffet. I piled a selection of Sophie's favorite cold cuts, liverwurst and raw smoked ham, and a few pickles on her plate, added a radish flower and some cucumber petals as well as a few slices of sourdough rye. When I checked back after dinner, her place was empty and her plate was clean. I found her in the foyer entertaining her cousins by passing around the key chain sized electronic Donkey Kong I bought her for the trip. Cousin Rainer's sons - I was shocked to see they were all old enough to have beards - were trying out their English with her. She certainly had no interest in calling it a day. I retired to the bar with Ulrike and the rest of my cousins. It was only after the last child left, some time around eleven at night, that I could persuade Sophie to follow me to our nearby hotel room. As I peeled off her party clothes, she chattered about cousin Till and cousin Jan, and how much fun it had been to swing in the willows with Kerstin and Lisa, and how she taught Jan a joke in English and he got it, and ... she would have kept talking, but I handed her a toothbrush. She finally fell asleep around midnight.

The next night, half the family showed up at Tante Bärbel's dacha for a round of *Rostbratwürste*. Sophie ate two, and sneaked a few sips of Opa's beer. She picked raspberries in the vegetable garden and hid in a nearby wheat field with her cousins. As we left Gera, I had to promise Sophie we would see both Lisa and Kerstin again soon.

Our next destination was a Bavarian farm that rented rooms to summer visitors. There were bunnies to feed in the barnyard and two old ponies that grudgingly carried Sophie across the pastures. Although Sophie was really too old for the sandbox, she used it to make friends with a little girl named Franziska staying in the rooms below us. Together with Franziska's family we spent a day at a swimming beach and an evening at a small festival centered on dance music, beer and marinated pork chops. Sophie and Franziska climbed onto the elevated dance floor and fused with the music.

A few days later, we encountered a street festival in the pedestrian zone of nearby Weilheim. The festival celebrated Weilheim's friendship with its Provençal sister city. The market square brimmed with food booths selling pretzels and tapenade. Sophie loved the party atmosphere, the colorful flags suspended above the city streets, the stores selling trinkets on the sidewalk, the huge communal tables where everyone consumed French wines and Bavarian sausages, the bands alternating between German folksongs and French.

The room we rented at the farm had a small kitchen, adequate for breakfast and lunch, but in the evenings we usually ate out. The *Bauersfrau* - farmwoman - recommended her favorite local restaurant, *Am Eibenwald,* for dinner. We liked it so much we returned again and again. The restaurant's deck overlooked a valley rimmed by Bavarian mountains. Our last time there, Sophie sat across from me. She had just finished a hill of mashed potatoes. Remnants of a child size portion of *Schnitzel* dotted her plate. I reached over to stab a piece with my fork. I couldn't shake my training not to waste meat.

A private party spilled out of the restaurant. Forty men and women dressed in *Trachten* - traditional Bavarian dress. The women wore dirndls with lacy white bodices. Heirloom silver brooches and pendants glinted in the early evening light. The men sported dark green knickers and richly embroidered suspenders. A group of them carried band instruments. They formed a line behind a man with a ceremonial staff and processed across the deck, down the stairs and into the meadows. Sophie ran to the railing's end to get a better look. She bounced to the music until it faded.

The next morning, we loaded up our rental car and headed for the Munich airport. Time to go home. I settled in the front seat with the map in my lap. Just as we entered the artery that skirts the central city, Sophie said, "Mama, can we move to Germany?"

"No," I said, before I even had a chance to think. The speed of my answer took me by surprise. I turned to look at her.

"Why not?" she said. A rush of contradictory emotion rocked me. I was thrilled that she loved it here but that feeling of joy collided with: who knows what she means by that, she loves everything when she's immersed in it, besides it's impossible, and I don't even want to anymore, and she'd be just as miserable as I was. I didn't say any of these things.

"Why would you like to move here?" I asked, glancing at Ron to check his reaction. He was busy sizing up the chance to merge into a passing lane at 140 km/hr.

"I like that you can go swimming naked," Sophie answered, giggling.

Oh. "Is that the only reason?"

"No. There's Kerstin and Lisa, and I love the food, and walking in the cities and the street festivals. So, can we, Mama?"

So, it was more than going to the beach. She connected with my cousins' children. I had given thought to making that possible. That she loved the food was no surprise. She had managed to turn our vegetarian household back toward omnivore with her love of meat and potatoes.

"No, Sophie we can't," I answered. "We can visit, maybe even for a few months in the summer once Daddy retires, but we aren't going to move to Germany."

"Why not?"

I sighed. I couldn't imagine leaving behind the place I had finally carved for myself in Minnesota. How could I wrap the complexity of my life into a simple answer she would understand? I ended up with mundane practicalities.

"I've got my pottery studio and Daddy has his job - we can't just drop all that and come here. And we wouldn't be able to afford a house as nice as ours."

"Why can't Daddy get a job here?"

"It's not that easy." I decided to try a different tack. "Wouldn't you miss your friends and your school?"

"We could bring my friends with us?" She laughed to show she knew that wasn't really possible. I turned back to my map; we were getting close to the airport and I needed to guide Ron to the proper exit.

Later, I settled into my coach class seat, stuffing a pillow behind my lower back to try to make it bearable, and closed my eyes. I barely heard Ron helping Sophie to set up a round of solitaire on her tray table.

I wondered when it had happened. I had balanced for so long on that edge of wishing I could move, but never quite getting around to it. When had I slipped off? It wasn't that I felt I had exchanged one home for another. Governments were too simplistic. They pretended that you could turn in your passport, exchange it for a new one, and your loyalties transformed. Either you were German or American. Make a choice. For too long I was caught in the same trap.

When I first realized that the Germany I grew up in no longer existed, I thought: "Now I have no home." But home could be more than either/or. Home could be more than one place. My home is a series of places: a vanished, divided Germany, Upstate South Carolina, and now Minnesota. I carry memories from each inside me. On a bad day, I still have that sense that I've left a piece of myself everywhere I've lived, and I'll never be able to heal them together again. But, I belong a little bit more in Minnesota than anyplace else.

Each of my homes has shaped me. My first impulse when I'm confronted by an authority figure in uniform will always be dictated by my experiences of East Germany. I harbor a distrust of the future that grows directly out of German history. I am certain that people can be brutal, that systems can be subverted, and I'm also sure that hope is possible. That knowledge will keep me an outsider in America. But I'm not the only one. And one of the gifts of America is that I can build a comfortable place for myself with other outsiders.

Years ago, when I was trying to understand my father's reasons for moving us, I asked him what home meant to him. He hesitated for a moment, then swept his eyes around the room from my mother to my sister to me. He said: "Home is being with my family, with the people I love."

I thought he was trying to justify himself, and refused to consider his answer. I open my eyes and see Sophie's blonde head bent over her tray table. Ron watches her fingers slide over the cards, then looks up to meet my eyes. I am sure no one on earth is as lucky. I am at home here on this airplane, right now. And that will have to do.

ACKNOWLEDGMENTS

As any memoir writer can tell you, crafting a story from life is a long and laborious process. I relied on the teaching and support of family, writing instructors, and fellow writers. My writer's group, the Widening Gyre, has kept me going with critique and companionship over the close to twenty years we've been together. A special thanks to Sue Hamre, Erin Hart, Lynda McDonnell, Cheryll Ostrom, and Liz Weir. I'd like to thank the Loft Writer's Workshop in Minneapolis for providing the impetus and courage to begin. Myrna Kostash, who selected me for a Creative Nonfiction Mentorship based on an early piece, boosted my confidence. I benefited from the generosity and skill of numerous teachers at the Loft and in the University of Minnesota Creative Writing Program. Thank you Pat Francisco, Mimi Sprengnether, and Patricia Hampl. Cheri Register helped me find the heart of the book and Paulette Bates Alden read and edited entire versions of the manuscript. I am grateful to them for their insight and patience. Thanks to Cami Applequist and Sue Hamre for their keen editorial eyes. My husband Ron was the guinea pig for every draft and an invaluable reality check. Sophie, my daughter, provided both inspiration and an appreciative audience. Misha, my departed Golden Retriever, kept my feet warm during many writing sessions. And last, but not least, I'd like to thank my mother who nourished me with stories of the past, and my father whose heart and self-confidence are big enough to read this book, supply facts, and cheer me on.